The Smart Girl's Guide to SPORTS

A Hip Handbook for Women Who Don't Know a SLAM DUNK from a GRAND SLAM

LIZ HARTMAN MUSIKER

HUDSON
STREET
PRESS

HUDSON STREET PRESS
Published by Penguin Group
Penguin Group (USA) Inc., 375 Hudson Street, New York, New York 10014, U.S.A.
Penguin Group (Canada), 90 Eglinton Avenue East, Suite 700, Toronto, Ontario,
Canada M4P 2Y3 (a division of Pearson Penguin Canada Inc.)
Penguin Books Ltd, 80 Strand, London WC2R 0RL, England
Penguin Ireland, 25 St. Stephen's Green, Dublin 2, Ireland
(a division of Penguin Books Ltd.)
Penguin Group (Australia), 250 Camberwell Road, Camberwell, Victoria 3124,
Australia (a division of Pearson Australia Group Pty. Ltd.)
Penguin Books India Pvt. Ltd., 11 Community Centre, Panchsheel Park,
New Delhi – 110 017, India
Penguin Books (NZ), cnr Airborne and Rosedale Roads, Albany, Auckland 1310,
New Zealand (a division of Pearson New Zealand Ltd.)
Penguin Books (South Africa) (Pty.) Ltd., 24 Sturdee Avenue, Rosebank,
Johannesburg 2196, South Africa

Penguin Books Ltd., Registered Offices: 80 Strand, London WC2R 0RL, England

First published by Hudson Street Press, a member of Penguin Group (USA) Inc.

First Printing, November 2005
10 9 8 7 6 5 4 3 2 1

REGISTERED TRADEMARK—MARCA REGISTRADA

HUDSON
STREET
PRESS

LIBRARY OF CONGRESS CATALOGING-IN-PUBLICATION DATA
Musiker, Liz Hartman.
    The smart girl's guide to sports : a hip handbook for women who don't know a slam
dunk from a grand slam / Liz Hartman Musiker.
        p.   cm.
    Includes bibliographical references.
    ISBN 1-59463-011-9 (hardcover: alk. paper)
1. Sports—Miscellanea.   2. Sports—Terminology.   I. Title.
GV707.M73   2005
796'.03—dc22   2005018858

Printed in the United States of America
Set in Avenir Roman
Designed by Daniel Lagin

To Bob and Jake, who make me feel like I've won the Super Bowl every day

Sports gets into everything . . .

—John Steinbeck

Acknowledgments

I am in awe of my editor, Danielle Friedman, who made this a far better book and was a joy to work with. I couldn't, in my wildest imagination, have dreamt up an editor with whom I could be more in sync. Thanks also to Laureen Rowland for her keen insight and her support of this project. I am indebted to Fred Lief, sports editor at the Associated Press, for reading hundreds of pages of stuff he doesn't need to know anything more about, all in the interest of saving me from embarrassing myself. And thanks to Sheila Norman-Culp for finding Fred for me. For hockey and car racing, Jack Falla and Jim Wright, respectively, were invaluable and abundantly generous with their time and expertise.

Love and thanks to my lifelong friend and agent Lisa Ekus (how fitting that we would share this, too); and to Kara Welsh for sharing the excitement and for having a husband who's a sports fanatic; to Nancy Pines for helping get the whole thing going; to Sue Nadel, who made sure that I didn't lose my perspective; to Don O'Hagan for cheering me on. And thanks to those I tortured via e-mail or cell phone with annoying sports questions: David Hochhauser, Stephen Cohen, Louis Biblowitz, Dan De-Beer, and Bill Rosson. Okay, and Jimmy Neisloss, even though he doesn't know anything about sports.

I owe a huge debt of gratitude to my colleagues at Long Island University, Catherine Larkin and Donna Marciano. I don't know how they put up with me when they both had far more important things to do. I am especially grateful to Donna for her extraordinary help with the diagrams.

More love and thanks to my sister Vicki, who has never wavered in her support of everything I do (but sometimes what I wear). I am grateful for the love and support that I received from the rest of my coast-to-coast family—from the Rochester contingent, Dad, Fran, Sarah, and Jeff (and

Bogey and Marley, too!); from the desert, Judy and Mike, who are a constant source of encouragement. Thanks to my bro-in-law, Jimmy Musiker, for taking time for sports chats and being opinionated, and to his wife, Jill, for not being mad at me for leaving the Mother's Day BBQ early to finish my edits. And thanks to their wonderful children: my spunky, sassy, charming nephew, Casey, for all his hockey tips (but most of all for all the great hugs and kisses), and to my beautiful and equally sassy niece, Ashley, for not blowing up the chemistry lab with her cousin (my son), thus enabling me to concentrate on my book instead of making an emergency trip to school.

There are no words to express my love and gratitude to my husband, Bob, and my son, Jake. Suffice it to say that without them, nothing is possible.

Contents

Introduction

One morning, circa 1995, I was sitting in the conference room at the New York book publishing company I worked for, waiting for our weekly marketing meeting to begin. Having arrived early, it was just me, the director of publicity; our patronizing director of sales, who never gave me the time of day, and who we'll call "Ward"; and two of Ward's underlings.

As we sat waiting for a few of our colleagues to arrive, the guys began talking about, of course, sports—specifically, the previous night's football game between the San Francisco 49ers and the New York Giants. It just so happened that football was the one sport that, even then, I knew a thing or two about. This wasn't even by choice, really—having gone to a football-obsessed high school and college in which most of my Friday and Saturday nights were spent in bleachers (or on an actual field, when I was going through my baton-twirler phase . . .), football got into my veins. Anyhow, without even giving it much thought, I jumped right into the boys' conversation with something like, "Yeah, Jerry Rice was even more amazing than usual. That catch he made in the second quarter was so clutch!"

Silence.

Then the wall came tumbling down—the gender wall, that is. The men were stunned, shocked, and most important, *impressed*. Ward then started to chat it up with me: "I didn't know you were a football fan, Liz! And by the way, your team did a great job with Walsh's book." Ward and I suddenly became allies, right then and there, bonded through football. From that day forward until he left the company, he sat next to me at every marketing meeting and even shared his top-secret, totally indecipherable spreadsheets with me. We even made a point of meeting for an after-work drink from time to time.

Jeez, I thought. That's it? That's the tool? More than a dozen years of toiling up the corporate ladder, and all I needed was to know that Jerry Rice could catch a football?

That's when I decided to learn more than just the little bit I knew about football. Aside from the professional motivation, there was the fact that the two most important men in my life—my husband, Bob, and my teenage son, Jake—were always watching various games, hooting and hollerin' and high-fiving, and I felt, well, *left out*. Why should they have all the fun? (Hey, I didn't strap on thirty pregnancy pounds and go through labor to fall behind in the Mommy vs. Daddy competition because of *sports!*)

And on top of that, I was tired of hearing jokes and all manner of sports references and not knowing what they meant. Aside from my precious football knowledge, my lack of sports knowledge made me feel, well, a little dumb about something that the vast majority of our country's males seemed to understand. If so many men have been able to figure this whole sports thing out, I reasoned, it can't be difficult to learn. . . .

And it wasn't. All it took was watching, asking, listening, and reading, and in small doses. If a big game was on (an NBA finals game, or a World Series game for example), I would watch. My modus operandi was to listen to the commentators, watch the replays, ask Bob and Jake tons of questions, and then read a sports column here or there. It all happened kind of naturally. And, as I became more and more sports savvy, I discovered that sports were actually fascinating and entertaining, and that being a sports fan who actually understood what was going on was *really, really fun*. That's when I got the idea to share everything I'd learned with you, smart girls of the world.

Welcome, ladies.

WHY BOTHER?

"Why bother?" you might ask. Well, as you've likely noticed, sports are *everywhere*—in the news, in our living rooms, all around us. Aren't you tired of seeing and hearing sports headlines—that might even *lead* the news—and having no idea what the big deal is? The *New York Times* gives a *daily* section to sports—the food section doesn't get that, the home section doesn't get that, and religion doesn't get that, yet you would think that food, shelter, and religion are more important than sports. With a little sports knowledge, you'll substitute a lifetime of boring sports moments for a big dose of entertainment, and vicariously live the thrill of victory and the agony of defeat.

Also, as my experience in the boardroom can attest, there are numerous reasons to learn about sports that fall under the heading of LET'S LEVEL THE PLAYING FIELD. Yeah, yeah, yeah, we've come a long way. (Thank you Gloria, Betty, Simone, Germaine, et al.) But we have a long way to go. We're still getting only seventy-seven cents to the male dollar, and there are still a paltry four female CEOs in the Fortune 500, so all is *not* quite right in the gender game. Being twice as smart and working twice as hard as our male colleagues still hasn't broken the glass ceiling, so what's left? Sports! If you're the only woman in the room who knows why Randy Johnson pitching a perfect game is such an extraordinary event (and it is), you *will* stand out.

A LITTLE BIT OF KNOWLEDGE GOES A LONG WAY

The beautiful thing about sports, unlike, say, neurosurgery, is that a little bit of knowledge is not a dangerous thing. A little bit of knowledge goes a long way, in fact. If you're amidst a herd of men (in a boardroom or sports bar alike) and the topic turns to sports, all you need to know are a few key points, and you're in. If the discussion turns to home runs, for example, and you say, "Yes, but there has never been anything more exciting than when McGwire and Sosa were after Maris's record," you instantly win a new kind of respect from the testosterone crowd. And that's really all you need to say. You can drift out of the conversation and go back to thinking about what you're going to wear tomorrow, how to achieve world peace, or whatever it is you would rather be talking about.

We don't need scientific evidence to know that men have a sports gene—that most men are genetically engineered to remember all sports information they have come in contact with throughout their life. This, in spite of the fact that men can't remember birthdays, anniversaries, to pick up the dry cleaning, to be home for the kids even though you said a hundred times that you had a meeting, or a plethora of other basic facts.

We don't have this gene. (We have other, better ones.) So this book does not try to teach you everything, or cloud your brain with endless streams of sports statistics. It aims to give you the most fundamental, most fun, most entertaining information—the tools to enjoy sports, or simply to participate in the game in whichever way you choose.

HEY, BUT WHERE ARE ALL THE GIRLS?

I know that I do not speak for all women. I know there are vast, *ever growing* numbers of women who either: (1) know sports very well; (2) play sports very well; (3) know and play sports very well. But this means that it is even more crucial for the rest of us to not necessarily catch up, but to *have a clue*.

You'll notice that women athletes are conspicuously absent from this book. *But how can a book* for *women* ignore *women so blatantly?* you're probably wondering. If it makes you feel any better, and it shouldn't, I don't cover college sports either (for men or women). The reason I stick to men's professional sports is because they are what capture the most headlines; they inspire the water-cooler chitchat; they are the universal language among sports fans. Right or wrong, this is the way it is right now—and this book aims to help you negotiate the sports universe as it is now.

WARNING: USE THIS BOOK ONLY AS PRESCRIBED

1. Read It All at Once or 2. Don't Read It All at Once

I have aimed to make this book a low-stress, easy-to-use guide. Thus, if you choose to read the book all at once, I promise that not only will you become well versed in the world of sports, but you'll also be entertained—I've geared the book toward us, the women, the enlightened sex (i.e., I make sex jokes; I'm disrespectful to men's intelligence).

If you choose not to read this book all at once, you can use it as a handy reference. Say, for instance, you pick up the paper on the way to work and the headlines are about Peyton Manning breaking Dan Marino's record for touchdown passes. You realize that you: (1) don't know who Peyton Manning is; (2) don't know who Dan Marino is; and (3) don't know what a touchdown pass is. You can find this information easily by flipping to the profile of Marino or Manning or going to the glossary or the main text of the football section. Then you can march into the office, grab a cup of coffee, and say, "Manning made breaking Marino's record look so easy!" and your previously smug male colleagues will be in awe—of you.

Each chapter has the following components to help make learning about the various sports as streamlined, and enjoyable, as possible:

* A **Here's How It Works** section at the beginning of the chapter that offers a brief overview of the sport being discussed. This section lays the groundwork for the lengthier explanation of the sport that follows, which will cover timing, rules, positions, and so on.

* A **Just Know This** section at the end of the explanatory section, which is a final, brief summing-up of the sport. Go directly to this section if you want a quick handle on the very basics before you dash off into a sea of men where sports chat is likely to arise.

* **Profiles** of each sport's legends and legends-in-training, highlighting only the most interesting aspects of each player's career and life (see below for more about the player biographies). They are arranged in easy-to-find-your-favorite alphabetical order.

* A **glossary** of terms for each sport. Also arranged alphabetically. (Throughout the text, any word or term found in the glossary is in bold.)

* A lot of fun stuff, such as the fiercest rivalries, the hottest men on the field, and even a section about who had the biggest Afro in professional basketball.

ALL ATHLETES ARE NOT
CREATED EQUALLY

. . . nor are the profiles of the athletes in this book. What makes an athlete great—or, more to the point, what makes him capture the attention of a nation or the world? You might as well ask why people fall in love. So what are my criteria for profiling the players in this book? First, I've made sure to include the icons, the names that have transcended their sport and have become part of history, from Babe Ruth to Tiger Woods. Then there are the athletes whose talent speaks for itself, who even if lobotomized would stand head and shoulders above the others. I have included only those evil geniuses whose accomplishments in their sports cannot be diminished even by their idiotic, asinine behavior. And then there are those whose personal stories—or smiles, dimples, abs, or buns—are simply irresistible. But no one got into these pages on looks alone. No way. (That's so *male* to choose someone based only on appearance!)

The lengths of the various profiles are calibrated to prevent boredom and overload. If the individual's statistics are important, they're there. If a player's triumph-over-adversity story is more interesting than his stats, that's what's there. My mantra is to give you the juicy tidbits, the most delicious bites, not the whole damn piece with all the gristle and fat.

ALL SPORTS ARE NOT CREATED
(OR, AT LEAST, NOT WATCHED) EQUALLY

I have selected for inclusion the most watched, most popular professional spectator sports. Yes, I am aware that soccer is *the most popular sport in the world*, as its three fans here in America will tell you, emphatically. (The truth is, Americans are interested only in people under the age of eighteen playing the sport; once it gets to the professional level, no one in the United States really cares.) Anyhow, tennis isn't included either. Neither is lacrosse, bowling, or darts. I focused on sports that continually obsess men and capture the headlines.

SEEING IS BELIEVING

One of my most important pieces of advice to you as you read on is: after you read, *watch*. While you're reading, you may find that you have a vague idea of what a particular position does or how a rule is applied, but not a full grasp. If you watch the sport on television and listen to the commentators, however—or go to a game (or match or race) in person—it will all come together. Each time you watch, you'll see something new, you'll learn something new, and more of the concepts you've read about will come into focus. This book, and watching a *little*, not a lot, will release the sports goddess within you.

On a related note, you'll notice that, in each chapter, I've included a list of the most popular, most classic films about that sport. Watching great sports movies can be an excellent way to form a stronger emotional connection with the sport, and to further "get" what the big deal is. (It also can provide a great date activity!)

HIP TIPS TO ENJOY SPORTS

It's clear that we women can and do enjoy sports, but not necessarily in the same way men do. What's crucial for us is to learn the basics, then form some sort of an emotional attachment to the various sports, even if we have to create one. Here are some tips to help you enjoy sports:

1. Set your sights on a "hottie," and root for him and his team. If you need some guidance to get you started, do a quick Google search on Derek Jeter, Tom Brady, or Jeff Gordon.

2. Attach yourself to a team. You can always root for the hometown team, but if you don't have one, or that doesn't get your engine going, root for your father's favorite team, or your lover's, husband's, son's, or brother's.

3. Find a team to passionately dislike. This is the reverse of no. 2. Here's an example: A very good friend of mine's ex-boyfriend was a huge fan of the Philadelphia Eagles (football). Therefore, since he's an ex, I

will never, ever root for the Eagles. This is the way it is, even though she wound up with a spectacular man, couldn't care less about her ex, and is surprised when I mention this. It works for me, though.

4. Watch the bigger games, when something is really at stake. These usually occur as the season progresses—playoff games, conference titles, and so on—or when there is a game between teams that share a classic rivalry (e.g., the New York Yankees and the Boston Red Sox).

5. Watch games on television whenever you are so inclined, and pay attention to the instant replays—this is when you can really see what's going on and learn from what the commentators are saying.

6. Listen to the commentators. You really can learn a lot from them. The play-by-play guys are usually professional broadcast journalists (as opposed to ex-players), and they provide a lot of detail about what's going on. They are teamed with "color" commentators who often *are* ex-players and provide great insight into the personality of the game and the personalities of the players on the field.

7. Tips nos. 5 and 6 require that you watch games on television, but actually going to games—for any sport—is a blast (unless you're watching the Buffalo Bills in Buffalo anytime after, say, September—ditto for the Green Bay Packers, or the Florida Marlins in August).

8. Ask questions. Men who like sports like to show off their sports knowledge. You're guaranteed to get way more information than you want or need, but take the little nugget you were looking for and smile politely through the rest.

9. Don't try to figure out every rule, every foul, every nuance. Go with the flow and enjoy the rhythm of the game.

10. And most important, remember that a little knowledge goes a long way. Again, sports are not neurosurgery. A little knowledge is not a dangerous thing, and, best of all, you only need to know a little to be able to enjoy the games.

So, L-E-T-S G-O! Come on, girls, let's GO!

Basketball

THE SOUND: *Squeak.* (Sneakers* pivoting on a gym floor.)

THE LOOK: Tall—really tall—men wearing long, baggy shorts and sleeveless shirts.

THE PLACE: Basketball courts—always indoors.

THE ORGANIZATION: The NBA (National Basketball Association).

(**very expensive* sneakers)

> There are really only two plays: *Romeo and Juliet,* and put the darn ball in the basket.
> —Abe Lemons, former University of Texas basketball coach

Basketball is hip-hop in style and attitude. It's fast, it's dynamic (you can almost always see the ball in motion), and it's fairly straightforward. The main idea, as the name says, is to get the ball into the basket, and to prevent the opposing team from doing the same.

There are a million (okay, maybe a few dozen) ways to get the ball into the basket: there's the **layup,** the **fadeaway**, the **jump shot**, the **dunk**, and the **alley-oop**, to name a few, and countless variations of each. Each shot has a distinct style, and each becomes even more distinct and stylized when executed by individual players. Then there's the dance of the players on the court—players perform all kinds of quick moves and fakes to outmaneuver one another. Finally, there are the coaches standing on the sidelines who are *always* dressed in exquisitely tailored suits and ties (not an essential component of the game, but an added bonus nevertheless).

With its quickness and cunning, basketball's attitude is urban, its rhythm, jazzy. And even though many pro players are, in fact, from the inner city, and the whole "white men can't jump" theory may prevail, if you take a drive around Any Suburb USA you will likely see a basketball hoop in almost every driveway. Hoop dreams are everywhere, and nowadays there's a new crop of abundantly talented, tall, tall, tall, players from all over the world joining the pros: Yao Ming, currently playing for the Houston Rockets, is from China; Manu Ginobili, from Argentina, just led the San Antonio Spurs to victory in the 2005 NBA Finals; Dirk Nowitzki, who plays for the Dallas Mavericks, is from Germany. Like the new M&Ms, the NBA has become wonderfully more colorful in recent years.

HERE'S HOW IT WORKS

The team that gets the most points by getting the ball into the basket wins. Period. You've probably caught enough games out of the corner of your eye at the gym or at a bar to know this. And you can follow a game knowing only this—which is why basketball is such a great spectator sport. But to *enjoy* the game, to understand why Nike would pay LeBron James $90 million to endorse its products, to understand why Michael Jordan is worshiped even now that he's retired from the game, to know why the names Bird, Kareem, and Magic bring grown men to their knees, you need to know a little more.

MISSING MICHAEL'S MAGIC

If you ever find yourself caught in the crossfire of a heated basketball discussion but have nothing specific to contribute, you can always just sigh and lament missing Michael Jordan. To basketball fans, Michael Jordan is a god. You didn't have to be a Chicago Bulls fan to be in awe of him. In fact, you didn't have to be a basketball fan to be in awe of him. When Michael played, America, and the world, watched—including lots of people who didn't previously care about basketball and who haven't cared since he retired. More on Michael's magic later, but suffice it to say that, right or wrong, the NBA hasn't had quite the same "zing" since Michael. (Like Cher or Madonna, he only needs one name.)

Basketball courts are appealing because they always have beautifully tended wooden floors in excellent condition. If only my floors at home

THE COURT

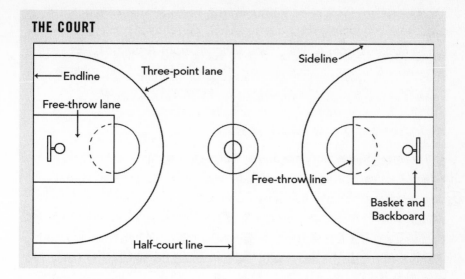

could look so good. A basketball court is a rectangle, 94 feet by 50 feet. At each end there is a basket, ten feet off the floor, in front of a backboard that measures 6 feet by 4 feet. Painted lines near each basket delineate the free-throw line and the three-point line (see below). There is also a half-court line, which designates the middle of the court.

The *free-throw lane* is the rectangle that extends from the free-throw line to the basket. The "lane" is usually painted a color (not just plain wood), so in b-ball lingo it is referred to as "the paint." A player in this area is said to be **in the paint**.

TIMING: Five Minutes Is All You Need

A basketball game is divided into four periods of twelve minutes each, with a fifteen-minute halftime in the middle. However, nothing really exciting usually happens until the last five minutes of the game. The first three periods of a b-ball game are like Ping-Pong, back and forth, back and forth, at a pretty even (read: dull) tempo. Even if a team is considerably behind, it always seems to miraculously catch up in the last five minutes, and then, suddenly, you have an exciting, tense competition.

For the players and for hard-core fans, though, the clock matters very much, and every second of the forty-eight minutes (which usually stretches to about two hours due to **fouls**, **free throws**, and time-outs) counts. There are two primary rules regarding timing that are helpful to know: the *twenty-four-second rule* and the *three-second rule*.

The Twenty-Four-Second Rule

The twenty-four-second rule states that, when a team has the ball, it *must* attempt a basket within twenty-four seconds or it's charged with a violation. In short: the twenty-four-second rule is your friend. *Why, exactly, would a basketball rule be my friend?* the intelligent woman might ask. Because without it, the game would be intolerably, interminably boring. Without this rule, the team with the ball could do all kinds of fancy, protective, defensive ballhandling, preventing the other team from ever getting the ball. Simply put, without the twenty-four-second rule, there would be no offense—no one would ever shoot. The twenty-four-second rule was instituted in the 1950s when the NBA was trying to attract an audience—at the time, everyone was snoozing through the games.

The Three-Second Rule

The three-second rule states that an offensive player cannot be in "the lane" (the area down near the basket, also known as "the paint": see diagram on page 3) for more than three seconds. Not even a finger or a toe can be in the lane for more than three seconds. Sounds strict, but it's very loosely applied—it's not usually called that closely by the refs. Recently, during the 2001–2002 season, the NBA added a similar rule for defense: A defensive player cannot be in the lane for more than three seconds if he is not closely guarding an offensive player. A bit vague, yes, but the general idea is that neither side is allowed to hang out in the lane.

Breaking either of these rules is a called a **violation**. When a team commits a violation, it loses possession of the ball. (When a team loses possession of the ball, the ref gives the ball to a player on the opposing team, who stands on the sidelines and throws it to one of his teammates

THE DIFFERENCE BETWEEN FOOTBALL
AND BASKETBALL, ACCORDING TO ANNA QUINDLEN

"I do not like football, which I think of as a game in which two tractors approach each other from opposite directions and collide. Besides, I have contempt for a game in which players have to wear so much equipment. Men play basketball in their underwear, which seems just right to me." (From a 1988 essay reprinted in *Living Out Loud*.)

on the court.) Violations aren't as bad as fouls (discussed below). They're like parking tickets versus moving violations.

The twenty-four-second rule and the three-second rule are the most common types of violations. (Other, non-timing-related violations such as *ballhandling errors* are covered later in the chapter.)

SCORING: Easy as 1-2-3

No, really, I mean it—it's that easy:

* After some *fouls*, the player who was fouled upon gets to go "to the line," which is the *free-throw line*, and shoot one, two, or three free throws at the basket. Each basket results in *one point*.

* A ball that is shot from the area *within* the arc (the three-point line) results in *two points*. This is the most common shot, and it's referred to as a *field goal*.

* A basket—also called a *field goal*—will result in *three points* if it is shot from beyond the three-point line. (Don't worry, if you can't tell whether a shot was made from behind the line or not, the announcer will always indicate whether it was a two- or three-pointer.)

(See diagram on page 3 for the location of the various lines and boundaries described above.)

SHOTS: The Black Pants Theory

There are ten basic shots, and then numerous variations from there. Look at it this way: shots = black pants. Let me explain: As women, we know that it can be necessary to own at least ten pairs of black pants. *We* know that each pair is completely different from the others—tight, loose, shiny, cottony, for dress-up, for dress-down, for work, for play, for yoga, downtown funky, uptown chic, and let's not forget the essential capri. But to men, one pair of black pants will suffice, and they are baffled and confused by our ebony array. It's the same, in gender reverse, with basketball shots. Until now, you might have been thinking, *Okay, so the ball gets in the basket. The team that made the basket scores. End of story.* Au contraire! There are almost as many varieties of shots as there are black pants.

Some shots sound exactly like what they are—the ***dunk***, for example. When a player dunks the ball, he "dunks" it into the basket like one might dunk a doughnut into a cup of coffee, or an Oreo into a glass of milk (except, unlike the doughnut or the Oreo, the ball comes out the other end).*

For our purposes, there's no need to learn the details of all the specific shots (see below)—a basic familiarity will suffice. Note that after a team makes a shot, the opposing team automatically gets the ball.

OFFENSE AND DEFENSE

In basketball, players play both offense and defense. When a

TYPES OF SHOTS

There is no such thing as a bad shot, unless it doesn't go *in*.
                —Larry Bird, legendary Boston
                                  Celtics player

1. Jump Shot
2. Fadeaway (or Fall-away)
3. Bank Shot
4. Hook Shot (or Sky Hook)
5. Layup
6. Dunk
7. Set Shot
8. Tip-in
9. Free Throw
10. Finger Roll

See Glossary for description of shots.

---

*For normal people, the dunk is exceedingly difficult. For seven-foot basketball pros, if near the basket, they can usually dunk it, even with an opponent in their face.

team has possession of the ball, it is the offense; when it loses possession of the ball, its opponent becomes the offense, and it becomes the defense. Players may have better strengths on defense or offense, but in the pros, they need to be talented in both.

For the first half (the first two quarters) of the game, Team Swoosh defends the basket at one end of the court and aims to score points in the basket at the opposite end of the court (the basket that their opponents are defending). After halftime, the teams switch sides, so if Team Swoosh was defending the basket at the north end of the court and scoring in the south basket before halftime, now they defend the south basket and attempt to score in the north basket.

> ## SIGNATURE SHOTS
>
> Michael Jordan and Kareem Abdul-Jabbar (another one of basketball's most elite Hall of Famers) were closely associated with one particular type of shot:
>
> **Michael Jordan:** the *fadeaway, or fall-away.*
> On this shot, the player bends or drifts backward, away from the basket, as he shoots the ball. A sports-savvy thing to say is: "You can argue that other players may be as good as Michael, but no one has ever made the fadeaway look as easy." As long as you're saying good things about Mike, no one will argue.
>
> **Kareem Abdul-Jabbar:** the *hook shot, or sky hook.*
> On this shot, the player stands sideways in relation to the basket (he doesn't face it), and shoots the ball over his head with one hand in a sweeping, arcing motion, forming a *hook* shape with his arm. Another sports-savvy thing to say is: "You know, neither in the NCAA* nor in the NBA have I ever seen anyone approach the art of the hook shot like Kareem." No one will argue with you because Kareem is a basketball god.

BLOCKS, STEALS, AND REBOUNDS

Aside from shooting, three key b-ball moves to know about are **blocking**, **stealing**, and **rebounding**. All of these moves essentially revolve around shooting. Shooting is like the queen bee of the game; the other actions are the worker bees.

---

*The NCAA stands for the National Collegiate Athletic Association.

Blocking

A defensive player aims to block his opponent's shots as they fly toward the basket, or prevent his opponent from even attempting a shot. He can use his torso, arms, and hands to distract his opponent and block shots, but he has to do this without actually touching his opponent or impeding his forward progress (if he does one of the latter, he is in danger of committing a *foul*).

Stealing

A defensive player can also legally steal the ball away from his opponent by swatting it away or grabbing it (again without touching the opponent), or by intercepting a pass from one offensive player to another.

ROUNDBALL RIVALRIES

Los Angeles Lakers vs. Boston Celtics: The rivalry between these two teams dates back to 1979, when Earvin "Magic" Johnson, playing for the Michigan State Spartans, led his team to the NCAA Championship, defeating Larry Bird and the Indiana State Sycamores. Shortly thereafter, Magic and Bird were drafted into the NBA by the Lakers and Celtics, respectively. In the 1980s, the east-west/Magic-Bird rivalry ignited the NBA. Magic would lead his Los Angeles team—which was often referred to as "Showtime"—to face Bird's blue-collar Celtics in the NBA Finals three times during the decade (the Lakers won two of the three meetings).

New York Knicks vs. Miami Heat: Maybe it's because the Heat are the newcomers on the block (the team was created in 1988), infiltrating the Knicks' territory—the Eastern Conference. Or maybe it's because Pat Riley, who coached the Knicks for three successful seasons, left them to head south—to coach the Heat. Whatever the deep-rooted psychological reasons were, the sparks fly when the Knicks play the Heat.

Rebounding

Only the defense is concerned with blocking and stealing, but everyone wants to get the rebound, which means to get the ball after a shot has been attempted and missed (by either team). Put differently, whoever attains possession of the ball after a shot has been attempted and missed is said to have "gotten the rebound."

BALLHANDLING: Dribbling and Passing

Ballhandling is the fancy term for bouncing the ball, passing it and, of course, *dribbling* it. (Couldn't they have picked a more appealing word than *dribbling*? It makes me think of drooling toddlers.)

Dribbling

Just because you can bounce a ball, it doesn't mean you can compete in the NBA. Bouncing a ball is to professional basketball dribbling as coloring in a coloring book is to painting the Sistine Chapel. What makes it even more challenging is that, while dribbling, players are *not* allowed to:

* use two hands at once.

* turn the ball over in one hand between dribbles (called *palming*).*

* dribble, stop (i.e., hold the ball), and then dribble again (called **double dribbling**).

* **travel**—meaning, you can't walk or run while holding the ball. The ball has got to be bouncing up and down at all times. (A player is allowed to take only one-and-a-half steps once he has "picked up his dribble"—in other words, once he has stopped dribbling the ball.)

---

*While palming is technically illegal, it's called maybe once a month. All the players do it.

FUN—BUT FAIRLY USELESS—FACTOID

For years, Bob Lanier, the 6'11" Hall of Famer (who played for the Detroit Pistons and the Milwaukee Bucks) had the biggest feet in the NBA—he wore size 22 sneakers. He has since been tied by Shaquille O'Neal, who also wears a size 22. I wonder if what they say is true. . . .

If a player does any of these things (and is caught), the refs call a *violation*, and his team loses possession of the ball. Players must, therefore, perfect a whole rainbow of legal dribbling techniques. These techniques help make basketball fun and unique—dribbling is a big part of what gives the game its hip-hop feel, its rhythm, its urban beat.

Passing

Passing is simply throwing the ball to your teammate, which can be done with a regular throw (from the chest, over the head) or a bounce pass. There are a lot of variations on this theme, though—fancy passes thrown behind the back, for instance, and "no-look" passes where the guy throwing the ball fakes out his opponent by not looking at the teammate to whom he's passing the ball. And there's the always-delightful **alley-oop**. An alley-oop is when the ball is thrown very high from one player to a teammate who is either running down the court toward the basket or waiting right near the basket. The player then catches the ball and dunks it into the basket. Always a crowd-pleaser!

FOULS

Fouls are what slow down the game and extend it from forty-eight minutes to close to two hours (or more, occasionally). When fouls are called, the clock is stopped (it is also stopped when a team calls a *time-out*, when the ball goes out of bounds, and/or when a violation is called).

On the one hand, fouls make the game far more interesting and complex. But they can also ruin the wonderful rhythm that basketball can offer. I'll let the late writer George Plimpton expound upon this idea as he recounts a conversation with the Boston Celtics great, Bill Russell:

BASKETBALL FLICKS FOR HIP CHICKS

White Men Can't Jump (1992): A brilliant satirical comedy starring Wesley Snipes, Woody Harrelson, and Rosie Perez. It's at the top of everyone's hoops movie list.

Hoosiers (1986): Based on the story of a small-town high school team in Indiana that went all the way to the state finals in 1954. This classic story of redemption has a star-studded cast, including Gene Hackman, Barbara Hershey, and Dennis Hopper.

Hoop Dreams (1994): A riveting documentary, *Hoop Dreams* follows two boys from inner-city Chicago along their perilous quest for basketball stardom.

I'll always remember Bill Russell talking to me about "levitating," a phenomenon which today's athletes describe as being "in the zone." On rare occasions, he told me, players from the opposing team get in the zone and "we'd all levitate," as he put it. He would get so involved in the magic of what was going on that chills would go up and down his spine and he'd think, "This is it! We've got to keep this going!" The whole flow of the game had a near balletic feeling to it. . . . Once during a run of this sort, the referee had blown a foul against the opposing team, and Russell had complained. The referee's jaw dropped. What Russell couldn't explain was that the foul call had broken the spell and everything had dropped back to normalcy.

Fouls are as fundamental to basketball as getting the ball into the basket. They happen constantly and give the person fouled upon a chance to score from the free-throw line. It's not uncommon for a baseball game to be played without errors. It is *not possible*, though, for a basketball game to be played without fouls. In any case, if basketball games *were* played without fouls, there wouldn't be time for enough commercials. Or to check out which celebrities were sitting courtside. Or to check out the duds on the dapper coaches.

What Is a Foul?

A foul is any kind of illegal contact between players. Once a player commits six fouls, he "fouls out" and must sit out for the rest of the game.

In basketball, players are not supposed to touch each other—the old "keep your hands to yourself" rule. You're probably thinking, I've seen games where *players touch each other all the time*. And they do—but fouls are not always called. Fouls result in either a change in possession of the ball or a free throw from the free-throw line (one, two, or three free throws, depending on the type of foul), and games can be won and lost at the foul line. There are three categories of fouls: ***personal fouls***, ***flagrant fouls***, and ***technical fouls***.

PERSONAL FOULS

The personal foul is the most common foul. It's your run-of-the-mill getting a little too "hands on" with your opponent. If a player is fouled while in the act of shooting the ball, that player gets two free throws. If that player was attempting a three-point shot, then he gets three free throws. If, despite the foul, the player who was fouled manages to make the basket, he still gets a free throw. This is called an **"and one"** because the player gets the points for the basket and then a chance to score one more point with a free throw. If a foul is committed upon a non-shooting player, or if a player commits a ***loose-ball foul*** (when neither team has the ball), the consequence is only a change of possession—possession goes to the team that did not commit the foul. If the non-offending team already had the ball, it simply retains possession of it.

By the way, a personal foul can be unintentional, but it's still considered a foul.

FLAGRANT FOULS

A flagrant foul is a nastier, more intentional foul defined, according to the NBA, as "unnecessary and/or excessive contact committed by a player against an opponent, whether the ball is dead or alive." It's not always easy to define a flagrant foul, but you'll know it when you see it. When a flagrant foul is called on a player, the opposing team gets to send a player to the free-throw line all by himself to shoot two free throws, with no defenders around. In addition, the fouled-upon team gets possession of the ball after shooting its free throws.

TECHNICAL FOULS

A player is given a technical foul for unsportsmanlike conduct—cursing the ref, for example, or punching an opponent. It's also not unusual for technical fouls to be called against coaches when they get overwrought about something and start throwing temper tantrums. When a technical foul is called, the opposing team gets to send a player to the free-throw line for one free throw, all by himself, with no defenders around. The fouled-upon team gets possession afterward as well.

Or, if the unsportsmanlike conduct is severe enough, the player can be immediately ejected from the game and later disciplined by the league (in the form of a suspension and/or fines).

In sum, fouls can result in a loss of possession of the ball, a free throw or throws, or, very rarely, ejection from the game.

You Say Foul, the Ref Says Fair: *Inconsistency Is the Name of the Game*

Remember in elementary school when *everyone* in class was talking and only *you* would get caught and have to go stand in the coatroom during recess? (Maybe that was just me.) In any case, the calling of fouls in basketball has about the same level of consistency as "talking during class" discipline. Sometimes they call 'em, and sometimes they don't. Commentators will occasionally speak of a game being called "tight," meaning the refs are being strict about calls. Other times, the refs will let a lot of potential fouls go by early in the game, and then the game will start to spiral slightly out of control, at which point, they will step up the vigilance and begin calling it more tightly.

It can be very frustrating when, as a viewer (especially a new viewer), you're trying to figure out what counts as a foul and what doesn't. Bear in mind that if one moment you see a particular move and a foul is called, and then, a little while later, you see the same exact move and no foul is called, you're not going crazy, and you do not need glasses—this is simply the way the game works.

POSITIONS

The good news is that there are only five basic positions in basketball. (There are five players on the court from each team at any given time.) The even better news is that knowing the differences between them is not crucial to understanding the game. Positions in basketball are very different from those in football or baseball, for example, where there are enormous differences between a quarterback and a lineman, or a pitcher and a center fielder. When talking about basketball with those in the know, you'll never need to say that "so-and-so was a great point guard" or whatever—all you'll really need to say is that "so-and-so was a great player." For our purposes, a passing familiarity will suffice.

Great basketball players transcend their position—they do it all. Every position requires every skill—ballhandling, defensive technique, and shooting, shooting, shooting. There is an *emphasis* on different skills for different positions, but they all blend together. The worst shooter on an NBA team was likely the best shooter on his high school or college team. With that disclaimer voiced, let's now take a glance at the positions:

1 Point guard

2 Shooting guard

3 Small forward

4 Power forward

5 Center

The basic formation for a basketball game is two *guards*, two *forwards*, and a *center*. Sometimes coaches vary this arrangement to better defend or compete against their opponent, but it is the fundamental lineup.

Each position has a name and a corresponding number (see page 14). In general, the numbers correspond with the size of the player—in other words, point guards are usually the smallest guys on the team, centers are usually the tallest, and so on. When coaches are planning strategy and coming up with plays, they refer to the positions by their numbers, rather than their names. Unfortunately for those of us just learning the game, many announcers and commentators are starting to call positions by their number—rather than the position itself—as well. For now, though, it's safe to put these numbers in the back of your noggin—they are certainly not crucial to your understanding the game.

Point Guard

The point guard can be compared to a football quarterback, or a director on a movie set (or Martha Stewart arranging a dinner party—pre–criminal record). The point guard is almost like an on-court coach. Because it is his job to get the ball into the hands of players who are best positioned to score, the point guard generally ratchets up a large number of *assists* (i.e., he *assists* his teammates in making shots). He is also typically the one who brings the ball from one end of the court to the other, and he is usually the best ballhandler—the best passer and dribbler—on the team as well. A good point guard sees everything that is going on, interprets what he

DOES SIZE REALLY MATTER?

One of the greatest point guards of all time was Magic Johnson. Point guards have traditionally been smaller, quicker guys, but at six foot nine, Magic was among the first to move away from that notion. (Magic actually played all five positions at one time or another, but he was most known for his work as a point guard.)

sees, moves fast, and directs his teammates. Point guards are also known as the *1-guard* or *lead guard*.

Shooting Guard

The shooting guard has to be able to do everything the point guard does—although maybe not *quite* as well—but as you may have guessed, he is expected to shoot. In fact, more than any other position, he's relied on to score points—lots of them—directly. He is especially counted on for outside or long-range shooting (three-point baskets, as opposed to two-pointers). The major difference between the positions is that the shooting guard is not usually relied upon to bring the ball up the court, as the point guard does. Some shooting guards can do everything a point guard can do *and* shoot really, really well—these players are formidable. There's only one name you need to know in this category: Michael Jordan. He could do everything history-making well. A shooting guard is also known as the *2-guard* or the *off guard*.

Small Forward

Small forwards are not small—they are in fact quite huge. They are called small forwards because they are smaller than power forwards (see below) and are expected to do *some* of what power forwards do, but they also need to be quick, and this quickness is often equated with lightness. Like power forwards, they play close to the basket, but they also need to be able to play on the perimeter.

Power Forward

You're probably expecting me to tell you that power forwards are actually weak, but no, they are typically very powerful. They are big and strong and generally counted on for defense—for blocking the opposing team's shots and getting rebounds. They are among the most physical players and are sometimes called "big forwards." They tend to hang out near the basket in what is called a **post**, or **low post**, position, which explains why they are sometimes called *post players*.

Center

If you look at a basketball team like it's a mini solar system, the guards and the forwards revolve around the *center*. The centers are typically the tallest on the team, and they are counted on both as offensive and defensive players. Defensively, they are relied upon to block shots and get rebounds. Offensively, they are counted on to make baskets—namely to make shots from "inside," or close to the basket.

Nowadays, in the NBA, centers are often seven feet or taller. This explains why these guys are often the ones who seemingly just *put* the ball in the basket (by dunking it or laying it in). They can (like the point guard) set the tone and tempo for the team. And they need to be aggressive and tough—willing to get pushed around to get to the basket.

THE NBA FINALS

The NBA Finals is the annual championship series for the NBA. It is the equivalent of the Super Bowl (football), the World Series (baseball), or the Stanley Cup Finals (hockey). It is a best-of-seven game series that is played in June.

HOW BIG IS *YOUR* AFRO?

If you really want to make an impression (not necessarily a good one) during a conversation about basketball, pose the question of who had the biggest hair in the sport's history. That special honor goes to Darnell Hillman. Hillman played for the American Basketball Association (the ABA), the more flamboyant renegade league that, for nine seasons, competed with the NBA but never reached the audiences that the NBA did. According to *www.remembertheaba.com*, Hillman was the runaway winner of the coveted "Biggest ABA Afro Award" at the 1997 ABA Reunion. For a walk down the memory lane of big male hair from the seventies, check out this site's photo gallery.

THE EVOLUTION OF THE HIGH FIVE IN BASKETBALL

Nowhere will you witness more "high fives" in two hours than in a basketball game. Players give each other high fives when they make a basket and when they don't make a basket; when they are winning and when they are losing; when a lot is at stake in a game and when there is nothing is at stake.

The act of the high five has evolved tremendously over the years. In the old days, the classic, palm-to-palm slap was all that was exercised. Now, there are a variety of choices:

The *three-bump fist move:* Fists are bumped on top of one another three times.

The *horizontal-one-tap fist bump:* It's self-explanatory, and it's currently widely used, as watching any NBA game, college game, or group of guys at a bar will reveal.

The *palm-to-palm-with-the-thumb-interlock-release-and-swipe move:* This is the most complex variation on the high five, and it has been adopted by men, young and old, everywhere (yet try to teach these same men a single dance step . . .).

The *full-body bump:* Players first bump their chests, with emphasis, then roll off each other's bodies and jump backward.

JUST KNOW THIS

The team that gets the most points, which is achieved by getting the ball in the basket, wins. There are two kinds of baskets: *field goals* and *free throws.* A field goal (regular basket) scores two points; a basket earns three points when it is thrown from farther away, from beyond the line designated as the "three-point field goal line."

Fouls—no-no's—are an essential, strategic part of the game. Games are won and lost at the foul line. There are three main types of fouls: *personal fouls*, *flagrant fouls*, and *technical fouls*. The personal foul is the most common foul. It's your run-of-the-mill getting a little touchy-feely with your opponent. Flagrant fouls are more malicious or egregious personal fouls.

Technical fouls are called for bad conduct, fighting, abusive language, and/or other actions that diminish the sport in general. Fouls result in a change of possession of the ball, and/or in one, two, or three free throws. (And technical fouls can sometimes result in a player or coach being ejected from the game.) Each free throw that lands in the basket earns one point.

Watch the last five minutes of a game and you'll be all set for tomorrow's water-cooler chat. No matter what has happened in the previous hour or two of play, the score always ends up being really close at the end of the game—this is when the action heats up.

For the players, timing counts—the game is designed so that no one player or team can hold on to the ball for too long (the *twenty-four-second rule*) or hang out in the lane for more than three seconds (the *three-second rule*).

Shooting is king. Shooting, *passing*, *blocking*, *stealing*, *rebounding* (and flying through the air) are the basic elements of the game, but the remaining four revolve around the shooting. Shoot-

NBA TEAMS	
Atlanta Hawks	New Jersey Nets
Boston Celtics	New Orleans
Charlotte Bobcats	Hornets
Chicago Bulls	New York Knicks
Cleveland Cavaliers	Orlando Magic
Dallas Mavericks	Philadelphia 76ers
Denver Nuggets	Phoenix Sun
Detroit Pistons	Portland Trail
Golden State	Blazers
Warriors	Sacramento Kings
Houston Rockets	San Antonio
Indiana Pacers	Spurs
Los Angeles Clippers	Seattle
Los Angeles Lakers	SuperSonics
Memphis Grizzlies	Toronto Raptors
Milwaukee Bucks	Utah Jazz
Miami Heat	Washington
Minnesota	Wizards
Timberwolves	

ing is like the queen bee of the game; the other components are the worker bees. To *shoot* is to throw the ball toward the basket, with the intention of getting it *in* the basket. To *pass* is to throw the ball to your teammate. To *block* is to block, or prevent, your opponent from shooting the ball. To *steal* is to take the ball away from your opponent. And to *get the rebound* is to get the ball after a shot has been attempted and missed by either team. (After a team *makes* a shot, the opposing team automatically gets the ball.)

The NBA is divided into two conferences, the Eastern Conference and the Western Conference. The Conferences are further divided into divisions: the Eastern Conference is comprised of the Atlantic, Central, and Southeast divisions; the Western conference has the Northwest, Southwest, and Pacific divisions. For a team to get into the NBA Finals, they first have to win their division, then their conference, and then they go to the Finals.

Players You Need to Know

A NOTE ON HEIGHT AND WEIGHT . . .

You'll notice that I've included height and weight for the basketball players. In basketball, height, and to a certain extent overall size (nowadays more than ever as we see men like Shaquille O'Neal), is such a big part of the game, I thought such measurements were important to include.

The Legends

KAREEM ABDUL-JABBAR, 1947–

   7'2", 267 lbs.
   1969–75: Milwaukee Bucks
   1975–89: Los Angeles Lakers

I'll begin with a brief personal Kareem story:

   If you were to ask my husband, Bob, what the best day of his life was, he would dutifully answer, "Well, there are two: the day I got married, and the day my son was born." That would be a big fat lie. The best day of his life was when Kareem Abdul-Jabbar high-fived him. It was the early eighties, and as we were walking into the Hyatt Regency hotel in Boston, Kareem and his teammates were leaving to board the team bus. As Kareem passed by, my husband said, "Hey, Kareem, have a good game." To my husband's shock and joy, Kareem turned to him, said, "Thanks, man," and gave him a high five. (For the record, it was an old-fashioned, palm-to-palm one.) My husband was transformed into a little boy with a dropped jaw, overcome with awe and rapture. If he could have avoided ever washing his hands again, he would have.

Kareem Abdul-Jabbar scored *38,387* points—more points than any other basketball player in history. If you ever want to talk about Kareem, just throw out any basketball move or honor and then say "more than any other player in NBA history." Kareem blocked more shots, received more MVP* awards . . . yada, yada, yada.

Kareem's signature shot was the sky hook, which he used to great effect with the Milwaukee Bucks and the Los Angeles Lakers—the two teams for which he played. His signature *look* was his glasses—you can always recognize Kareem in photos by his goggle-like specs.

Although Kareem enjoyed a brilliant twenty-year career (he played until he was forty-two!) unmarred by drugs, rape charges, fights, or anything scandalous, he has had his struggles. As an intellectual and something of a loner, Kareem wasn't a fan favorite—he didn't kowtow to the fans or the press and was perceived as aloof. As his career was winding down he did begin to open up, though, at which point the fans embraced him.

Kareem was born Ferdinand Lewis Alcindor in New York City and was known as Lew Alcindor when he first started playing pro ball for the Milwaukee Bucks. He changed his name in the early seventies when he converted to Islam. If a conversation about Kareem ensues, and you casually drop a comment about the "former Lew Alcindor," you will rule.

LARRY BIRD, 1956–
NICKNAME: "BIRD"

6'9", 220 lbs.

1979–92: Boston Celtics

Larry Bird—"Bird" is enough when talking basketball—is a legendary Boston Celtics player, and he is one half of a great NBA rivalry with Magic Johnson of the L.A. Lakers.

---

*MVP = Most Valuable Player

In the 1980s, the Magic Johnson/Larry Bird show revitalized the Celtics and the NBA. Their competitive duet started in college when Bird was at Indiana State University and Magic was at Michigan State. In the 1979 NCAA tournament, Indiana State was undefeated until the national championship game, where they faced Magic and the Spartans. That game still stands as the most widely watched college basketball telecast ever. And that was just the beginning. Magic and Bird both went pro later that same year, and at the end of their first pro season in 1980, Bird was named Rookie of the Year and Magic was named MVP of the NBA Finals (as a rookie!).

In his thirteen years with the Celtics, Bird led his team to three NBA championships—and he really did *lead*. As a player, he truly used his skills and abilities to make those around him better.

Bird grew up dirt poor in French Lick, Indiana, and entered big-time basketball as "the hick from French Lick," with a five-year, $3.25 million contract. According to *Sports Illustrated* writer Jackie MacMullan, Bird "won the affection of his fans with a disarming frankness and a fierce determination to offset the glare of stardom by stubbornly remaining true to himself." Once, as recounted by *Sports Illustrated* writer Gerry Callahan in 1998, Bird was at a pub in Dallas with *Boston Globe* writer Dan Shaughnessy, when the streets became filled with roaming young people. Bird asked Shaughnessy what was going on, and Shaughnessy told him that Bruce Springsteen was playing in town.

"Who's he?" asked Bird.

"Who's he?!" repeated Shaughnessy, stunned. "Larry, he's the you of rock and roll."

Bird shrugged and returned to his beer.

"He must be pretty good, then," he said.

In the eighties, there was a fairly popular belief that if Bird had been black, he would have been just another player. But Magic Johnson helped put the silliness to rest when he said, "It's hard to look at a white man and see black, but when I look at Larry, that's what I see. I see myself." While he couldn't fly like Michael Jordan, and he doesn't hold records for the most points scored, Larry Bird is one of the best *all-around* players basketball has ever seen.

WILT CHAMBERLAIN, 1936–1999
NICKNAME: "WILT THE STILT," "THE BIG DIPPER"
7'1", 275 lbs.

1959–62: Philadelphia Warriors

1962–65: San Francisco Warriors

1965–68: Philadelphia 76ers

1968–73: Los Angeles Lakers

I could go right into Wilt's extraordinary career and why his name always comes up in talking about the greatest legends of all time, but that would mean ignoring the pink elephant in the room: In his 1991 autobiography *A View from Above*, Wilt claimed that he slept with 20,000 women.* I've done the math so you don't have to: Based on Wilt Chamberlain's claim, and assuming he started sleeping with women at age fifteen (he was fifty when his autobiography was published), he had to have averaged 571.42 different women a year, or 1.56 women a day (no days off). In calculating this figure, I have determined that the entire math section of the SAT could be based on Wilt's sexual prowess (which would no doubt increase the scores of high school boys everywhere). Think of the possibilities:

If NBA basketball great Wilt Chamberlain left Los Angeles at 8:00 P.M., after having sex with two women that day, arrived in New York at 6:00 A.M., and had sex with three women before 9 A.M., calculate Mr. Chamberlain's new lifetime average, considering the time change. Please show all your work (pictures are not necessary).

Okay, enough of that. The most important *basketball* detail of Wilt the Stilt's career is that he scored *one hundred points* in a single game. He's the only player ever to do that in the NBA. It happened in Hershey, Pennsylvania, on March 2, 1962—final score: Philadelphia Warriors 169, New York Knicks 147. (Yes, Wilt was on the winning team.) Aside from

---

*Note that no one took this exaggerated number seriously . . . although, with his talent, his sexy goatee, and his muscular 7'1" frame, it may not be as exaggerated as one might think. . . .

being known for scoring (pun intended), Wilt was also known for his amazing endurance (pun also intended). During the extraordinary 1961–62 season—of which his one hundred-point game was the highlight—Wilt was just eight minutes shy of playing every minute of every game—including seven overtime games. That's like triple back-to-back spin classes.

Wilt was so good, so big, and so dominating that NBA rules were actually changed because of him. The "lane" (the rectangular painted area under and in front of the basket) was widened, and the offensive goal-tending rule was instituted. So if anyone tries to dis Wilt, just come back with the fact that he literally changed the rules—and that, in more than three decades, no one has come close to doing what he did in Hershey, Pennsylania.

JULIUS ERVING, 1950–
NICKNAME: "DR. J." "DOCTAH"
6'7", 210 lbs.
1976–87: Philadelphia 76ers

If you call Julius Erving "Julius Erving" (à la "My name is Forrest Gump. People call me Forrest Gump"), you will sound like a giant sports dork. He was and always will be "Dr. J."—or perhaps "Doctah!"—but never just "Julius Erving."

As you've learned, Wilt Chamberlain changed the game near the basket (*low post*); Dr. J. changed it *all over the court*. In a game of jazzy, hip-hop rhythms, Dr. J. was a star performer. He added razzle-dazzle acrobatics to the game, and was the first to spend seemingly endless moments in the air, levitating toward the basket. (Michael Jordan became the master at this, earning the moniker "Air Jordan," but the Doctah supplied the original formula.) As *Washington Post* sportswriter Tony Kornheiser observed: "Doc took the game off the ground and into the air—reinventing it with each flight—playing a kind of jazz that was as accessible as it was futuristic." Before Dr. J., it was more common for the ball to be directed toward the center (the big guy near the basket), who was then expected to go for the shot. Not so once Dr. J., a forward, entered the game. Dr. J. ushered pro basketball forward from competition to *entertainment*.

Dr. J. was the MVP in the 1980–81 season. He took the 76ers to the NBA Finals three times (1980, 1982, and 1983), but they didn't win the championship until 1983, when another great player, Moses Malone, joined the team. The Dr. J./Malone duo was an unstoppable force.

Dr. J. remains one of only a handful of players to score more than 30,000 career points* (the others are Kareem Abdul-Jabbar, Karl Malone, Michael Jordan, and Wilt Chamberlain). And on top of his enormous skill, Dr. J. possessed grace and dignity. When more and more black players began playing professional basketball in the 1970s, fewer whites began attending and viewing games. Dr. J. changed that—he was a black superstar embraced by whites. The Basketball Hall of Fame says of him, "Erving is simply known as basketball's ambassador to the world."

FUN FACTOID

Here's a handy little piece of Dr. J. trivia to toss around when you're bored, or perhaps when you want to gain the immediate respect of male sports fanatics: Howard Stern, Eddie Murphy, and Dr. J. all went to Roosevelt High School in Hempstead, Long Island.

EARVIN "MAGIC" JOHNSON, 1959–
NICKNAME: "MAGIC"
6'9", 225 lbs.
1979–91, 1995–96: Los Angeles Lakers

"What do Mary Tyler Moore and Magic Johnson have in common? Both could turn on the world with their smile."

Sounds like a woman said that, right? Nope. It was Larry Schwartz of

---

*Dr. J.'s 30,000 points include the points he scored in both the ABA and the NBA.

ESPN.com, and it just goes to show the effect that Magic's warmth, strength, and sweetness has on people.

If you Google Magic Johnson, the first item that comes up out of almost a million hits is the Magic Johnson Foundation, which is dedicated to the needs of minority youth and their underserved communities throughout the nation. Scholarships, the fight against youth AIDS, community development—Magic's organization is involved with all of these causes.

Oh, and the other important thing that you need to know about Magic is that he has HIV, which, magically, hasn't taken the smile off his face. When he announced this news on November 7, 1991, he immediately transformed attitudes toward this scourge: Being who he is, Magic took the shame of having HIV away for many people, and he also demonstrated that a diagnosis of HIV was *not* a death sentence.

In the NBA, it didn't take long for Magic to make his mark. During his 1979 rookie season with the L.A. Lakers, he scored 42 points in an NBA Finals game and went from rookie to legend right then and there. His legacy isn't as a shooter, however, but as an all-around player. He took the position of point guard to new heights with his no-look passes and his drives (moving the ball toward the net) that went from end-to-end on the court. He electrified the game with his passing, rebounding, shooting, and showmanship.

Smiling up and down the court and leading in assists, Magic reminded us all of the point of and the fun in teamwork. His team spirit and overall expertise earned him the NBA Most Valuable Player Award three times, and he led the Lakers to five NBA championships in his twelve seasons with the team.

MICHAEL JORDAN, 1963–
NICKNAME: "AIR JORDAN"
6'6", 216 lbs.
1984–93, 1994–98: Chicago Bulls
2001–03: Washington Wizards

I'm convinced that an alien could land on earth, watch Michael play, and know he was great. You don't have to know a thing about basketball to be mesmerized by him. As Baryshnikov was to ballet, as Pavarotti was to opera, as Johnny Carson was to late-night TV, so was Jordan to basketball.

While some basketball fans will debate whether he is the *greatest* player of all time, Michael was, and still is, the most *famous* hoops man ever. This is largely due to the fact that he was the right man at the right time. As you read about the great players, a pattern emerges—the truly great, those who transcend their sport, were those who had a symbiotic relationship with history. Football quarterback Joe Namath was the perfect personality for the newly dominant TV era, for instance, and Muhammad Ali was the force needed to ratchet up the stature and pride of blacks in sports and America in the 1960s. Michael unleashed his talent in the global age, the satellite age, and thus became the biggest *international* sports star. He was known and adored by people all over the world.

Much of Michael's fame and fortune were superheated by marketing and his sponsorships with Nike, Gatorade, and numerous other companies and products. In 1992, Jordan earned $3.8 million playing basketball and a whopping $21.2 million from endorsements; but as Nelson George noted in *ESPN SportsCentury*, "Nobody . . . questioned Jordan's right to every damn dollar . . . because he gave America something it so desperately craved and so rarely received: soul-satisfying artistry and undiluted excellence. In an age of hype (and commensurate disappointment) Jordan delivered and delivered."

So just what did he deliver? you might be getting impatient to know. Dunks galore, breathtaking fadeaway shots, ethereal hang time. He could shoot, pass, rebound, and soar. He wasn't the *best* shooter, or the *best* rebounder, or the *best* passer in history, but he was fierce and breathtaking all at once, and he was magnificent with the game on the line.

Michael took the Chicago Bulls to six championships. He was a five-time NBA MVP and a six-time NBA Finals MVP. He worked and worked at his craft and never took his gift for granted—he is widely quoted as saying: "I have missed more than 9,000 shots in my career. I have lost almost 300 games. On twenty-six occasions I have been entrusted to take the game-winning shot . . . and I missed. I have failed over and over and over again in my life. And that's precisely why I succeed." And that's precisely why he is a true role model.

Michael prematurely retired from the Bulls in 1993 following the tragic death of his father. James Jordan, whom Michael often referred to as his best friend, was driving home from a wedding on July 23, 1993. He had apparently pulled over to the side of the highway near Wilmington, North Carolina, to take a nap. Days later his body was found in a nearby river with a fatal gunshot wound. Michael was inconsolable.

After leaving the Bulls and having his number 23 retired, Michael decided to try his hand at professional baseball, but he lasted only a brief time in the minor leagues. He then decided to return to basketball in 1994, but wearing a different number, 45. Whether it was because of bad karma from switching numbers, or because he hadn't fully recovered from his loss, or because he only played in seventeen games that season, the Bulls did not win the championship in 1995.

When Michael returned for the following season, he decided to don number 23 once again. Maybe he was just more fit mentally, or maybe there is just some magic behind that number, but that year the Bulls went all the way and won the championship (against the Seattle SuperSonics) at home in Chicago's United Center on June 16, 1996, which happened to be Father's Day. At the final buzzer, Michael wrestled the ball from the hands of teammate Randy Brown and struggled through the crowd to the locker room where he lay down and wept for his father. As David Halberstam wrote, "This was a key image of the era, and one for the ages. After a career of on-court highlights and poised on-camera appearances to hawk products, here was Michael Jordan, emotionally naked, overwhelmed by a mix of grief and satisfaction beautiful in its truth."

After retiring from the Bulls in 1999—this time as a winner—Jordan was appointed president of basketball operations for the Washington Wizards, and he became a partial owner of the team. After two years of management, however, he was lured back onto the court. He signed on as a player for two years—which meant giving up his ownership and executive position—after which, in 2003, he decided that he was retiring for good.

KARL MALONE, 1963–
NICKNAME: "THE MAILMAN"
6'9", 259 lbs.

1985–2003: Utah Jazz

2003–04: Los Angeles Lakers

The Mailman. This is the nickname that was given to him in college (Louisiana Tech) because he *always* delivered. He delivered for a long time, playing past the age of forty. Malone spent eighteen years with the Utah Jazz and then joined the L.A. Lakers in 2003. During the 2004–05 season, he was a free agent (i.e., he didn't have a contract with a team) and was sitting out the season because of an injury. Ultimately, in February 2005, he announced his plans to retire.

Malone is considered one of the greatest power forwards ever. Among his many accomplishments, he:

* is the second-highest all-time scorer in the league (behind Kareem Abdul-Jabbar);

* holds the records for most free throws attempted and made in the NBA;

* and was a two-time league MVP (1997, 1999).

We usually think "city kid" when we think of basketball players, but Malone is more of a country boy. He has a ranch in Arkansas and is a passionate hunter *and* environmentalist. Malone is also a model citizen. He was selected by *The Sporting News* in 1999 as one of the "99 Good Guys in Sports," due primarily to acts such as helping to pay off a mortgage for a family with four sick children; donating $200,000 worth of supplies to Navajo Indians; and building a playground for handicapped children at an elementary school. He won the 1998 Henry B. Iba Award for athletes who go out of their way to help others, and founded the Karl Malone Foundation for Kids, which helps children and families through difficult times.

SHAQUILLE O'NEAL, 1972–
NICKNAME: "SHAQ"

> 7'1", 325+ lbs.
> 1992–96: Orlando Magic
> 1996–2004: Los Angeles Lakers
> 2004–present: Miami Heat

"Shaq" is considered the dominant force in basketball today. In 1996, when the NBA announced the fifty greatest players in NBA history, Shaq—who had played only *four seasons*—was already included on this list.

There are many reasons to love Shaq. *Sports Illustrated*'s Rick Reilly used his column of June 5, 2000, to send a thank-you note of sorts to the legend, enumerating the reasons why we should love him. Reilly pointed out how Shaq doesn't show up in the sports pages kids read with a bowl of cocaine and a gun. Nor has he ever been accused of a D.U.I. Nor has he been accused of abusing women in any way. Reilly also reported that Shaq quoted Aristotle a few days before he wrote his column, saying, "You are what you repeatedly do."

What Shaq does is give away a lot of money—in big chunks of, say, a million dollars, to organizations like the Boys and Girls Clubs of America, and in smaller doses to friends in need. He also dresses up as "Shaq-a-Bunny" at Easter and "Shaq-a-Claus" at Christmas for charitable causes. Shaq refuses to take his celebrity and status for granted—he's made it his mission, it seems, to repeatedly make people happy, on and off the court.

It's this wonderful attitude that *Sports Illustrated* writer Jack McCallum summed up when he wrote, "Unlike most giants, he walks among us." And unlike most giants, he is agile, and can thus do spectacular things on the court. Shaq began his professional career with the Orlando Magic. Then in 1995, he began playing for the L.A. Lakers—the team he led to three consecutive NBA championships via three consecutive Finals MVP awards. At the end of the 2003–04 season, Shaq headed to Miami to join the Heat.

DAVID ROBINSON, 1965–
NICKNAME: "THE ADMIRAL"
7'1", 250 lbs.
1989–2003: San Antonio Spurs

When you hear the phrase "officer and a gentleman," ladies, you need to replace the image etched in your mind (of Richard Gere in a white uniform gallantly carrying Debra Winger into the distance) with that of David Robinson. Robinson, who retired in 2003 after winning a second NBA championship for the San Antonio Spurs, has a reputation for being an exceptionally good guy.

Robinson is a real-life officer—he's a graduate of the United States Naval Academy (hence his nickname, "The Admiral"). He was drafted by the Spurs in 1987, but he made them wait for two years while he fulfilled his commitment to the Navy. He was definitely worth waiting for. The Spurs were playing pretty pathetically before the Admiral came on board. In his rookie season, for which he earned rookie-of-the-year honors, Robinson led the Spurs to fifty-six wins, a thirty-five-game improvement over their previous season and the greatest single-season turnaround of any team in NBA history. He was technically a center, but like all great players, Robinson could do it all. He was named MVP of the NBA in 1995 and is the Spurs's all-time leading scorer.

And *then* the great Tim Duncan joined, and this commanding duo led their team to two NBA championship victories (1999, 2003). The Robinson-Duncan twosome is amazing both on and off the court. Because of their talent and decency, they were named *Sports Illustrated* Sportsmen of the Year in 2003. In the fifty-plus years that *SI* has been awarding this honor, only seven times have they given it to a twosome, and only once before to a twosome of teammates.* Upon bestowing the honor,

---

*In 2001, Randy Johnson and Curt Schilling, who at the time were both pitchers for the Arizona Diamondbacks, received this honor for leading their team—which had been in existence only for four years—to a World Series victory.

the *SI* editors said that Robinson and Duncan demonstrated "that achievement and citizenship are not mutually exclusive."

Robinson doesn't like a lot of hoopla. He is married with three kids, and he is a devout Christian who practices what he preaches. In 1992, he established the Carver Academy, an elementary school that serves many disadvantaged children in the San Antonio area. Not only has he shelled out about $9 million for the Academy, but he and his wife also devote countless hours and energy to the school. Upon his retirement from the Spurs in 2003, Robinson said that he preferred donations to the school rather than gifts or ceremonies, commenting, "Life is not all about making as much money as you can and being as famous as you can; it's about service."

BILL RUSSELL, 1934–

6'10", 220 lbs.
1956–69: Boston Celtics

The bio of Russell at the Basketball Hall of Fame's Web site (www.hoophall.com) states, "Without a doubt, Russell was the greatest defensive center in the history of basketball." Note that there are no qualifiers here, no "*one* of the greatest"s, no disclaimer stating this is *arguably* so. He was simply, without a doubt, the best.

Russell was king of the rebound and the block, and like his rival, Wilt Chamberlain, he changed the game. Before Russell, the prevailing thinking was that championships were won by offense, but he changed all that by making *defense* a winning strategy. The proof is in the pudding—Russell won eleven NBA championships with the Boston Celtics in thirteen seasons. (That's like finding the perfect pair of jeans, in your size, at fifty percent off, on eighty-five percent of your shopping trips—or something like that.) At the beginning of the 1967 season, Russell succeeded the legendary Red Auerbach as head coach of the Celtics, making him the first black coach in the NBA. (He played *and* coached from 1967–69.)

When writing about Russell, race cannot be ignored. He entered the NBA in 1956, less than ten years after Jackie Robinson broke baseball's racial barrier. Then, and for years to come, the country was gripped by paroxysms of the changing tides of racism, and nowhere more harshly than in Boston, home of the Celtics. In *ESPN SportsCentury*, Tony Kornheiser notes that "it's intriguing . . . that the great Celtic dynasty was fueled by Russell and Red Auerbach, a black and a Jew, two outsiders in clannish, Catholic Boston." Kornheiser goes on to say that Russell differed from Robinson, "who courageously endured the virus of racism in silence as part of the pact he made with [his team's president and general manager] to be the perfect pioneer and martyr if need be. Russell represented a new type of black athlete: the educated, outspoken, defiant star, seeking—no, expecting—respect just for who he was."

Russell's coolness on the court and his unfathomable ability to rebound and block shots captivated fans. His dignity and intelligence earned him respect. Russell also knew how and when to retire from the game. He played with passion, and when that ebbed, he quit with the same dignity with which he played.

Legends in Training

KOBE BRYANT, 1978–

6'6", 220 lbs.

1996–present: Los Angeles Lakers

"What do you see when you see Kobe Bryant? The best player in the NBA? An accused rapist? An intelligent, charismatic, twenty-five-year-old athlete? A spoiled superstar?"

Karl Taro Greenfeld posed these questions in the March 24, 2004, issue of *Sports Illustrated.* Unfortunately for Kobe—with headlines such as THE COLLAPSE OF KOBE (the *New York Times,* December 2004) far outnumbering the positive ones these days—it seems "spoiled superstar" is winning in popularity.

Kobe's fall from grace wouldn't have made headlines if his fall hadn't been from a rather spectacular height. The youngest player ever to play in an NBA game, Kobe Bryant, as an eighteen-year-old, made his NBA debut on November 3, 1996, with the Los Angeles Lakers. By the time he was twenty-four, he had helped the Lakers win three NBA championships (2000, 2001, 2002). In March 2003, he became the youngest player in NBA history to reach the 10,000-point mark. And 2003 was looking like a great year for this abundantly talented young man.

But in the summer of '03, Kobe seemed to forget that he was considered to be the next Michael Jordan; that he was paid handsomely by both the NBA and numerous companies whose products he endorsed; and that he was a husband and father. On June 30, 2003, at a hotel and spa in Colorado, Kobe had a sexual encounter with a woman who was an employee of the hotel. Shortly thereafter, she accused him of rape, and Kobe was charged with felony sexual assault. Kobe admitted to being an adulterer, but maintained his innocence regarding the rape charges. In the fall of 2004, the charges were dropped. Whoopee—he's only an adulterer, not a rapist. The thing is, the public—and the companies who want to sell products to that public—don't really like adulterers much.

Then the Lakers fell apart in the 2004 NBA Finals against the Detroit Pistons, and the team imploded. Shaq was traded to the Miami Heat, and uber-coach Phil Jackson left.* Although it's never been proven, the widely held belief is that Kobe was responsible for convincing the Lakers management to ditch Shaq and Jackson, in an effort to commandeer the spotlight for himself.

TIM DUNCAN, 1976–

6'11", 260 lbs.

1997–present: San Antonio Spurs

Tim Duncan doesn't fit the stereotypical persona of "NBA cool." He is quiet to the point of stoicism; he lacks your typical NBA charisma. But if coolness is measured in talent, then it's a whole different matter.

Duncan is one of today's greatest players and is sure to earn a place in the Basketball Hall of Fame. He's won three NBA Finals MVP awards

---

*In an unexpected turn of events, Phil Jackson will return as coach of the Lakers in 2005, it was announced in June 2005.

(1999, 2003, 2005), and he also won back-to-back NBA MVP awards in 2002 and 2003, the first player since Michael Jordan to do so.

Sportswriters seem to struggle with Duncan because he's everything everyone claims that a sports hero/role model/professional should be—pure, honest, loyal, talented, and hardworking—and yet, while they know he's good, his extreme shyness and his refusal to accept the spotlight have made it difficult for many to articulate exactly *why*. In 2003, during the NBA Finals, William Rhoden of the *New York Times* wrote: "Duncan lacks Shaquille O'Neal's presence . . . Kevin Garnett's sense of theater, and Allen Iverson's penchant for playing on the edge. But Duncan takes consistency to a new level." That same week, Jack McCallum noted in *Sports Illustrated* that "Duncan doesn't seem to be stronger or quicker or more explosive than the average player; the prosaic economy of his game is, paradoxically, its most distinctive characteristic."

"Consistency"? "Prosaic economy"? Unfortunately, words seem to diminish his talent. In 2003, he received one of the highest accolades in sports when he and fellow Spurs teammate David Robinson were chosen as *Sports Illustrated*'s Sportsmen of the Year.

ALLEN IVERSON, 1975–

6'0", 165 lbs.
1996–present: Philadelphia 76ers

Allen Iverson is an amazing basketball player, but he's had his troubles. Let's get the ugly stuff out of the way first.

Iverson has been arrested for gun possession, marijuana possession, and assault (although many of the charges have been dropped). A lot of his friends have died way too young. His father is serving time for assault. A surrogate father for Iverson named Tony Clark was killed by Tony's girl-friend.

Less bad, but still not good, is that Iverson produced and performed a rap CD (while playing for the NBA) with lyrics that featured offensive terms for women and gays and that set off a storm of criticism and prompted some civil rights groups to demand an apology.

Even as a basketball player, Iverson was a renegade—he was repeatedly late for practice and unconcerned about what his teammates, coaches, the NBA, or the fans thought of him.

You'll notice that everything I've written about Iverson thus far has been in the past tense. This is because, when Iverson turned twenty-five, he made a resolution to change his bad-boy ways. A year later, on his twenty-sixth birthday, he was able to say: "For the first time in my life, I'm conducting myself on and off the court like a professional. And it just took some growing up, you know?" He made this statement in June 2001, and he's maintained the good behavior ever since.

On the court, Iverson has always had his act together—despite the disrespect he showed toward his profession and toward the NBA in his earlier years. He's scored more than forty points in a game more than fifty times, and he's known for his fearlessness, his toughness, his energy, and, of course, his ability. And let's remember that at 6'0" and 165 pounds, he's competing against many guys a foot taller and a hundred pounds heavier than him. Iverson was the reason the 76ers were able, after a six-year drought, to get into the Finals in 2001. That same year, he was awarded league MVP honors.

LEBRON JAMES, 1984–

6'8", 240 lbs.

2003–present: Cleveland Cavaliers

LeBron James = $100 million. For better or worse, this is what comes to mind when I hear his name. He's a kid, literally—born in 1984—who traveled at the speed of light from high school to the NBA in 2003, passing "GO" along the way and picking up a neat $10.8 million contract (chump change in light of the endorsement deals worth more than $100 million that were also secured before he ever bounced an NBA ball).

So far, the ones who are paying him the big bucks can breathe a sigh of relief. James hasn't just lived up to everyone's expectations—he's shone. He achieved a remarkable first season with the Cleveland Cavaliers, earning the Rookie of the Year Award, the youngest winner ever. In addition:

* James's points, rebounds, and assists in his rookie year rivaled those achieved during Michael Jordan's rookie year.

* During one game against the New Jersey Nets he scored forty-one points, making him the youngest player in the league to break forty.

* In more than thirteen different games, he scored more than thirty points.

* Since he began playing for the Cavaliers, home attendance during the 2003–04 season soared from 11,497 to 18,288—the highest increase in a single season in the past twenty years for an NBA team that hadn't moved into a new stadium.

James's second season (2004–05) wasn't too shabby either. He played even better, impressive enough for the February 2005 issue of *Sports Illustrated* to feature him on the cover with two words: "Best Ever?"

JASON KIDD, 1973–

6'4", 210 lbs.
1994–97: Dallas Mavericks
1996–2001: Phoenix Suns
2001–present: New Jersey Nets

Jason Kidd is the savior of the New Jersey Nets. Until Kidd joined the team in 2001, the Nets were "more laden with lameness than any other team," as *Time*'s Joel Stein put it. But then Kidd came along and took the lameness out of this team in a hurry.

Kidd is a point guard who is often compared to his hero, Magic Johnson. He has the same ability as Magic to command the court—he knows where every player is at all times and is a genius at passing the ball to whatever guy is in the best position to make the basket. As John Hareas wrote in *NBA's Greatest*: "There aren't many players in the history of the NBA who can dominate a game without scoring a single point. Jason Kidd is one of those players."

But don't be mistaken—the man can shoot, too. He, again like Magic, is referred to as a "triple-double," a player who racks up double-digit points, rebounds, and assists in a single game. He does this a lot.

However, Kidd's reputation as an NBA celebrity has not always been stellar: A few years ago, Kidd was arrested for punching his wife in the face, and the public's impression of him changed forever. But the ordeal seemed to serve as a transforming event for Kidd. He accepted full responsibility, went for counseling, and apologized publicly and privately. It appears he's making his marriage work—Jason and his wife have remained together and are raising three children.

What didn't seem to work for Kidd was Phoenix, where he was playing for the Suns at the time of the incident. He was traded to the Nets not long afterward in 2001, and he seems to have been a new man ever since. Kidd led the Nets to back-to-back Finals in 2002 and 2003.

DIRK NOWITZKI, 1978–

7'0", 260 lbs.

1997–present: Dallas Mavericks

Nowitzki is an international import—from Germany—which automatically makes him NBA cool. More important, he is big, agile, and versatile. He can shoot from anywhere—particularly from outside the arc (three-pointers)—he's quick, and he's an excellent passer. He's technically a forward, but he can pretty much do it all.

Some hard-core American basketball fans originally cast a skeptical eye on European imports, claiming that they were too soft, too silky smooth, to play in the rough, tough NBA. Nowitzki put these Ameri-centric notions to rest once and for all. Nowitzki is sometimes compared to Larry Bird, and even if this were only because they're both blond, it would be an undeniably awesome comparison. But the comparisons are in fact made because Nowitzki exhibits the same versatility, the same touch and feel for the game, that Bird once did. Lucky Nowitzki. Lucky Dallas Mavericks. Lucky NBA. Lucky spectators.

YAO MING, 1980–

> 7'6", 310 lbs.
> 2002–present: Houston Rockets

Yao Ming is from China. Yup, he was born and raised in Shanghai, where he played basketball for the Shanghai Sharks and was voted the MVP of China's national league twice before moving to the United States and joining the Houston Rockets. Even among the many international players the NBA has recently signed, Yao stands out. One obvious reason is that he is 7'6" and 310 pounds, the tallest player in the NBA.

The NBA in particular loves Yao Ming because they see him as a way of sparking not just national but *international* interest in NBA games. According to *Sports Illustrated*, "in the eternal search for the It Guy, Yao is now." The marketeers share this view: Yao earned about $4 million for the 2003–04 season, and by the fall of 2004, with endorsements from McDonald's, Gatorade, Pepsi, and Reebok, he was already earning $25–$30 million in addition to his contract.

But the truth is, no one really knows yet if Yao will be a great player or simply a good one. Cultural differences influence the way he plays the game. Early in his NBA career, for instance, he didn't dunk—even though he's 7'6"! In China, players are taught not to embarrass opponents, and a dunk, especially a slam dunk, is an in-your-face move partially designed to rattle your opponents' mojo. Still, despite his less aggressive approach, Yao, as of the 2004–05 season, ranks seventh in field-goal percentage and among NBA leaders in both blocked shots per game and rebounding average. And, as starting center, he was a big reason why the Rockets made it into the postseason in 2004 and again in 2005.

Glossary

Air Ball: A shot that doesn't hit the rim, the net, the backboard, or anything. Just air. (Think "totally embarrassing"—and by the way, air balls were my forte during my short-lived high school basketball career.) I suppose if a player is only, say, 6'6" and is being defended by seven-footers, it's bound to happen now and then, but still—it looks so . . . well . . . *lame.*

Alley-oop: When a player lobs the ball high in the air to a teammate who is either running down the court or right near the basket, who then catches it and dunks it or otherwise gets it into the basket. It's as fun to watch as it is to say.

And One: If a player is fouled in the act of shooting the ball, and the ball goes into the basket anyway, he is still entitled to a free throw. So, the player gets two points for making the basket *and one* more if he makes the free throw. In order to not sound dorky, it must be said with emphasis—aaand *one!*

Bank Shot: Any basket that is made by first deflecting the ball off the backboard (i.e., a shot in which the ball first hits the board and then plops into the basket). There's a small square painted on the glass in the center of the backboard, just above the basket. If the ball hits this square, it is likely to fall into the basket.

Block (a Shot): A defensive player can legally block the shot of an opponent as long as he doesn't make physical contact with the opponent nor impede the opponent's progress. He can flail his arms wildly, keep his body positioned in a way that makes it difficult for the player with the ball to get a good shot at the basket, but he can't push, shove, or hold his opponent.

Blocking: A type of personal foul. A defensive player cannot impede the progress of the player with the ball. The defensive player can be all over him, and/or do the hokey pokey to force the player with the ball to miss the shot, pass badly, or just lose the ball, but he can't set up a road block.

Box Out: Boxing out is crucial to defensive basketball strategy—primarily to getting the rebound. To box out is to stick your tushy in front of your opponent's . . . well, crotch, I guess. It's like spooning among giant athletes, while standing up.

Charging: What you do when you *must* have the new Coach handbag that you really can't afford. Or, if we assume that basketball players aren't interested in Coach handbags, what happens when an offensive player (usually with the ball) runs into a defensive player who is correctly positioned and just trying to do his job. Charging is a personal foul that results in a change of possession of the ball.

Deep Threat: 1. Misspelling of a well-known porn movie. 2. Misspelling of the source in the Watergate scandal story. 3. Women who are smarter, more capable, and earn more than their male counterparts. 4. A player who is really good at making long shots and three-pointers.

Dribble: Not the same as to drool. Dribbling is the art of bouncing the ball on the floor. (Oh yes, bouncing a ball is an art.)

Drive in Traffic: See *Traffic*, below.

Double Dribble: This often happens to a nonathlete after receiving Novocain at the dentist. For basketball players, a double dribble is a violation. When a player double dribbles, it means that he dribbles, stops (and holds the ball in his hands), then dribbles again. A player must continuously dribble while he is moving with the ball.

Dunk: When a player literally dunks the ball into the basket, like a doughnut into a cup of coffee (albeit a cup of coffee that has no bottom and in which the doughnut would fall right through). This doughnut dunk would have to be pretty splashy, too, because the basketball dunk usually has a bit of drama to it. It's a definitive motion—it carries an *I'm puttin' the ball in the basket, so take that!* kind of attitude.

Fadeaway (or Fall-away): When a player is attempting a fadeaway, he bends backward, away from the basket, as he releases the ball. It is one of the more difficult shots, and it is almost impossible to defend when done properly. This was Michael Jordan's signature shot. Like everything he did, he made it look easy.

Field Goal: A regular basket that is made while the ball is in play—i.e., not from the free-throw line. Field goals are worth two points, except for those that are made from beyond the aptly named "three-point field goal line" (aka, the perimeter, or arc). From there, baskets earn three points.

Finger Roll: A shot in which the ball is rolled off the fingers and into the basket.

Flagrant Foul: As you now know, basketball players are supposed to avoid touching each other on the court at all costs. They're not homophobic (some might be, but that's not my business), they're just following the rules. Illegal contact results in a foul. When it's obviously intentional and more than just a minor touchy-feely moment, the ref will deem it a flagrant foul.

Foul: The umbrella term for any kind of illegal contact between players (during the game, at least). There are three main categories of fouls: *personal fouls*, *flagrant fouls*, and *technical fouls*. The most common is the personal foul. Sometimes (and always when it's a shooting foul) fouls result in a free throw (or throws) for the player who was fouled. Other times they result in a change in possession of the ball.

Foul Out: A player cannot commit six personal fouls during a game. If he commits six, he "fouls out," meaning he cannot continue playing in that game.

Free Throw: After certain types of fouls, the player who was fouled goes "to the line," which is the free-throw line, and gets one, two, or three free throws at the basket, depending on the situation. The clock is stopped during free-throw opportunities.

Give-and-Go: Like the alley-oop, the give-and-go is as snazzy as it sounds. This is when a player, let's call him Hottie #1, passes—*gives*—the ball to his teammate, Hottie #2. Hottie #1, now ball-less (I guess he wouldn't be too hot then, huh?), then moves toward the basket. Hottie #2 passes—*gives*—the ball back to #1 who (when it works) shoots and scores a basket.

Goaltending: Defensive goaltending occurs when a player blocks an opponent's shot just as it's about to go in the basket, which is not allowed. In short, the ball cannot be blocked once it starts its downward trajectory at the basket—i.e., a defensive player's hands cannot be directly above the basket, or right at the rim. The player needs to do the blocking of the ball *before* it reaches its highest point in the air or is directly over the basket, where Newton's theory of gravity tells you that it's going in. Goaltending automatically results in two points for the non-offending team.

Hook Shot (or Sky Hook): In this shot, the ball is thrown with the arm in a sweeping, arcing motion over the head, forming a *hook* shape. The hook shot is executed while the player's body is not facing the basket, but is slightly sideways. It's often executed over an opponent's head. Kareem Abdul-Jabbar was a master at this shot.

 In the Paint: If a player is "in the paint," it means that he is in the rectangular area closest to the basket, also called "the lane" (or, more generally, "the key"—see below). This area is always clearly marked and usually painted a color that contrasts with the rest of the court, hence the expression "in the paint." To casually comment that a player is in the paint sounds very cool. See the diagram on page 3 for a visual.

Jump Ball: At the start of a game, or when possession of the ball is under dispute, the ref will call for a jump ball to begin or resume play. To execute a jump ball, the ref tosses the ball up into the air between two opponents, who then swat at it in hopes of getting the ball to a teammate, thereby gaining possession.

Jump Shot: When a player jumps up and shoots the ball toward the basket. It's a basic shot made with one hand. It's not fancy, but it works.

Key: The key is the "lane" (see below) plus the free-throw circle area. It's shaped like a key if you've recently taken hallucinatory drugs. In the old days, it was narrower and really did look something like a key, but the players got so big that the dimensions of the court had to be changed.

Lane: The rectangular area directly under and in front of the basket. It is usually painted a color that contrasts with the rest of the court, and is thus also referred to as *the paint*.

Layup: The layup should be called a "layup and in" because it's a shot where the player reaches up toward the basket with one arm and puts the ball into the basket. It's an up-and-in motion (almost the upside down version of a dunk) that is executed close to the basket. It is often also a type of bank shot, where the player reaches up and banks the ball off the backboard.

Loose-Ball Foul: A foul that is committed when neither team has possession of the ball. The team that was fouled against (i.e., the non-offender) gets possession of the ball.

Nothing but Net: (aka, "nuthin' but net," or "nutten-but-net.") Totally cool. "Nothing but net" is the b-ball way to describe what happens when the ball is thrown perfectly into the basket—it doesn't touch the rim or the backboard—just the *net*.

Offensive Foul: Most often, fouls are committed by defensive players who are trying to block shots, to block passes, or to steal the ball. But sometimes, an offensive player commits a foul. A typical offensive-foul scenario is when the player with the ball charges ahead and plows right into an opponent who was simply doing his job, minding his own business (called "charging," see above). Offensive fouls result in a change of possession.

On the Line: "On the line," "at the line," "go to the line"—they all mean that a player is in position, or getting into position, for a free throw. The "line" is the free-throw line.

Personal Foul: Most fouls are personal fouls. A personal foul is any illegal contact between players. A player can't poke, prod, tickle, or trip (duh) another player. Very minimal touchy-feely is allowed—sometimes the refs are strict about fouls, other times they are not. Depending on the situation, personal fouls can result in a change of possession or one, two, or three free throws.

Post or Low Post: This refers to the location near or under the basket. If a player is in a post or low-post position (also known as "posting up"), he's playing near the basket, in the paint.

Press: Pressing is an "in your face" kind of move. Typically, once a ball is in-bounded (i.e., put in play after a basket, or thrown in from the sidelines) the defense will run down court to defend their basket. Sometimes, however, teams use a full-court or half-court strategy, which means that they cover the opposing offense tightly as it tries to move the ball up the court—this is pressing. It has its risks, though, because if an offensive player breaks free, then there is no one down near the basket to defend against him. You might hear a commentator say something like, "Team Swoosh likes to use the full-court press early in the game."

Rebound: What you do when you've been dumped—or a term used in basketball for the act of grabbing the ball after a missed basket (by either team). Whoever attains possession of the ball after a shot has been attempted and missed is said to have "gotten the rebound." Note that after a team *makes* a shot, the opposing team automatically gets the ball.

Ride Him While He's Hot: I'm not even going there—I'll just let you, gentle reader, let your imagination run wild. I'll wait until you're ready to hear the basketball definition . . . still waiting . . . still waiting . . . okay: It's simply when the ball is passed repeatedly to a player who is on a scoring streak.

Set Shot: Utilitarian, not glamorous. A set shot is when a player physically sets himself up before the shot. He stands, bends his knees, and doesn't jump, but gently pushes off the floor as he releases the ball. (Yeah, pretty boring.) With the increase in the game's pace over the years, and the increase in the size of the players, the set shot is not as effective as it once was, and it isn't used much at all—if ever anymore in the NBA. It is, however, what is used at the free-throw line.

Sixth Man: There are five *starters* on a basketball team. The sixth man is the equivalent to the number-one runner-up in the Miss America pageant. He's the first one to come off the bench when it's discovered that Miss America posed nude for *Playboy*. Wait, I've tangled things. He's the first one to come off the bench as a substitute for one of the starters who comes off the court. A starter might come out for a rest, or because he's not playing well, or because he has fouled out.

Slam Dunk: A dunk with *emphasis*, a dunk executed in bold with a dozen exclamation points.

Steal: A defensive player steals the ball away from his opponent by either intercepting a pass from one offensive player to another, or by simply swatting it away from the offensive player. Stealing in basketball is perfectly legal.

Swingman: Could be a jazz musician, or a man who's married but likes his neighbor's wife. On the court, however, it's a versatile player who can play several different positions well. The sixth man is often a swingman.

Swish: A swish is similar to "nothing but net"; it's a word used to describe a ball that goes smoothly through the basket. It's also a way for commentators to practice the literary convention of onomatopoeia: "Bob passes to Jake who shoots and *swish!* What a beautiful shot!"

Technical Foul: A technical foul is called for unsportsmanlike conduct—in short, for abusive language and fighting. If a player or a coach has more than one technical foul in a game, he is ejected from the game. If the foul is deemed egregious by the ref, a player or coach can be ejected with just one technical foul. When a technical foul is called, the opposing team gets to send a player to the free-throw line all by himself to shoot one free throw, with no defenders around. In addition, the fouled-upon team gets possession of the ball after shooting its free throw (because there is no one to get the rebound)—this is not the case with all free-throw situations. A technical foul is also called if a player tries to call a time-out when his team has already used its allotted number of time-outs.

Thread the Needle: The expression used when a ball is passed from one offensive player to another, right between two defenders. It's a tight squeeze. You might hear an announcer say something like, "Wow, did you see Tall Tom thread the needle to Taller Tony? What a perfect pass."

Tip-in: A tip-in is, in a sense, a two-man basket. It is when one player shoots the ball, but it doesn't quite go in, and then his teammate tips it into the basket just as the ball is about to fall out. It is sometimes called a "tap-in."

Traffic: To "drive in traffic" means that the offense penetrates an area crowded with several opponents (which is usually the *lane*). Because the three-second rule prevents players from spending too much time in the lane, "driving in traffic" doesn't happen all that often. (Herein lies the fundamental difference between the real world and sports. In the real world—especially when you really need to be somewhere on time, like a wedding, or a job interview—you are *always* driving in traffic.)

Traveling: A player cannot "travel"—run or walk—with the ball without dribbling it. The ball has to be bouncing up and down at all times—a player is allowed to take only one and a half steps while holding the ball. If a player stops dribbling and takes more than a step, it's a traveling violation, and this results in a change of possession. Traveling is sometimes called "walking." (Traveling is not called that tightly, however; players often take two steps without being called for the violation.)

Violation: A lesser crime than a foul. It's like getting a parking ticket instead of a moving violation. When a team commits a violation, they must give up possession of the ball to the other team. Common violations are breaking the clock rules: the twenty-four-second rule, the three-second rule, and a few others not discussed in this book. Other violations are ballhandling errors such as traveling, double dribbling, and palming.

Wipe the Boards: To wipe the boards is to get a rebound. Instead of hearing an announcer say, "Tall Tom got the rebound," you're more likely to hear, "Tall Tom wipes the boards and passes to Taller Tony."

Football

THE SOUND: *Crunch!* (Big shiny helmets colliding.)

THE LOOK: BIG guys, both in height and girth, that look even bigger because of the pounds of equipment they wear (most notably, Joan Crawford-on-steroids type shoulder pads).

THE PLACE: Football fields, sometimes called "gridirons," in football stadiums. Most football stadiums are outdoors, but some are played in indoor domes.

THE ORGANIZATION: The NFL (National Football League).

> **Dancing is a contact sport. Football is a hitting sport.**
> *—Vince Lombardi, legendary Green Bay Packers Coach*

Football is weird. It's complex. It carries this aura around it. It's crazy, it's rough—okay, you could say *violent*—but it is also exciting, dizzying, and spellbinding at times. Football is the opposite of baseball, "America's pastime," which is so much a part of Americana—hot dogs and Cracker Jack, grainy black-and-white images of neighborhood ballparks. If baseball is apple pie, football is red-hot chili. Baseball has become the darling sport of intellectuals and other so-called serious writers because it is a sport of nuance, of subtlety—yet, the game itself is quite simple; the basics of baseball are easily understood from the get-go. Not so with football, which can look like a big blur until you learn a little bit about the nuts and bolts. Football is by far the most complicated, the most *psychological* sport we will discuss in this book. But because football has been forever linked (unfairly) with the image of the dumb jock and its dependence on brute strength, it has often been forsaken by the intelligentsia—and by many women.

One could argue that you have to be a little dumb to play a game where guys who can weigh 300 or more pounds—most of it muscle—come charging at you with all their might to bash into you and knock you down. Human instinct would compel you to run for your life in the opposite direction. But the truth is that football is too complex to be played by dumb players. Of course, some players are smarter than others. (But this is also the case with our esteemed presidents. Need I remind you that our current president has trouble staying conscious and eating pretzels at the same time?) As you will see, there's much more to football than just violence and strength. What looks like random tackling, pushing, hitting, and all-fall-down-and-go-boom is really a finely orchestrated endeavor, the ultimate purpose of which is to score points by marching through the opponent's territory and getting past their goal line.

HERE'S HOW IT WORKS

Now that I've made you queasy talking about the complexity of the game, let me just say, DON'T PANIC. The great thing about football is that you don't have to know every layer, every subtlety, or even the names of the specific positions to enjoy (yes, *enjoy*) the game—all you need is a basic understanding. Here's the overview:

The primary aim in football is to score **touchdowns** (worth six points), which are achieved when a player runs the ball into the **end zone**, or when a player catches a ball thrown to him in the *end zone*. In order to reach the end zone, the guys with the ball must penetrate—get by—the guys on the opposing team and successfully progress all the way down the field with the ball. If a team is in a situation where they cannot pull off a touchdown, they may settle for a **field goal** (worth three points), which is scored when the ball is kicked between the *goalposts* in the end zone. There are a few other ways to score points as well. For those of you who care deeply about scoring (and don't we all?), these methods are described in more detail below.

As with most sports, in football you've got your offense and your defense. However, unlike, say, baseball, where players play both offense *and* defense (hitting = offense; fielding = defense), football players play either offense *or* defense—not both. There are twenty-two players on the field at any given time—eleven on offense and eleven on defense. The offense of Team Macho will be on the field with the defense of Team Manly. Then, after Team Macho either scores or loses possession of the ball, the teams will switch and the offense of Team Manly will be on the field with the defense of Team Macho. The offense and defense of the same team are never on the field at the same time.

Here's where it's gets a little complicated: The team with the ball—the *offense*—gets four tries (called **downs**) to move the ball forward ten yards or more (toward the opposing team's goal), by running with it, or throwing it to a teammate. Each time an attempt is made to move the ball down the field—whether it's a pass, a throw, or a kick—it's called a *play*. If a team fails to progress ten yards in four downs (four tries), they lose possession of the ball, and the other team gets a chance to move down the field in the other direction and score. Progressing ten yards may not sound so difficult—ten yards isn't that far, after all. However, while the offense is trying to move the ball forward, eleven gigantic men of steel (the defense) with the words **tackle**, *pummel*, *push*, **block**, **blitz**, **sack**, *knock unconscious*, and *cowabunga* running through their minds are trying to *prevent* the ball (and essentially the offense) from going anywhere, and also trying to gain possession of the ball for their own team. On the *fourth down*, if the offense doesn't think they have a good shot of moving the ball forward the whole ten yards, they will usually give up and **punt** (kick) the ball to the other end of the field. Now the other team gets the ball and has a chance to score. The offense of Team Macho (the **quarterback** among them) leaves the field and is replaced with Team Macho's defense. Conversely, Team Manly, the team that was just punted to, brings on their offense.

And that's the big picture. You're well on your way to becoming a football goddess.

THE FIELD

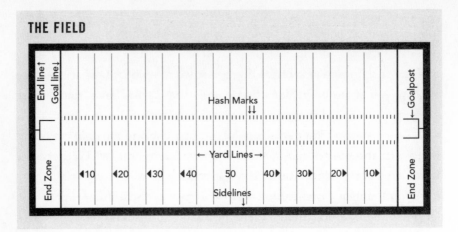

For a complicated game, a football field, also referred to as the *gridiron*, is relatively simple. It's a rectangular field of grass (or artificial turf) one hundred yards long, with a ten-yard *end zone* at either end. Technically, this means the entire rectangular area is 120 yards from goalpost to goalpost, but in casual conversation, the football field is spoken of as one hundred yards from end zone to end zone.

The field is divided into ten-yard chunks marked by *yard lines*. The 10-yard line on either end of the field is ten yards from the end zone; the 20-yard line is twenty yards from the end zone; and so on. The 50-yard line is the center of the field. (If some big shot claims he has the "best" seats, ask if they are on the 50-yard line. This is the ideal spot for viewing the game.) The yard lines allow the progress (or not) of a team to be kept track of.

Another thing you'll notice on the field are the *hash marks*—those small dashlike lines that run lengthwise down the field. Each play must be started within the two lines of hash marks. If the ball winds up outside this area at the end of a play, it is moved to the nearest hash mark to begin the next play.

A player is considered to be out of bounds when any part of his body touches the ground outside the *sidelines,* which run the length of the field on either side, or the *end lines,* which are at the back of the end zone.

TIMING: How Sixty Minutes = Four Hours, or, the Timing of the Game

 Football may have rhythm (you'll often hear broadcasters say something like, "Now that the Bears have found their rhythm, the game is looking up for them"), but it never really flows. The game is made up of a choppy series of plays that begin with the quarterback handing off or throwing the ball. Occasionally, the quarterback will run with the ball himself.

There are four *quarters* in a football game, each fifteen minutes in length. Be warned, though, that this is not a continuous fifteen minutes—the clock is stopped *a lot*. Every time a player goes out of bounds, or a pass is incomplete (the ball is thrown but not caught), or when players call a time-out,* or a player commits a penalty, to name just a few possibilities, the clock is stopped. Also, after the first two quarters of the game—"at the half," or *halftime*—there is a twelve-minute break. At halftime, the teams go into their respective locker rooms, get yelled at (unless they're winning by a

> The reason women don't play football is because eleven of them would never wear the same outfit in public.
> —*Phyllis Diller, comedienne*

lot), get their steroid shots (just kidding), get their painkiller shots (not kidding), and get psyched for the second half.

A football game will generally last anywhere from two and a half to four hours. But with so many commercials and interruptions, there's plenty of time to get snacks, pee, do your nails, get the kids into bed, read *War and Peace*, and more. It's the multitasker's dream sport.

If, at the end of the four quarters, the score is tied, the game goes into a fifteen-minute *sudden death overtime* period to determine a winner. "Sudden death" simply means that whichever team scores first during overtime immediately becomes the winner, and the game immediately ends.

---

*Each team is allowed three time-outs per half.

KICKING OFF: Getting the Party Started

At the very beginning of the game, after halftime, and to begin any over-time periods the ball is put into play via a **kickoff**,* during which the *kicker* kicks the football off a tee. (A football tee is similar to a golf tee, in that it is a type of support for the ball that keeps it slightly above ground—one inch, to be exact.) The kickoff takes place at the kicking team's 30-yard line (see diagram), and the kicker tries to kick the ball as far as possible, so the opposing team will have to travel a longer distance to get to the end zone/goal.

Just before the game starts, a coin toss takes place (usually flipped by the ref), and the team that wins the coin toss opts to either (1) choose be-tween receiving the kick or kicking (teams almost always choose to re-ceive, putting them on offense and thus giving them the first chance to score); or (2) choose which end zone his team will defend first. After half-time, the loser of the coin toss gets first choice on the options. Almost without exception, if Team Manly received at the start of the game, Team Macho will receive after halftime.

When the kicker kicks the ball, a designated offensive player on the opposing team catches the ball and then takes off with it like a bat out of hell. This act of catching and running is known as a **kick return** (which refers only to that one play). Meanwhile, right after the kicker kicks the ball, he and his teammates start sprinting down the field toward the guy with the ball. The first *down* starts at the place where the guy with the ball is brought down or forced out of bounds by the opposing team.

---

*A kickoff is also used after every score (we'll get into this later).

SCORING

Touchdowns, Extra Points, and Two-Point Conversions

When a player throws the ball to a teammate (called a *receiver*—because he, um, *receives* the ball . . .) in the end zone, and the teammate catches it, or if any offensive player runs with the ball past the *goal line* and into the end zone, the player's team scores a **touchdown**, and the offense gets six points. After a touchdown, the offense is given a chance to earn an *extra point* by kicking the ball through the goalposts.* The offense also has the option of going for a **two-point conversion**, which yields—yep, you guessed it—two points (see, you're already a football genius). For a two-point conversion, instead of kicking the ball through the goalposts, the offense tries to run the ball into the end zone or throw it to someone in the end zone. It's just like a touchdown, except it's attempted from a very short distance from the end zone (from the 2-yard line).

A two-point conversion is much more difficult to pull off than the kick for an extra point, so it's usually only done when the team that has just scored the touchdown is behind and desperate for more points to win or tie the game. Thus, a touchdown is almost always followed by the kick for the extra point—and since the extra point isn't that difficult to achieve (the average success rate in the NFL is ninety-five percent), a team will usually rack up seven points as a result of the touchdown (six for the touchdown itself, and one for the extra point).

Field Goals

Another way to score is by a **field goal**. A field goal is a kick through the goalposts (it's sometimes called "splitting the uprights"). It yields three points. The method and the aim is the same as a kick for the extra point, but the field goal is

---

*The extra-point kick can be taken from any spot that's at least two or more yards from the goal line. Usually it is placed around the 10-yard line.

attempted from the spot at which the offensive team's last play ended, which can be anywhere from the 1-yard line out to about the 45-yard line. A team will go for a field goal when its chances of getting a touchdown are slim to none. A field goal is easier to achieve than a touchdown, depending on how far the kicker is from the end zone. A thirty-yard kick is easy (well, it is for the NFL kickers who get paid lots and lots of money to kick); a fifty-five-yard kick is not (even for someone getting high six figures). In short, anything over forty-five yards is challenging. (The longest field goal ever kicked is sixty-three yards.) Field goals are usually executed when it's *fourth down*; if the kicker misses, the other team takes possession of the ball from where the kick attempt was made.

Safety

Finally, there is the **safety**, which, on its Web site, the NFL describes like a precious gem, calling it the "rarest of all the scoring opportunities." A *safety* occurs when the defensive team tackles an offensive player in the offensive player's own end zone (that is, *not* the end zone that the offense is trying to get into to score a touchdown), or when the offensive team fumbles the ball in its own end zone and the ball then goes out of bounds. A safety yields two points for the *defense*, and it only happens for a team a couple of times a season. When it happens, it's almost always a happy accident (for the defense) because the team with the ball screwed up.

After a touchdown (and the extra-point kick or two-point conversion) or a field goal, the offense of the opposing team receives the ball via a *kickoff*. This cuts down on a lot of "it's our turn now" bickering or having to resort to eeny-meeny-miney-mo to determine who gets the ball.

WAYS TO SCORE: A QUICK RECAP

If it doesn't matter who wins or loses, then why do they keep score?

—Vince Lombardi, legendary Green Bay Packers coach

* **Touchdown** (six points) = Achieved by running the ball past the goal line into the end zone, or catching the ball while in the end zone.

* **Extra Point** (one point) = A chance for the offense to earn one extra point immediately following a touchdown by kicking the ball through the goalposts.

* **Two-Point Conversion** (two points) = A chance for the offense to earn two extra points immediately following a touchdown. The ball is run or thrown into the end zone just like it is on a regular touchdown play, but success is rewarded with only two points. A two-point conversion is more difficult than an extra-point kick. It's like a mini-touchdown.

* **Field Goal** (three points) = Achieved by kicking the ball through the goalposts from anywhere on the field.

* **Safety** (two points for the defense) = Earned when an offensive player is tackled by the defense in his own end zone, or an offensive player fumbles the ball out of bounds in his own end zone.

Other Ways to Score

There are no guarantees, but dinner by candlelight, flowers, and jewelry usually help.

THE MOVES

As you read about the push and pull of the offense and defense, keep in mind that most actions, or moves, in football are relatively straightforward. (As complex as football is, remember that millions of men follow games while drinking a six-pack of Bud.) On the next few pages, some of the most common football moves are discussed.

Blocking

Blocking is done by the offense. The point of blocking is to try to block defenders—their opponents—from tackling the guy with the ball.

Tackling

Women tackle problems. Men tackle each other. Tackling is what defense in football is all about; the defense wants to tackle—that is, wrestle to the ground—the player with the ball.

Passing

Passing, in football, is throwing the ball from one teammate to another, and it is almost always the *quarterback* who does the passing (more on the quarterback below). A forty-yard pass is a pass that is thrown across a distance of forty yards (pretty impressive). A *completed pass* is one that is caught by a receiver. An *incomplete pass* is a pass that is not successfully caught by a receiver.

Hitting

Hitting isn't really a proper football term, but it's one you'll hear frequently, as in, "What a hit!," "Man, that was a rough hit," or "What a nasty hit." In short, it is the act of one solid, supersized body smashing into another. Hitting is (for better or worse) the essence of football. (The humorist Dave Barry captures this essence beautifully: "I have seen women walk right past a TV set with a football game on and . . . not stop to watch, even if the TV is showing replays of what we call a 'good hit,' which is a tackle that causes at least one major internal organ to actually fly out of a player's body.")

Forcing a Player Out of Bounds

To avoid being tackled, a player may run out of bounds. This can be advantageous for the offense, which may be running out of time to score, because the clock is stopped when a player goes out of bounds, and because the player avoids being tackled (which hurts, no matter how much padding you have on). A player may also be pushed or shoved out of bounds by the

THE GIPPER REVEALED

During Ronald Reagan's presidency, and throughout his political career, he used the phrase "win one for the Gipper" ad nauseam, and I was always clueless as to what it meant. . . .

Throughout the first half of the twentieth century, Knute Rockne, a renowned college football coach, pregame motivator, and orator coached Notre Dame to 105 wins, 12 losses, and five ties. In 1920, one of his star players, George Gipp, died of pneumonia. Football legend has it that, eight years later, Rockne repeated Gipp's dying words to his team to motivate them against Army: "Rock, I know I'm going . . . but I'd like one last request. . . . Someday, when the going isn't so easy, when the odds are against us, ask a Notre Dame team to win one for me, for the Gipper. I don't know where I'll be then, Rock, but I'll know about it, and I'll be happy." Notre Dame won the game, 12–6.

After Rockne's death in a plane crash in 1930, Hollywood made a movie, *Knute Rockne All American*. And guess who played George Gipp? That's right, the fortieth president of the United States, while he was still in his acting phase (as opposed to his political phase, which didn't require any acting at all . . .).

defense. All of these instances are called being "forced" out of bounds, because a player would certainly rather progress forward given the choice.

WORKIN' THE FIELD

To score in football, you have to first make your way all the way down the field until you reach the *end zone*. It's very difficult for the offense to get too far, to gain territory, however, before the defense goes into action and tackles the guy with the ball, or forces him out of bounds.

Downs

As we discuss the nitty-gritty of the offense's march down the field, remember that the physical field, as well as the scheme of the game, is divided into ten-yard chunks, and that the offense is given four *downs* to move the ball forward (toward the opposing team's end zone) ten yards. If the offense fails to do this, they lose possession of the ball, and the opposing offense gets a chance to score. A *down* is just a football-y term for a "try" or a "chance," and players move the ball forward by running with it, or by throwing (*passing*) it to a teammate. Note that while the offense *must* gain at least ten yards in four downs, they can also gain much more than ten yards. The desire is to gain as many yards as possible on each down. As long as the offense gains *at least* ten yards in four tries or less, they keep the ball and get a "fresh set of downs."

Now on to the more niggling stuff. The phrase "first-and-ten" means that it's the first down and the offense must move the ball forward ten yards to get a new set of downs and keep its **drive** going. Say the offense of Team Macho successfully throws or runs the ball ten yards or more on the first try—it will then be "first-and-ten" again. Or maybe Team Macho gains only three yards (a "three-yard gain")—then it will be "second-and-seven." If they then get five yards, then it's "third and two." Let's say on the third down, Team Macho doesn't get any yards, because when the quarterback handed off the ball to a **running back**, he was immediately tackled. Now it's fourth and two. The fourth down gets a little dicey. If Team Macho doesn't get those last two yards, Team Manly will get the ball at the exact spot where Macho has it, which could make it much easier for a player on Team Manly to eventually get into the end zone. So, on fourth down, Team Macho (aka, the offense) either wants to attempt a field goal, as discussed above, or, if they don't think they can make a field goal, they at least want to drive Team Manly back farther away from their goal before Team Manly's offense takes over. This is done by *punting*. To execute a **punt,** a player drops the ball toward his foot and kicks it before it hits the ground. Punting is a kind of surrender with compromise. "Okay, we didn't get the ten yards, but we can't have you so close to our goal, so we're kicking it and pushing you back." This prevents the team who just got the ball from having great "field position."

Similar to a kickoff situation, when the punter kicks the ball, a player on the opposing team will catch the ball and then run with it—this is called *fielding the punt*, and the run itself is called a *punt return*. The receiving team's first down will start at the place where the guy with the ball (the guy who fielded the punt, who's also known as the *punt returner*) is brought down or forced out of bounds.

Reversing It: Switching Sides and Directions at the End of a Quarter

If at the end of the first *quarter* it's third-and-five at the 42-yard line, then when the second quarter starts, it will be third-and-five at the 42-yard line on the opposite side of the field, and the teams will switch directions and head toward the opposite end zone. This was instituted so that in outdoor conditions such as wind or blinding sunshine, the advantages and disadvantages are borne equally by both teams.

At halftime, however, the game temporarily ends, then starts anew "after the half"—that is, in the second half. If a team is one inch away from the end zone when the clock runs out at halftime, tough noogies—they don't score, and when the game resumes after the half, play is started with a *kickoff* near the kicking team's 30-yard line, just as it is at the beginning of the game.

FOOTBALL FLICKS FOR HIP CHICKS

Remember the Titans (2000): This movie stars Denzel Washington, so that should be enough for you to drop this book and go rent it. It's a wonderfully inspirational movie based on a true story of a Virginia high school team that strove to fight racism after their school had been desegregated.

Brian's Song (1971): In the mood for a good cry? This one'll make you weep buckets. It's a true story about Chicago Bears running back Brian Piccolo, who befriends Gale Sayers (another Bears running back) and then dies from cancer. One of the most memorable tearjerker lines of all time is when Sayers, upon accepting an award, announces, "I love Brian Piccolo . . . and I want you to love him too."

Any Given Sunday (1999): A somewhat over-the-top Oliver Stone movie starring Al Pacino as an aging, beleaguered coach. (Okay, I know football can be rough to the point of violence, but a scene in this movie involving a knocked-out eyeball is, in my opinion, gratuitous and just plain gross.)

THE LINE OF SCRIMMAGE

The *line of scrimmage* is the term for where the ball ends up when a play is finished, and where the next play begins. The line of scrimmage is really an imaginary line—the offense lines up on one side of it, the defense on the other. The players who are standing within a yard of this line are said to be *on the line*. Other players farther back are said to be in the *backfield*.

THE HUDDLE

 Before each play, the offense will get into a *huddle*. This allows the viewing audience (women in particular) to appreciate those tight pants stretched over the players' tight glutei maximi. In addition, I suppose you could say *more important*, the huddle is when and where the quarterback tells his teammates what play they will be executing, and on what count (hut, hut, hut, or hut, hut, grunt; and some numbers, too). These seemingly unintelligible rants are codes for the numerous plays that have been designed, studied, and practiced by the coach and team.

You've learned how a team penetrates the end zone; now it's time to learn more about positions. Penetration and positions—I told you football was a great sport!

POSITIONS

In football, positions are annoying and, frankly, not worth learning too much about, because they're fluid—the job of each position often changes according to the whims of the coach. On different teams, different players in the same position do different things, and that's way too many "differents" to contend with. A cursory understanding is enough for our purposes and will not give you a headache. But do remember that, unlike many other sports, such as basketball, hockey, and soccer, in football, offense is offense and defense is defense and never the twain shall meet.

The Offense: Touching Tush and Other Key Football Strategies

Here's the overview: The offense is led by the *quarterback* (say "QB" if you want to be hip). He's the one with his hands under the other guy's tushy. Weird, I know. The tushy (or "tush" if you prefer, or "bum" if you're British) that the QB's hands are under belongs to the **center**, who "snaps" (a little throw under his, um, you know) the ball right into the quarterback's hands. The center is usually a really big guy whose tush might be too big to be considered cute—but the QB almost always has a desirable derriere. **Tight ends**—really, this is what they're called—also have nice ones, but that's not why they're called tight ends. (More on tight ends in a moment). The other positions that are part of the offense are *guards*, **tackles, receivers**, and **running backs**.

> ### THE OFFENSE: POSITIONS
>
> Quarterback (QB)
> Running backs (RB)
>   halfbacks (HB)
>   fullbacks (FB)
> Receivers (R)
>   wide receivers (WR)
>   tight ends (TE)
>   split ends (SE)
> Offensive linemen
>   center (C)
>   tackles (T)
>   guards (G)

THE QUARTERBACK

The quarterback is undeniably the most important player on the team. Yeah, yeah, you gotta have that teamwork thing going on, but you cannot win games without a great quarterback. Former player and sportswriter Sam DeLuca, in his book *Football Made Easy*, describes the quarterback as "the man who makes it all go."

Quarterbacks used to call their own plays, meaning that they would decide whether or when to pass (throw) the ball or to hand it off and to whom. Nowadays the coaches usually call the shots. Nevertheless, the quarterback needs to be quick, quick-thinking, strong, agile, and above all, confident. The best quarterbacks exhibit a cool confidence that commands the respect of their teammates. Each play starts with the snap to the quarterback, who must then make something happen.

RUNNING BACKS

Running backs, as you might guess, usually, but not always, run with the ball (toward the goal)—the quarterback will *hand* the football to the running backs (as opposed to throwing it), and the running back will then run with it. Running backs also block. Running backs are generally shorter and more compact than their teammates because they have to be FAST to avoid the big, huge, giant defensive guys coming at them to crush them to the ground. They're the guys who often zig and zag in cool formations as they run down the field. Just watching running backs makes my hip joints ache. They must all be great dancers. (Actually, professional football players have been known to take ballet classes to improve their agility and flexibility. Shoulder pads and tutus—wow.)

WIDE RECEIVERS

Wide receivers, who are often simply called *receivers* or *wideouts*, receive—that is, they catch the ball from the quarterback.* (The term *wideout* is perhaps why very few women play football. Who wants to be known as a *wideout*?) In spite of the name, wide receivers tend to be tall, lean, and graceful. ("Wide" refers to where they line up on the field.) They have to leap, stretch, and reach for the ball. Over the years there have been certain notable quarterback-receiver partnerships. Dance had Fred and Ginger, comedy had Abbott and Costello, and football (the San Francisco 49ers) had Joe Montana and Jerry Rice, to name just one pair. The quarterback comes to depend on certain receivers—a "go to" guy on the field. Currently, Peyton Manning and Marvin Harrison of the Indianapolis Colts are doing a beautiful football

---

*It is almost always the quarterback throwing (passing) the ball to a receiver, but there are some rare occasions when the QB will throw it to another player first, who will then throw it to a wide receiver.

tango, as are the Philadelphia Eagles' Donavan McNabb and Terrell Owens. Passing the ball, when successful, is a quicker, more efficient way to gain yards than running the ball. A good receiver can catch balls in the tightest situations (when he is being defended by one or more opponents) and can also catch balls that look uncatchable to mere mortals.

TIGHT ENDS

A tight end is a receiver and a blocker. Tight ends have it *all* goin' on. They are lean but mean; they are agile but tough; and they have strong hands (to catch the ball) and strong bodies (to block their opponents). They are usually bigger all-around than wide receivers.

SPLIT ENDS

Split ends: hair problem or football player? Both, in fact. A **split end** in football is a kind of wide receiver, but he positions himself farther away from the line than a wide receiver would. He is *split* away from the line. For our purposes, just know that a split end is a receiver; like all receivers, they are counted on to catch the ball.

THE OFFENSIVE LINEMEN: THE CENTER, THE TACKLE, AND THE GUARDS

Okay, put your seat belts on, ladies. Here is one reason why football can make your head spin: The **offensive linemen**—the **center**, **tackle**, and *guards* (left and right tackles, left and right guards, etc.) are on the offense, but they sort of *defend* the offense. In short, the offensive linemen have two jobs: (1) to protect the QB. You'll often hear a broadcaster say something like, "Brady has had excellent protection here in the first quarter." Or conversely, "Coach can't expect his quarterback to make plays with such lousy protection." (2) to protect the running back once he has been given the ball by the quarterback. For these reasons, the offensive linemen need to be massive.

As discussed, the *center* stands directly in front of the QB, and his job is to snap the ball back to the QB, then block. The *guards* line up on either side of the center. And the *tackles* line up on either side of the guards. The offensive lineup might look like this:*

WR TE T G C G T TE WR

QB

RB

The Defense: Big, Bigger, Biggest

THE DEFENSE: POSITIONS
Defensive tackles (DT)
Defensive ends (DE)
Linebackers (LB)
Cornerbacks (CB)
Safeties (S)

The defensive positions can get really confusing, because their jobs are even more interchangeable than the offensive positions. So, to keep it simple, we'll look at all the defensive positions and how they interact at once, so you get an idea of the big defensive picture. The defensive positions are: **defensive tackles, defensive ends, linebackers, cornerbacks**, and **safeties.**

The *defensive tackles* and *defensive ends* are types of **defensive linemen**. One of the reasons defensive linemen were put on this earth is to make us women always feel oh-so-petite. If you're having a fat day, just conjure a mental image of a linebacker's arm, whose circumference is quite possibly bigger than your waist, and *voilà*, you're a skinny-minny again. The *tackles* and *ends* line up on the defensive line; the linebackers, cornerbacks, and safeties stand a little farther back than the linemen. A defensive line-up might look like this:†

DE DT DT DE

CB   LB LB   LB LB   CB

S

---

*Or it might not.
†Or it might not.

Very simply, the *defensive tackles* and *ends* try to get to the *quarterback*. The *ends* and *linebackers* are also responsible for stopping the *running backs* or short passes. *Cornerbacks* try to make sure the *receivers* of longer passes don't catch the ball, or that they get knocked down as soon as they do. And *safeties* also defend the *receivers*, functioning as a safety valve, or extra protection. The permutations of how a coach will use these guys is as confusing as trying to keep straight sandal toe, control top, sheer, very sheer, matte, microfiber, control-top microfiber, opaque, and the thousands of other types and cross-types of pantyhose available. Just hang on to whatever you know and go with it.

If learning about all the various positions makes your head spin, you're not alone—positions in football are confusing. Remember that men are born with a special gene to process this information.

ON LINEBACKERS, BY ARTHUR KRETCHMER, *PLAYBOY* (1973)

"The question of linebacking is an interesting one to consider. To play that position, a man must be strong enough in the arms and shoulders to fight off offensive linemen who often outweigh him, fast enough to cover receivers coming out of the backfield, and rangy enough to move laterally with speed. But the real key to that position is an instantaneous ferocity— the ability to burst rather than run."

DEFENSIVE STRATEGY

While the job of the offense is, essentially, to score, the various strategies of the defense warrant a little more explanation.

In any sport, the defense wants to prevent its opponents from scoring. This is true in football as well, but, as you've learned, before the offense even comes close to scoring, the defense tries to prevent them from gaining any territory. The quicker and more effectively they do this, the quicker they get the ball and give their offense a chance to score for themselves.

The basic defensive maneuver is to tackle, force out of bounds, or pummel the guy with the ball (usually the running back or the receiver). But they also try to prevent these guys from getting the ball in their hands in the first place, by attacking the quarterback.

Bringing Down the QB

A key defensive strategy in football is to tackle the quarterback before he even has a chance to release the ball to a teammate (by handing it off to a running back or passing it to a receiver). It takes a lot of effort to get to the quarterback, because he is protected by the other set of big guys—the offensive line (guards, tackles, and the center). If the quarterback isn't successfully protected enough to make plays—to get the ball into the hands of one of his teammates—his team cannot win. The quarterback is like the president—he gets the most Secret Service detail.

So, needless to say, getting to the quarterback is exactly what the defense wants to do. This is variously called *blitzing the quarterback*, **rushing the quarterback**, and when they succeed, *sacking the quarterback*—otherwise known as the *blitz*, the *rush*, and the *sack*. Sacking the quarterback is a very cool achievement for the defense, because not only has the offense not been able to gain any yards, it has actually *lost* yards, since the quarterback moves backward before he releases the ball. It is often accompanied by a funky, self-congratulatory, celebratory dance on the field by the guy or guys who accomplished the sack.

The blitz is not executed on every play, however, because if it fails, the quarterback probably *did* get the ball to a teammate, and since the defense was using most of its guys to get to the quarterback, that teammate is probably running joyously toward the end zone. So it's often a trade-off: concentrate on the quarterback, or concentrate on the guy who the quarterback is going to throw the ball to. The challenge is to do both.

Turnovers: Interceptions and Fumbles (Whoops and Oops)

Another key aim of the defense is to cause *turnovers.* A turnover occurs when the offense loses the ball unexpectedly through an **interception** or a **fumble**. When turnovers happen, the team that has intercepted the ball or recovered the fumble now takes possession of the ball (that team's offense will come on the field). Turnovers are a huge boon because otherwise, in order for the defense to gain possession, they must wait until the other team's offense fails to gain ten yards in four downs.

INTERCEPTIONS

An interception is every quarterback's nightmare. It is when the quarterback tries to throw the ball to one of his receivers (a play that, if successful, constitutes a *completion*, or a complete pass), but OOPS, it lands in the hands of the defense instead. Big oops. Big !@#$%^ oops. The offense then loses possession of the ball and the defensive team immediately gains possession—so immediately, in fact, that they can try to run with the intercepted pass to the other end of the field for a touchdown. Interceptions can be very exciting, dramatic, and entertaining to watch. Sometimes the ball is caught by one of these behemoths who are built for demolition, not speed, and they go clunking down the field in their version of a run. An interception can turn an oft-forgotten defensive player into the hero of the day.

FUMBLES

Another way a turnover happens is when the guy with the ball *fumbles* it—he drops the ball or the defense successfully knocks it out of his hand. When the ball is fumbled it becomes a *loose ball*—neither team has possession of it and both teams will try to recover it. Often you'll see a huge pileup following a fumble, because every player is trying to get to the ball. In these cases it's not always clear who has it until the pile is disassembled. Whoever is left with the ball gains possession of it.

GRIDIRON GROWLS: THE RIVALRIES

Washington Redskins vs. Dallas Cowboys

It is *de rigueur* for a Redskins fan to despise the Cowboys, and vice versa. It's part of the fabric of both teams. It began in the 1970s with Washington hating Dallas coach Tom Landry, the Dallas cheerleaders, and everything else about the team. In return, Dallas hated Redskins quarterback Joe Theismann and the team's (some would say politically incorrect) logo of a Native American. It's classic, really—Cowboys vs. Indians.

Green Bay Packers vs. Chicago Bears

Not as intense as it once was, because lately, the Bears haven't been in a position to compete with your local high school team, much less the Packers. But when they were both at the top of their game, it was a well-known classic rivalry.

Cleveland Browns vs. Pittsburgh Steelers

For these two teams it's more of a love/hate thing—they love to hate each other. Separated by only 143 miles, they have one of the longest-running rivalries in the NFL. The sense of competition dates back to when the cities were both budding industrial steel giants. Now, instead of competing for manufacturing, these hardworking towns compete for touchdowns.

New York Jets vs. Miami Dolphins

New York and Miami have a long-standing rivalry based on a long-standing history of vicious hits and fierce competition. According to sports legend, Jets fans would be happy with a 2–14 season as long as the two wins were against the Dolphins. Those New Yorkers—always willing to sacrifice for the good cause of a lively rivalry.

Special Teams: So No One Has to Work Too Hard

You now know that each team has an offense and a defense that are on the field at different times. But—God forbid these players have to do more than one job to earn their exorbitant salaries!—every team also has *special teams*, in addition to the offense and defense. These groups come on the field only for kicking situations: kickoffs, field-goal attempts, extra points, and even the punt on fourth down. These situations require unique kicking skills, to which specific players devote all their time and energy. Although it is rare, some starting players from the offense or defense also play on special teams.

Even though kickers on football teams don't do anything but kick, they can win or lose games—namely when they're trying to kick a field goal or an extra point. For example, say it's 21–20 with only seconds remaining, and Team Macho is behind. Team Macho's kicker holds the fate of the game in his hands . . . I mean, his feet. So, needless to say, you want to have a reliable kicker.

PENALTIES: No-nos

Even a game as wild and crazy as football has its no-nos. Football is controlled madness; it is not all-out violence. Some **penalties** are designed to make the game fair, others are designed to protect the players from injury—the latter fall under the subheading of *personal fouls*. I know, I know, it seems ridiculous in this game of total roughness to designate rules against rough behavior, but you'll see that they do make sense. For example, a player cannot grab another player by the face mask (the wiry part of the helmet that protects the face) and yank. This could cause the grabee's head to be wrenched into positions reminiscent of Linda Blair in *The Exorcist* (remember the pea soup?!), and nobody wants that. As in all sports, there have been horrendous injuries that have left players severely injured or paralyzed. Rules like the face-mask penalty are designed to minimize such risks. Other personal fouls include:

* *Roughing the passer* (being very, very mean to the quarterback).

* *Roughing the kicker* (being very, very mean to the kicker).

* *Late hit* (when a guy is hit, blocked, or tackled after the play is called dead or is out of bounds).

* *Clipping*, which is when a blocker hits from behind.

✷ *Unnecessary roughness.* As you can imagine, in a rough game like football, this is often a subjective call by the ref. The point is that contact is supposed to stop the offense, or block the defense—not mercilessly punish the players.

Some common penalties that are *not* personal fouls but are designed to ensure fairness are **holding** and **offsides**. *Holding* is when a player literally holds on to another player for too long. You just can't do that. You gotta hit, or tackle, or block, and then move on, buddy.

The *offsides* penalty happens when the teams are lined up waiting for the ball to be snapped. (To be completely accurate, the term "offsides" only applies to the defense; for the offense, this penalty is called a "false start.") It states that no one on the line is allowed to move until the ball is snapped, and if you prematurely jump (premature activity is always a drag, isn't it, ladies?) the ref will call a penalty. If they do, a penalty is called against the team that moved early. Football players are masters at trying to provoke their opponents to try to move prematurely—the slightest move, an eyebrow wiggle, a lip twitch—can draw the opponent offsides.

The backfield—the players not lined up at the line of scrimmage—*are* allowed to move, but only one at a time. Hence the expression "backfield in motion," which became the theme (and title) of a 1969 Motown hit. It could also signify that you need to get to the gym and spend some time on the butt-blaster machine.

I've mentioned only a few fouls. There are more than a *hundred* fouls, and mentioning them would surely make you throw this book in the trash. Furthermore, penalties often fall into a gray area, left to the refs' discretion, so it's not worth trying to learn them all. You'll learn by watching. If you hear savagelike noises coming from the crowd (or the couch potato in front of your TV), you can assume that the screamer disagreed with the ref. "Bad calls" can incite extremely loud, bizarre, and scary behavior among viewers.

The Punishments

If a penalty is called against the *offense*, it results in lost yardage—five, ten, or fifteen yards, depending on the severity of the crime. Loss of yardage means that the offense is pushed farther back; if they were on the 30-yard line and got a 5-yard penalty, the line of scrimmage becomes the 25-yard line. If it's against the *defense*, *penalty yards* are assessed and the offense gets to move forward; or the offense gets to repeat the down; or, if it was a good down for the offense despite the penalty, and it doesn't want to repeat the down, the offense can *decline* the penalty and proceed. If the defense committed a really bad penalty, the offense may also get an automatic first down. The permutations are endless.

When a penalty occurs, the ref will blow his whistle, throw a yellow flag on the field, and call the penalty.

CHALLENGING A CALL: Hey, We Want a Do-Over

A team has the option of challenging some of the referee's calls. (Penalties, however, can*not* be challenged.) For example, if the ref called a player out of bounds when he caught the ball, but the player (and his coach) thinks he was inbounds, the call might be challenged. Because things happen quickly in football and because refs don't have eyes in the backs of their heads, what happens on the field isn't always crystal clear. These types of questionable calls also elicit volatile behavior among viewers—this is another instance when men become apoplectic and start raving madly about "no !%#$%*! way that was out of bounds," and so on. When a call is challenged, the ref reviews the play on videotape. He goes under a little tent on the sidelines and watches replays from a million different angles and decides whether the call was right or wrong. It's a bit of a gamble for a team to challenge a call, because if it does, and the call stands (that is, if the ref decides that the correct call was made and does not reverse it), the team that challenged the call will lose a **time-out**, which is not good (a team only gets three time-outs per half). On the other hand, after reviewing the tape, the call may well be reversed, and then it was worth risking losing the time-out. (Calls are reversed roughly half of the time they are challenged.)

The challenge is a recent development. When the NFL first allowed coaches to challenge calls in 1996 there was no connection to giving up a time-out. Teams had nothing to lose by challenging calls, and it seemed as though there was a challenge every two seconds. The games took forever, and the momentum of the games was ruined. So, a few years later, the NFL changed the rules by limiting the number of challenges permitted to two per game, and tying the challenge to the possible loss of a time-out. This means that a team will challenge a call only when it really, really, really thinks an egregiously erroneous call has been made.

THE SUPER BOWL: *Including a Special Plea to the NFL to Nix the Roman Numerals*

The Super Bowl is the grand finale, the big final championship game of the NFL, viewed by millions of people worldwide. If this chapter hasn't convinced you that football can be fun to watch, then go get theater tickets or make reservations at the restaurant that you've been trying to get into for months on Super Bowl Sunday, because most of America watches the event.

It's a long road to the Super Bowl. The thirty-two NFL teams are divided into two conferences—the AFC (American Football Conference) and the NFC (National Football Conference). The AFC and NFC are further divided into four subgroups: the eastern, western, northern, and southern divisions. The teams at the top of their division then compete in playoffs for the conference championship. Then the AFC champion faces the NFC champion in the Super Bowl.

The game is usually played on the last Sunday in January or the first Sunday in February. This is the game where advertisers pay millions of dollars for commercial time (the over-the-top, entertaining commercials are as eagerly anticipated as the game). Not only is this aspect slightly ridiculous, but the halftime show has become an embarrassing spectacle of schmaltzy showbiz. Yes, the 2004 Super Bowl halftime show was the home of the infamous Janet Jackson "wardrobe malfunction." Another irritating aspect of the Super Bowl is that since 1967, when the first Super Bowl was played, it has been designated using Roman numerals—Super Bowl I, Super Bowl X, XI, etc. Now that we're up to XXXIX, can we *please* deep-six the roman numerals? Although I have the utmost respect and admiration for the fine young men of the NFL, I would venture to say that the majority are neither math whizzes nor scholars of the Holy Roman Empire. They're soon going to spend their practices deciphering what Super Bowl they're up to. It was clever; now it's silly.

Oh, yeah, sometimes the games can be really great. Other times, it's a rout and you'll wish you had gone out to dinner instead.

MONDAY NIGHT FOOTBALL

Why, you might be wondering, *is* Monday Night Football *such a big deal?* Here's why: Unless it's playoff time, football games are aired regionally. In other words, in New York, we'll see a game featuring the Giants or the Jets, but maybe not the Denver Broncos. It's not quite *that* simple, but suffice it to say that different games are aired in different regions, so not everyone is watching the same game. On Mondays, however, games are aired *nationally*; *Monday Night Football* is a big national showcase for the two teams playing. Since the schedule is planned in advance, the games usually feature the outstanding teams from the previous season. Also, *Monday Night Football* is a coveted spot for top sports broadcasters. It always receives huge viewership. As of the 2004 season, it was ranked among the top ten prime-time shows for the fifteenth straight season, with an average audience of roughly 16.6 million. *Monday Night Football* is part of football history and television history, past and present. Beginning with the 2006 season, *Monday Night Football* will move from ABC, its home since its debut in 1970, to ESPN.

JUST KNOW THIS

Here's the handy microwave version: The team with the ball—the offense—has four downs (tries) to move the ball forward ten yards or more. On fourth down, unless they're desperate, they usually give up and punt (kick) the ball, and now the other team gets the ball and has a chance to score. The offense of Team Macho (including the quarterback) goes off the field and is replaced with the defense. Conversely, Team Manly, the other team who was just punted to, sends their defense off and brings on their offense.

NFL TEAMS

Arizona Cardinals	New Orleans
Atlanta Falcons	Saints
Baltimore Ravens	New York Giants
Buffalo Bills	New York Jets
Carolina Panthers	Oakland Raiders
Chicago Bears	Philadelphia
Cincinnati Bengals	Eagles
Cleveland Browns	Pittsburgh Steelers
Dallas Cowboys	San Diego
Denver Broncos	Chargers
Detroit Lions	San Francisco
Green Bay Packers	49ers
Houston Texans	Seattle Seahawks
Indianapolis Colts	St. Louis Rams
Jacksonville Jaguars	Tampa Bay
Kansas City Chiefs	Buccaneers
Miami Dolphins	Tennessee Titans
Minnesota Vikings	Washington
New England	Redskins
Patriots	

The quarterback rules. He gives the ball to a running back, who will run with it toward the goal, or he passes (throws) the ball to a receiver who will try to catch it; if the receiver is lucky and hasn't been tackled yet, he'll run with the ball toward the goal. The defense will try to stop either the runner or receiver by tackling him. The defense will also try to sack the quarterback, or force turnovers by causing fumbles or intercepting the ball.

Plays begin at the line of scrimmage, which is an imaginary line on either side of the ball where players line up. Prior to going to the line, the offense gets into a huddle and discusses who the hottest cheerleaders are. Okay, maybe just at practice. What they really discuss is the strategy for the next play. The quarterback gets the information from his coach and passes it on to his teammates.

Scores are made by a touchdown (six points), which is achieved when someone runs with the ball into the end zone, or catches the ball and then runs into the end zone, or catches the ball while *in* the end zone. After a touchdown, the offense goes for an extra point—a kick from around the 10-yard line that must go between the goalposts. Or, sometimes, they go for a two-point conversion, which is attempted *instead of* the extra point. The two-point conversion is much harder to accomplish and is thus attempted infrequently. Instead of kicking the ball between the goalposts, the ball must be run or passed into the end zone (from the 2-yard line). It's like a mini-touchdown. Another way for teams to score is by kicking a field goal, which is a kick from varying distances that yields three points. This is usually attempted when it's fourth down and the offense doesn't think they can get a touchdown, or time is running out.

Now you're ready to go and enjoy the game, or to at least talk about it like you love it.

Players You Need to Know

FOOTBALL QUIRK

Professional football players are drafted only from college. This isn't the case in baseball, basketball, hockey, or other professional sports where they can be drafted right out of high school (or sooner in the case of soccer's whiz-kid wonder Freddy Adu, who went to the pros at age fourteen!). So football players are always and forever associated with their college. I mean, forever—even when the players turn thirty or forty, a player will be talked about as "Joe Schmo out of Texas A&M." (Their grade point average, on the other hand, is a nonissue!)

The Legends

JIM BROWN, 1936–
1957–1965: Cleveland Browns

Brown, who played with the Cleveland Browns beginning in 1957, is considered by many to be the best running back in the history of the NFL. He was a fast, explosive runner—as sportswriter Red Smith wrote in *ESPN SportsCentury*, "For mercurial speed, airy nimbleness, and explosive violence in one package of undistilled evil, there is no other like Mr. Brown."

Brown graduated from Syracuse University, where he was an All-American in football and lacrosse, and where he lettered in basketball. His first year in the NFL, 1957, he won the Rookie of the Year award.

In his stellar eight-year career, Brown:

* led the NFL in rushing for eight of nine years (i.e., he ran for more yards than anyone else during those years).

* scored 126 touchdowns (that's a s**tload).

* for a while was at the top of the list for career rushing yards (he has since dropped to eighth place—still, his 12,312 yards are none too shabby).

Another cool thing Brown did was retire at his peak. In 1965, he scored twenty-one touchdowns and was awarded his second MVP award (his first came in 1958), and the very next year, after nine seasons, he announced his retirement. Brown said, "For all the guys who stayed too long—Joe Louis, Muhammad Ali*—I thought it was embarrassing. People had sympathy for them and you should never have sympathy for a champion."

After he retired from football, Jim Brown had a successful, if undistin-

---

*Both legendary boxers.

guished, movie and television career. He appeared in such films as *The Dirty Dozen* (1967), *Black Gunn* (1972), and *Slaughter's Big Rip-Off* (1973), to name a few. His television guest spots included appearances on *I Spy* (1965), *CHiPs* (1983), *T.J. Hooker* (1984), and *The A-Team* (1986). He also devoted himself to urban causes: In the 1960s he created an organization called the Black Economic Union that helped black-owned businesses, and in the 1980s he began working with gangs, helping members move toward more productive lifestyles.

DICK BUTKUS, 1942–
NICKNAME: "THE ANIMAL"
1965–1973: Chicago Bears

With a name like "Dick Butkus," what else could you possibly be besides a ferocious football player?

Butkus is one of the greatest linebackers of all time. He played for the Chicago Bears from 1965 to 1973. In the words of Bears owner George Halas, "If God ever designed a man to be a professional football player, he had Butkus in mind." He became the most feared linebacker in the game, and he would do just about anything to get his linebacking job done. He is reported to have once said, "I sometimes have a dream where I hit a man so hard his head pops off and rolls downfield."

Butkus was characterized by his intensity on the field since he was a teenager. In high school, his coach wouldn't let him scrimmage* during practice for fear he would hurt one of his own teammates. During his playing years, Butkus stood at 6'3" and was 245 pounds. By today's giant standards for linebackers, those figures are no big whoop, but Butkus played almost forty years ago, when the Universal gym that he had in his basement was a novelty. At the peak of his playing Butkus was the subject of a *Playboy* magazine profile, which in 1970, was nearly the equivalent being on the cover of *Time* or *Newsweek*.† Arthur Kretchmer, who wrote

---

*A "scrimmage" is a game played during practice, during which teammates usually play against teammates.
†In those days, *Playboy* had a fine literary reputation to go along with its unique photographic reputation. It was a coup to write for, or be written about in, *Playboy.*

the piece, reported that Butkus was "built large and hard, big enough to make John Wayne look like his loyal sidekick. When he [walked], he [led] with his shoulders, and the slight forward hunch [gave] him an aura of barely restrained power. He always [seemed] to be ready."

JOHN ELWAY, 1960–

1983–1998: Denver Broncos

First of all, John Elway is really smart; he went to Stanford (where his father was the football coach) and majored in economics, which explains why he was able to develop a franchise of car dealerships across the country that has probably made him wealthier than his football career. On the field, he, like Dan Marino (see page 80), was known for last-minute, game-winning drives—but with forty-seven fourth-quarter comebacks, Elway holds the record.

Elway played for the Denver Broncos for fifteen years, from 1983–1998. He first wowed the football world in 1986 during a championship game against the Cleveland Browns with a ninety-nine-yard (that's from one end of the field to the other!), game-tying touchdown drive. This incident has become part of football legend, and it's referred to as "The Drive." If some guy mentions "The Drive," and you know what he's talking about, you will immediately be raised to goddess level, at which point this man will become putty in your hands—to use for business or pleasure or whatever purpose you have in mind.

Elway was a champion on the field for other reasons too. After doing a spectacular job leading the Broncos for nearly two decades—but never making it to the Super Bowl—he finally reached the promised land in 1998 and again in 1999. Elway also had the dignity to retire before he became decrepit. Among other reasons for retiring, he said that he no longer wanted to miss his children growing up, so he retired and began coaching his son's Little League team.

Elway exhibited a final note of grace with the timing of his retirement announcement: Every move Elway made was front-page news in Denver, so when his decision to retire fell right around the time that Colorado had to deal with the horror of the Columbine school shootings, he had the decency and presence of mind to delay the announcement about his retirement until Denver had recovered a bit.

BRETT FAVRE, 1969–

1991–present: Green Bay Packers

Favre (pronounced "farv"), the quarterback for the Green Bay Packers, is among the best quarterbacks of all time. But in my opinion, the best thing about him is his role in the movie *There's Something About Mary*. Favre has a tiny part (but one that's bigger than a cameo) in the movie. Ben Stiller does a bit where he goofs on Favre's hard-to-pronounce last name. Meanwhile, Favre delivers his three lines of dialogue kind of like a kid in a high school play, but it works brilliantly.

Oh, yeah, football. Favre has been leading the Packers and doing incredible things for them for over a decade, including taking them to victory in the Super Bowl in 1997. Favre is one of those quarterbacks (like Montana, Elway, or Marino) who can lead his team from a seemingly hopeless loss to a win. Even seasoned football watchers are left in awe of what he can make happen on the football field. (Never, ever bet against Favre.) Favre is the recipient of three MVP awards, but he is best known for his toughness, for overcoming adversity, and for being just a regular guy. On the toughness thing—Favre holds the record for the most consecutive games, more than 200;* he's played with a broken thumb (ouch!), and he played the day after his father died. "Any discussion of toughness in the NFL starts with Brett Favre because Brett Favre starts. Every game. Week after week. Year after year," wrote Larry Weisman in a 2005 *USA Today* article.

Favre is not a razzle-dazzle kind of guy. He's just a good ol' boy from Mississippi who loves to play football, and it shows. He's at the top of the pack of quarterbacks, and he is a shoo-in for the Hall of Fame.[†]

---

*As of February 2005, Favre had started in 208 consecutive games.
[†]At the end of the 2004–05 season, the possibility of Favre retiring was in the news, but as of this writing, he intends to be leading the Packers again for the 2005 season.

DAN MARINO, 1961–

1983–1999: Miami Dolphins

Dan Marino, the Miami Dolphins' quarterback for seventeen years, is one of the most recent enshrinees in the NFL Hall of Fame. Marino holds some of the top records—very impressive records—among quarterbacks; as of now he's the most productive quarterback ever. He holds the career record for most touchdowns passes (420), most passing yards (61,361), and until very recently, what was considered a staggering record of forty-eight touchdown passes in a single season. Peyton Manning, the new boy-wonder quarterback of the Indianapolis Colts (more on him later) broke this record in the 2004–05 season and is predicted to surpass more of Marino's marks in the future.

The heartbreaking aspect of Marino's career is not that Manning is on track to break his records, but that this crème de la crème quarterback never won a Super Bowl. He got his team there twice, but left in defeat both times. And it bothers him. As he told ESPN's Dan Patrick in an interview for *ESPN The Magazine*, "as far as giving some of [my records] up to win a Super Bowl, I would for sure."*

Nevertheless, Marino's reputation as a football superstar is solid. Among Marino's many talents was pulling his team out of a hole in the last few minutes of a game. His team could be down by two or more touchdowns with minutes to go, and Marino would perform miracles. At his Pittsburgh high school, he was a multitalented athlete and was also made an offer to play professional baseball with the Kansas City Royals. Instead, he followed his gridiron heart and went just down the road to the University of Pittsburgh, where he was a starter as a *freshman*.

Marino, who is a commentator on HBO's *Inside the NFL*, had a brief, exciting Hollywood stint playing himself in the hilarious 1994 flick *Ace Ventura: Pet Detective*, which starred Jim Carrey.

---

*Reprinted in the 2000 book *Outtakes*.

JOE MONTANA, 1956–

1979–92: San Francisco 49ers
1993–94: Kansas City Chiefs

You need to know two things about Joe Montana. First, along with Johnny Unitas, Dan Marino, and Joe Namath, he is one of the greatest quarterbacks of all time. Second (and more important?), he has the most gorgeous ice-blue eyes ever seen in the NFL. Writing about him in *Football Digest* in 2000, Chuck O'Donnell (a *guy*) called him "the matinee-idol quarterback." He played most of his career with the San Francisco 49ers, where he won *four* Super Bowls and was named the Super Bowl MVP three times.

Montana combined Marino's game-saving abilities and Joe Namath's charisma. He went beyond charisma and cool, though, exhibiting an astonishing steely grace under pressure that has been called "Montana's Magic." Thirty-one times in his NFL career he led his team in fourth-quarter comebacks.

HOW THE LATE, GREAT COMEDIAN JOHN CANDY AIDED JOE MONTANA

In Super Bowl XXIII, 1989, San Francisco was down 16–13 against the Cincinnati Bengals. They weren't just down in points—they were down the field on their own 8-yard line with only three minutes left to try to go 92 yards to tie or win the game. Montana, undaunted as usual by the oppressive odds, was focusing on something else instead. He sensed that one of his young linemen, Harris Barton, had a case of the Super Bowl jitters and looked for a way to calm him down. He surveyed the stadium and in the huddle—in the final three minutes of the Super Bowl—said, "Hey, look, there's John Candy," as if they were shooting the breeze over a beer. Montana successfully calmed Barton down, and then, in a dizzying span of two minutes and thirty-six seconds, completed eight of nine passes. In a total of eleven plays in less than three minutes, in a dazzling drive, Montana led the 49ers to one of their four Super Bowl victories.

You can't mention Montana's Magic without also mentioning his secret ingredient—Jerry Rice, the 49ers receiver who more often than not would catch Montana's soaring passes. Montana and Rice were a team within a team. (As of 2005, Rice, at forty-plus years old, is still a remarkable player.)

Montana grew up in New Eagle, Pennsylvania, a state with a penchant for rearing great quarterbacks (Dan Marino, Johnny Unitas, and Joe Namath, to name a few), then moved a bit farther west in his college years, attending Notre Dame.

JOE NAMATH, 1943–
NICKNAMES: "BROADWAY JOE," "JOE WILLIE"
1965–76: New York Jets
1977: Los Angeles Rams

Joe Namath, another one of the great quarterbacks, personified cool, both on the field and off. Known as "Broadway Joe," he embraced the glitz and glamour that came with professional football in the 1960s and 1970s, and he took New York by storm with his flashiness and playboy antics, which the media devoured. Throughout those years, his good looks and bold sixties style (his longish hair was in direct contrast to Johnny Unitas's crew cut) made him one of American sports' first sex symbols. The sportswriter Dan Jenkins, in 1966, called him "pro football's very own Beatle."

Namath's antics would have secured his reputation as a colossal jerk if he weren't monumentally awesome on the field. A defining moment in Namath's career was in 1969, three days before the Super Bowl, in which Namath's team, the New York Jets, would face the heavily favored Baltimore Colts with the legendary Unitas at quarterback. Namath, ignoring his team's serious underdog status, publicly proclaimed, "We're gonna win. I personally guarantee it." And they did, stunning the football world and assuring Joe Willie's place in football history.

Namath grew up in Beaver Falls, Pennsylvania, where, like so many great athletes, he excelled in more than one sport. Upon graduation from high school, he had several offers from major-league baseball teams but instead went with one of his many college football offers. The one he accepted was from the University of Alabama and their top-rated team, the Crimson Tide, with legendary coach Bear Bryant at the helm.

Later, Joe was plagued with knee injuries, but his reputation as an outstanding quarterback remains untarnished. The next time you're with a crowd of football fans, here's a sports-savvy thing to say: "I still haven't seen anyone who comes close to matching Namath's totally cool confidence—well, maybe Favre."

JOE, THE OTHER GEMINI

When I was twelve years old, I was invited to a Jets game at Shea Stadium in Queens, New York—the team's home back then. I knew nothing about football, but having nothing better to do, I went—and was struck immediately by Joe Willie fever. This infatuation was the spark that ignited my lifelong enthusiasm for football (and my lifelong crush on Joe). During the course of writing this book I discovered thrilling news (for me)—*Joe and I have the same birthday!* May 31. But please let the record show that I was born fifteen years after Broadway Joe.

WALTER PAYTON, 1954–1999
NICKNAME: "SWEETNESS"
1975–1987: Chicago Bears

Walter Payton is the other running back you need to know besides Jim Brown, whose career rushing record he broke. Several of Payton's records have subsequently been broken, but he remains number two in career rushing yards, with 16,726, and rushing touchdowns (touchdowns made by running into the end zone), with 110.* He was given the nickname "Sweetness" because he was known for always having a

---

*Emmitt Smith, who retired from football in 2005, broke both of these records. Marcus Allen, who retired from the NFL in 1997, also broke Payton's touchdown record.

kind word; for always being there to lift a teammate up when he was down.

Payton played for the Chicago Bears for thirteen years (1975–1987). Football fans loved him because not only was he skilled, he was tough, too—an essential quality for a star running back. The sign of a really great running back is one who won't scurry out of bounds (when he has the ball) to avoid being tackled (and thus gain a few extra yards), but one who will put his shoulder down, plow through the oncoming defenders, and take the hit. Not only was he was tough on the field, but he was always on the field. In his thirteen professional seasons, he missed only one game and was never seriously injured.

Payton began his high school career in the late sixties, in a segregated school that later became integrated. When it came time to decide among the many college offers he received, he chose Jackson State College, a historically black college (now Jackson State University). Football was only one thing he excelled in. By twenty, he had a bachelor's degree in communications and began work toward a master's degree in education for the deaf. In his autobiography, *Sweetness*, he wrote that he followed this path "to help dispel the myth that athletes in general, and black athletes in particular, don't have to work to get their diplomas, and that they don't learn anything anyway."

Tragically, in 1999, a few years after retiring from football, Walter Payton died of bile-duct cancer at age forty-five. In Payton's *New York Times* obituary, NFL commissioner Paul Tagliabue lauded Payton as "an inspiration in everything he did."

WILLIAM PERRY, 1962–
NICKNAME: "THE FRIDGE" OR "THE REFRIGERATOR"
1985–93: Chicago Bears
1993–95: Philadelphia Eagles

"The Fridge," so named because of his girth—he weighed more than 300 pounds—made football *fun*, and he made headlines for doing so. He was a lovable, giant teddy bear of a man who never let his fame go to his head. Although the 300-pounders are pretty common in today's NFL, he was somewhat of a novelty during his playing days in the eighties and nineties.

A defensive tackle who played with the Chicago Bears for ten years, Perry was among the reasons the Bears went to the Super Bowl in 1986. He could do anything on the field—which is surprising for a defensive lineman, and even more surprising for one so large. (According to his Web site—www.thefridge.net—his Super Bowl ring is the largest ever made.) During his tenure with the Bears, The Fridge, with his gap-toothed grin, became America's sweetheart.

So this big teddy bear of a guy who's getting all the glory—the endorsements, the money, the whole bit—then leaves the sport gracefully. After nine years in the NFL, he knew he was past his prime and retired in 1995. Profiled in a 2000 "Where Are They Now?" article in *Sports Illustrated,* The Fridge, wrote Austin Murphy, is "a brick-layin', bass-hookin' picture of contentment." For about five years after he retired back home in his native Aiken, South Carolina, The Fridge worked laying bricks in a subcontracting business with his father-in-law and brother-in-law. Now he spends his leisure time relaxing with his wife and four kids. Asked by Murphy if he missed celebrity and its trappings, he responded, "This is me now. Those things you're talking about, that's just stuff in the breeze."

Five years after the *SI* article, The Fridge's appeal remains strong. As of 2005, he is still featured in commercials for ESPN and Coors, among others.

JERRY RICE, 1962–

1985–2000: San Francisco 49ers
2001–03: Oakland Raiders
2004: Seattle Seahawks
2005: Denver Broncos

Jerry Rice is the greatest receiver in NFL history, and he has been playing longer than just about everyone. He began his professional football career in 1985, when "surfing" still only meant riding waves in the ocean. He is one of only two players from the 1985 draft class still playing—the other is Doug Flutie, quarterback for the San Diego Chargers. Yes, you've done the math correctly—Jerry Rice is over forty and is still playing, as of the 2005 season. While his longevity is astounding, what he has done in his more than two decades in the game is even more breathtaking. Here are the highlights:

* For twenty years, Jerry Rice caught a pass in every game he played— 274 straight games. That record-breaking streak came to an end on Sunday, September 19, 2004, but I don't think Rice has anything to worry about—it's not likely that anyone will surpass it anytime soon, if ever.

* He holds thirteen league records and ten Super Bowl records.

* He was league MVP three times, and Super Bowl MVP once.

* *ESPN SportsCentury* notes that at the end of the century, Rice "[owned] the receivers wing of the NFL record book." His ownership comes by having achieved the most catches, most yards, and most touchdowns for a receiver, ever.

Rice has an uncanny ability to "get open"—football-speak for getting away from defenders in order to catch the ball. For years it was quarterback Joe Montana throwing the ball to him, when they led the San Francisco 49ers, the team that dominated the league for years. In 2001, after the 49ers decided they wanted to develop younger talent, Jon Gruden, a former 49ers player who was then coaching the Oakland Raiders (and who, incidentally, was a year younger than Rice) picked him up. Gruden, whose banter typically isn't full of niceties, said of Rice, "Jerry is my idol. When I was with the 49ers in my first year in the NFL, I couldn't believe what I saw . . . the vibrance that he brought to the team. He is the best coach, the best role model you could ever be around."

Since then, both Gruden and Rice have moved on. Gruden is now the head coach of the Tampa Bay Buccaneers, and Rice was with the Seattle

Seahawks until they released him in February 2005. In May of 2005, Rice signed a one-year contract with the Denver Broncos. Word on the street is that he'll retire after the 2005 season but never say never. . . .

EMMITT SMITH, 1969–

1990–2002: Dallas Cowboys
2003–04: Arizona Cardinals

In 2002, Emmitt Smith broke Walter Payton's record to become the NFL's all-time leading rusher—meaning that, as a running back, he ran for more yards (with the ball) than anyone else in NFL history. He also holds the all-time record for rushing touchdowns, and he had eleven straight seasons where he rushed for more than 1,000 yards. Smith was a major factor in three Super Bowl victories when he played with the Dallas Cowboys in the nineties, and he was named Super Bowl MVP once.

Smith, since his earliest pro days, deliberately pursued Payton's record. "Rarely has any athlete relished his pursuit of history as much as Emmitt Smith. Unlike other contemporaries . . . Smith embraces the attention, courts the acclaim, understands the obligations generated by fame," wrote Paul Attner in *The Sporting News* (November 2002).

Smith's glory days (and they were glorious) were spent with the Cowboys, for thirteen years, from 1990–2002. At that point the Cowboys let him go and he signed a two-year, $7.5 million deal with the Arizona Cardinals. At the completion of his contract at the end of the 2004 season, having achieved his dream of being the all-time NFL rusher, Smith announced his retirement.

Smith may not have had the pizzazz that running backs Jim Brown and Walter Payton displayed during their careers, but he had extraordinary levels of determination, intelligence, and relentlessness that got the job done.

LAWRENCE TAYLOR, 1959–
NICKNAME: "L.T."

1981–1993: New York Giants

Lawrence Taylor—known as "L.T."—was a linebacker who, like Dick Butkus before him, made the linebacker position exciting to watch. If someone was tackled while L.T. was on the field, it seemed that nine out of ten times, L.T. had done the tackling. He was aggressive to an extreme, and he pioneered a move that involved swiping the ball out of the quarterback's hands.

The New York Giants have won the Super Bowl twice, in 1987 and 1991, and both times L.T. was on the field. In 1986, he was named the NFL's MVP, making him the first defensive player to be so honored since 1971.* Among his specialties was sacking the quarterback, which he did frequently and ferociously, accumulating an impressive career total of 142 sacks.[†]

When *The Sporting News* chose L.T. as one of football's one hundred greatest players (1999), they said this about him: "When Lawrence Taylor stepped onto the field, everybody noticed. The riveting eyes, imposing glare and intimidating, perfectly sculpted body were merely appetizers for the savage rage he would unleash on every play. . . . Linemen forgot counts, quarterbacks dropped snaps, and blockers jumped offside."

Sadly, L.T. made headlines not only for his on-field talent but also for his off-field problems. Although he was a consummate, if not fierce, professional on the field, he was a scofflaw off, and his incomparable career as an NFL defensive player is tainted by his suspensions for substance abuse and his subsequent arrests. He once said, "Sunday is a different world. It's like a fantasy world which I'd rather live in. Then I go back to the rest of the world and that's where the trouble starts."

A sports-savvy thing to say is: "All the talk today is about QBs. It

---

*Minnesota Vikings' Alan Page (now a justice on the Minnesota State Supreme Court) received the MVP honor in 1971.
[†]In a gruesome football moment, L.T. smashed into Washington Redskins quarterback Joe Theismann and broke Theismann's leg—a career-ending injury. L.T., though aggressive, was not vicious and always regretted this unfortunate accident.

would be nice if there was some excitement about the defense, like there was with L.T."

JOHNNY UNITAS, 1933–2002
NICKNAME: "JOHNNY U."
1956–72: Baltimore Colts
1973: San Diego Chargers

Johnny Unitas is considered one of the greatest quarterbacks of all time. He was a working-class hero who grew up in a blue-collar family devastated by the Depression, and he went on to become one of football's first superstars.

Unitas played from 1956 to 1973, all for the Baltimore Colts (now the Indianapolis Colts), with the exception of his final year. As his career was soaring, the power of television was sweeping the nation, and society was becoming more taken with celebrity. Unitas, however, cared little about the celebrity aspects of the game. It was the *game*, not the glitz, that was important. In many ways, his modesty and his old-fashioned values made him the opposite of the flashy QB, Joe Namath, who later became heir to Unitas's throne.

In 1958, in a game that is considered by many to be the greatest ever played, Unitas led the Colts to victory in overtime in the championship game against the Giants. The drama of this game—Unitas threw two long passes that clinched the game in both the final seconds of regulation and again during sudden-death overtime—is thought by some to have catapulted football into the forefront of American sports culture, competing with baseball for America's attention and making television an essential ingredient in the popularity of professional sports in America.

Unitas threw at least one touchdown pass in forty-seven consecutive regular-season games (i.e., not including playoffs and championship games). It's really, really hard to throw a touchdown pass—a touchdown pass is when the receiver not only catches the ball but runs it into the end zone, or catches the ball in the end zone. Anyway, no one since has come close to breaking Unitas's record.

Dome of Disgrace

O. J. SIMPSON, 1947–
NICKNAME: "THE JUICE"
> 1969–77: Buffalo Bills
> 1978–79: San Francisco 49ers

Before he was charged with the murder of his ex-wife, Nicole Brown Simpson, and her friend Ronald Goldman, O.J., who was once known as "Juice," was famous for being one of history's greatest running backs. As the years go by, his fabulous football feats are being forgotten, and he is becoming the guy who got way too much attention and presumably got away with murder. Here's what he threw away:

He was a black hero adored by both blacks *and* whites. In a mid-seventies poll of grade-schoolers commissioned by *Ladies' Home Journal*, Simpson was voted the nation's most admired figure, by both boys *and* girls. As a pitchman for Hertz during the same decade, he was the first black celebrity featured in a national corporate ad campaign.

Simpson was taller, stronger, heavier, and *faster* than most of the running backs during his playing days. In 1968, he won the Heisman Trophy (an annual award given to the most outstanding college football player), then went on to break Jim Brown's all-time single-season NFL rushing record, finishing with 2,003 yards in fourteen games.

Oh, well. Never mind.

Legends in Training

TOM BRADY, 1977–
> 2000–present: New England Patriots

Tom Brady's trajectory to the top has been unstoppable since high school. As a teenager in San Mateo, California, he was smart, nice, hard-working, and unbelievably talented at both football and baseball. Baseball's Montreal Expos wanted to draft him as a catcher right after high school, but Brady decided that his true love was football and went to the University of Michigan to pursue his gridiron dreams.

Although Brady wasn't a shining star at U of M, he was good enough to get drafted by the New England Patriots. He spent his first season with the team on the bench, but then, in 2001, when starting quarterback Drew Bledsoe got injured, Brady stepped in and calmly and coolly led his team to victory after victory. At twenty-four, he became the youngest starting quarterback ever to lead a team to an NFL championship—that's right, they won the Super Bowl that season! Brady has also led the Patriots to two *more* Super Bowls wins, in 2004 and 2005. He was named MVP in both of those Super Bowls.

One other thing to know about Brady: He is extremely good-looking. He's got classic, all-American (whatever that means), hunky good looks. But don't take my word for it—trust *People* magazine. Brady landed on their annual fifty most beautiful people list in 2002.

DAUNTE CULPEPPER, 1977–

1999–present: Minnesota Vikings

Daunte Culpepper, a quarterback for the Minnesota Vikings, is one of the best in the NFL today. He is a force for defenses to contend with because he is a master at scrambling (i.e., evading the defense and not getting sacked). And at 6'4", 265 pounds, he is BIG—much bigger than most other QBs in the league.

Culpepper's personal story is as amazing as his athletic abilities. He was born to an unmarried prison inmate in a Miami jail and was subsequently adopted by Emma Culpepper, who worked with troubled teenagers and volunteered at the prison where Daunte's mother was incarcerated. At the time of Daunte's birth, Emma Culpepper was sixty-two and had already raised a dozen children who were not her own, so she was reluctant to adopt another infant. But she saw something special in Daunte.

Culpepper attended the University of Central Florida, earning UCF a national reputation in football—but as is frequently the case, as you've seen, he was a multitalented athlete. In his senior year of college, Culpepper was also drafted by the New York Yankees, but football was his pro sport of choice.

PEYTON AND ELI MANNING

PEYTON MANNING, 1976–
1998–present: Indianapolis Colts

ELI MANNING, 1981–
2004–present: New York Giants

Sports do run in families, but you'll usually hear about a high school or college player or coach whose offspring goes pro, or perhaps the occasional set of brothers* who go pro—but a *father and two sons*, all pros in the same sport, all playing the same position, is pretty rare. That is the case, however, with dad Archie Manning (an excellent football player in the seventies) and his two sons, Eli and Peyton—the mighty Manning family.†

In July 2004, Eli Manning, a rookie just out of the University of Mississippi and the younger of the two brothers, signed a six-year contract with the New York Giants worth $45 million (along with another $9 million in incentives), making it the most lucrative rookie contract in NFL history. Of that figure, $20 million is signing bonus money, which is believed to be the second-largest signing bonus ever in the NFL. And guess who received the *first*-largest? That's right, older brother Peyton. In March of the same year, Peyton Manning, who had been playing with the Indianapolis Colts since 1998, signed a seven-year, $98 million deal with the Colts, $34.5 million of which was the signing bonus.

Peyton has proven he's worth it. In 2004 he was chosen as the NFL's

---

*The year 2004 was an exceptional year for brothers playing simultaneously in the NFL. That year, there were five sets of quarterback brothers alone.

†For the record, there is a third brother, Cooper Manning, who also played football for Mississippi before a spinal condition put a premature end to his football career.

co-MVP (along with Steve McNair, another star QB), and he became the *first* quarterback to achieve more than 3,000 yards passing (meaning that the total yards gained from his complete passes was 3,000) in each of his first six seasons, the first to get more than 4,000 yards passing in five straight seasons, and the first to toss twenty-five or more touchdown passes for six straight years. And he keeps on getting better. By the end of the 2004 season, he had broken Dan Marino's record for single-season touchdown passes (Manning, 49; Marino, 48).

Eli's rookie year with the Giants was not particularly impressive, but some of the greatest quarterbacks have had inauspicious beginnings. As with many athletes, time will tell.

DONOVAN MCNABB, 1976–

1999–present: Philadelphia Eagles

Donovan McNabb of the Philadelphia Eagles is among today's top quarterbacks. He has led his team to three divisional championships and, most important, in 2005, led his team to the Super Bowl against the formidable New England Patriots. (The Eagles didn't win, but it was a most respectable 24–21 loss.) McNabb has been rated as one of the best for several years:

* At the conclusion of the 2004 season, McNabb had the highest winning percentage (.709) of all QBs in the NFL (Favre is next at .658).

* He is one of only four players in NFL history to throw four or more touchdown passes in at least five games in a single season (the others are Manning, Marino, and Favre).

But it wasn't until the 2004 season, with the addition of Terrell Owens as a receiver, that his talent really began to shine—some predict that they will be the next enduring dynamic duo, à la Joe Montana and Jerry Rice.

McNabb's name may be familiar to you even if you don't follow football, because there was a big brouhaha perpetrated by radio talk-show host Rush Limbaugh that ultimately blew up in Rush's face. In the fall of 2003, on the ESPN show *NFL Countdown*, Limbaugh made some ridiculous remarks that smacked of racism and cost him his job as commentator on that television program—he basically said that McNabb was overrated because the media wanted black quarterbacks to succeed, and thus gave him more favorable attention than he deserved. Meanwhile, McNabb's performance on the gridiron has just been getting better and better, so Limbaugh's been forced to eat crow (and go into rehab). McNabb handled the whole episode with characteristic grace and dignity and never let it distract him.

CHAD PENNINGTON, 1976–

2000–present: New York Jets

Pennington's story is not unlike Tom Brady's. And let's cut to the chase here—I would put them both in the "hottie" category. While Brady has a more tall, handsome, athletic cool about him, Chad (may I call you Chad, Chad?) has an irresistible boyish charm. Watching him play or be interviewed may give you the sudden urge to bake chocolate-chip cookies for him, even if you've never baked a thing in your life.

Chad, like Brady, was a major sports success in high school and college, *and* an academic success—he was a finalist for a Rhodes Scholarship when he was a college senior at Marshall University in West Virginia. He was drafted by the New York Jets in 2000 but was forced to watch from the sidelines for more than two seasons. Then, during the fifth game of his third year (2002), Vinny Testaverde, the Jets veteran quarterback, was injured, and Pennington stepped in. He performed magically for the rest of the season, taking the Jets to the playoffs, something he repeated in the 2004 season.

MICHAEL VICK, 1980–

2001–present: Atlanta Falcons

When Michael Vick plays, the Falcons win; when he doesn't, they lose. Until Michael Vick started playing, the Falcons' stadium in Atlanta, the Georgia Dome, had never been sold out.

Vick's stats aren't the best in the league, but his unconventional style as a quarterback defies statistics. He's essentially changing the way QBs play: He's fast—he runs as much as he throws. Falcons general manager Rich McKay told the *Atlanta Journal-Constitution*, "You can't go by traditional quarterback ratings with him. He has a skill set that has not been seen."

It's a skill set worth a lot of money. In December 2004, Vick signed a ten-year, $130 million deal with the Falcons, essentially guaranteeing that his whole career will be spent with Atlanta. *The Sporting News*'s Dan Pompei in January 2005 called Vick a "fountain of hope" for his teammates.

KURT WARNER, 1971–

1998–2003: St. Louis Rams
2004–05: New York Giants
2005–present: Arizona Cardinals

In 1998, QB Kurt Warner became a huge name in football. His rise to NFL stardom was perceived by many to have happened "overnight"—although, in truth, he endured years of toiling and struggling in obscurity before gaining recognition. Warner started out playing for the lowly Arena Football League, which is played on a small indoor field the size of a hockey rink, before finally getting a break with the St. Louis Rams in 1998. Even then, he was only a backup quarterback, and there was every likelihood that he'd spend the season (and the seasons to come) on the sidelines. But when the starting quarterback, Trent Green, got hurt, Warner stepped in and—voilà—made magic happen on the field. He quickly became a star quarterback who, over the next few years, took his team to the Super Bowl twice, in 2000 and 2001, winning in 2000.

More important, Kurt Warner is the new millennium's knight in shining armor, and not because of football. Here's the short form: Warner meets his wife, Brenda, in 1992 at a country and western dance in Cedar Falls, Iowa. She tells him that she has two kids and that if he doesn't want to see her again, she would understand. The next morning, he shows up at her door *with a rose* and wants to meet the kids. Then Brenda tells him that her son, Zachary, had a horrible accident when he was four months old and suffers from neurological damage. Warner remains undeterred. Add to this the fact that neither of them at this point had a pot to piss in—he was stocking shelves in a grocery store and she was on food stamps. *And* then Brenda's parents died tragically in a tornado a few years later. Well, you can see why, even with Warner's football stardom, he says, "The things that are important are not throwing a bunch of touchdown passes."

Beginning with the game when he replaced Green, Warner adopted a ritual—a ritual of love you might say. At the end of every game, he goes over to the stands, finds Brenda, and kisses her.

Warner went through a slump with the Rams after 2002, with injuries largely to blame, and he was traded to the New York Giants in 2004. Then, in 2005 his star rose again when he signed a one-year, $4 million contract with the Arizona Cardinals to be their starting quarterback.

Glossary

Blitz: When defensive players in addition to defensive linemen (who always rush the quarterback) rush toward the quarterback as soon as the ball is snapped, in an attempt to sack (tackle) him. The blitz is not executed on every play, because if it fails, the rest of the offense (since the defense has used most of their men to try to sack the quarterback) is running down the field with the ball.

Block: To use your body to prevent opposing players from doing whatever it is they want to do, or to clear a path for the guy with the ball so he can run toward the end zone. The offensive line will try to block the defensive line from rushing the quarterback, for example, and the defense will try to block a kick (i.e., use their hands to try to deflect the ball as it whizzes past their heads) by the of-fense. A block differs from a tackle because, in a tackle, you physically grab, hold, or do whatever it takes to pull your opponent to the ground.

Center: The *center* is a member of the offense—he lines up right smack in the center of the offensive line, directly in front of the quarterback. At the begin-ning of a play, the quarterback puts his hands underneath the center's derriere, and the center "snaps" the ball back through his legs and into the quarterback's hands. The center also protects the quarterback by blocking the defensive guys who try to move forward and rush the quarterback. The center is usually a very big guy.

Cornerback: The *cornerback* is a defensive player. He stands toward the outside of the defensive line, usually opposite the receivers, and tries to defend the pass—that is, he tries to prevent the receiver from catching the ball, or even catches it himself for an interception. There are usually two cornerbacks on the field at a given time.

Defensive End: There are always two *defensive ends* on the defensive line. Their two main jobs are (1) to prevent the running back from running and (2) to rush the quarterback. They stand on the ends of the defensive line, hence the title *defensive "end."*

Down: A football-y term for a try or a chance. The offense has four downs to gain a minimum of ten yards either by passing (throwing) the ball or running with it. Each down is called a *play*.

Drive: A series of plays by the offense. A successful drive will yield a lot of yards, bringing the offense closer to the end zone and giving them a chance to score.

End Zone: The *end zones* are located on both ends of the football field. Between them is one hundred yards. When the ball is run or passed into the end zone, the offense scores a *touchdown*. When the ball is kicked through an opposing team's goalposts—which are in the far end of each end zone—the offense scores either a *field goal* or an *extra point*, depending on the situation.

Fair Catch: A guy who is nice, handsome, and does the housework—but has trouble holding down a job—rates only as a fair catch. In football, it's when the receiver of a punt decides—before the punt reaches him—to catch the ball but not run forward with it. The punt returner signals for a fair catch by raising one arm and waving it. This essentially means, "please don't hurt me," because when a fair catch has been signaled, the receiver cannot be touched, but he still *must* catch the ball. The punt returner chooses this option, essentially, to avoid getting hit. (Remember that once the punt has been executed, there is a veritable wall of human muscle heading straight toward him.)

Field Goal: A way to score three points by kicking the ball through the uprights of the goalpost. If the offense does not have a good chance of scoring a touchdown (i.e., it's fourth down, or time is running out, and the offense is too far from the goal line to risk attempting a touchdown and not making it), they will usually try to kick a field goal instead. The closer the kicker is to the end zone, the easier it is to accomplish.

Field-Goal Attempt: When the offense decides to attempt a field goal. It gets its own term, because members of the special teams come onto the field for the field-goal attempt, and there's a lot of rigmarole going on, and "field-goal attempt" gives the football broadcasters a fancy term to use while the teams get organized.

First-and-Ten: The phrase used to describe the situation in which the offense has a first down and ten yards to go. Each *drive* (possession) begins with a team having a "first-and-ten." If the offense gets the minimum ten yards in four downs, it becomes "first-and-ten" again.

Flea-Flicker: A term for the more advanced football student, but one that sounds so, well, cute that I had to include it. A *flea-flicker* is a play in which the quarterback hands off the ball to a running back, who then flicks it back to the quarterback, who then throws it to someone else, or maybe runs with it himself. The play fools the defense because they assume the running back is just going to run with the ball. This flea-flicker isn't used much, which is too bad—it's pretty cool to watch, and say.

Fumble: Oopsy-daisy. A *fumble* is just what it sounds like—a fumble, a bumble—dropping the ball. The worst kind of fumble is when the runner or receiver (or whoever has the ball) just kind of drops it for no reason. These moments are extremely embarrassing for the "fumbler," and they seem to immediately lead the owner of the team to think, "Why am I paying this #%;af*%! butterfingers $8 billion?" Slightly more redeemable is when the defense forces a fumble: When the guy with the ball is tackled, in theory, he is trained and paid well to hang on to that ball for dear life. But sometimes, the defense not only stops the offensive player (tackles him), it also wrests, punches, slams, or karate-chops the ball loose.

Hike: See *snap*.

Hit: When a player blocks or tackles another player. A good hit usually means a hard hit. If you've heard the sound of two helmets colliding, you'll understand why it's called a *hit*. A hit is really the same thing as a block or a tackle. Fans and broadcasters get excited about hard, tough hits, as in, "What a hit Joe Schmo just took! His brains must be scrambled."

Holding: *Holding* is a common penalty—it's when a player defends against another (who doesn't have the ball) by literally holding on to him and getting caught in the act. Holding can get into some very gray areas—it's difficult to tell after the fact whether a player did or did not hold. The bottom line is that you can't hold on to a player, unless he has the ball and you're attempting to tackle him. You gotta do your job—stop him or block and get on with it. You can't hold on and do a tango.

Interception: Every quarterback's nightmare. An *interception* occurs when the quarterback throws the ball, intending it to land in the hands of his own teammate, but it lands in the hands of the defense instead. The offense then loses the ball. Interceptions can be very exciting, dramatic, and entertaining—especially when a 300-pound defensive guy intercepts the ball and starts to run with it. These guys are not built for speed, and their runs are sometimes less than graceful but always fun to watch.

Kickoff: A *kickoff* happens at the very beginning of the game, after halftime, to begin an overtime period, and after a team has scored. To execute a kickoff, the kicker (a member of the "special teams") kicks the football off a tee, a stand upon which the ball sits just slightly off the ground. The kickoff takes place at the kicking team's 30-yard line (see diagram on page 48), and the kicker tries to kick the ball as far as possible, so that the opposing team will have a longer way to go to get the ball into the (kicking team's) end zone.

Kick Return: In a kickoff, or whenever the ball is kicked (on a punt, for example) the team that is kicking knows that the other team is going to get the ball, so they want to kick it as far as possible. By kicking it far, the opposing team has to travel a longer distance to get to the goal. The *kick return* is the act of catching and running with the ball. It refers to that single play only. Occasionally there are dramatic kick returns—Team Macho will kick the ball quite far, but Team Manly will catch it and run with it all the way down the field and score a touchdown. *Special teams* are used for kickoffs and kick returns.

 Linebackers: *Linebackers* are really big guys on the defense who are also fast and agile. (When you hear *linebacker*, think big, fast, and mean.) They are responsible for a variety of defensive tasks: They basically try to stop everyone—the running backs, the receivers, and occasionally the quarterback; they are usually in back of the line of scrimmage, behind the defensive linemen (hence "linebackers"); and they are usually the players who call the plays in the defensive huddle— think of them as the "quarterbacks" of the defense.

Line of Scrimmage: The line of scrimmage is where the ball ends up when a play is finished, and the point from which the next play begins. It is an imaginary line on which the offensive linemen and defensive linemen line up, facing one another.

Linemen, Defensive: The job of the *defensive linemen*—i.e., the defensive players who form a veritable wall of human muscle and face the offense—is to try to sack the quarterback and stop the running backs. To do so, they must penetrate the offensive line. The defensive line is usually made up of the defensive tackles and defensive ends. These guys line up directly across from the center and other offensive linemen on the line of scrimmage.

Linemen, Offensive: The *offensive line* is comprised of the center, the guards, and the tackles, who line up at the line of scrimmage. The offensive line is also a veritable wall of human muscle. They make football confusing, because their job is basically to *defend* the *offense*—they defend the quarterback against getting sacked, and they try to prevent the defense from defending and/or tackling the runners and receivers. The offensive line tries to make way for the runner to run with the ball, or the receiver to catch the ball. Even though they are part of the team with the ball (the offense), offensive linemen rarely have the ball in their hands.

Man-to-Man Defense: A defensive strategy that is the opposite idea of "zone defense." In man-to-man defense, the defensive players defend against individual players, as opposed to defending an area.

Offsides: A penalty, and the football version of premature ejaculation. Until the center snaps the ball (on the quarterback's call—hut, hut, grunt, grunt, etc.), no one on the line (either the defensive or offensive line) is supposed to move. (The backfield—receivers, etc.—can move [but only one at a time], hence the oft heard "backfield in motion.") If they do, a penalty is called against the team that moved. (To be completely accurate, the term "offsides" applies only to the defense; for the offense, this penalty is technically called a "false start.")

Passer: Another word for the quarterback, or the person who throws the ball (which is usually only the quarterback).

Penalties: Penalties are no-nos. There are different levels of severity, and the punishments are decided accordingly. A minor penalty will usually result in a loss of five to ten yards for the wrongdoer's team. Something really bad will result in a fifteen-yard penalty (a loss or gain of fifteen yards) and sometimes an automatic first down for the offense. When the offense commits a penalty, they lose yards—the offense is pushed back and the defense moves forward. When the defense commits a penalty, the offense gains yards—the defense is pushed back and the offense moves forward. When a penalty occurs, the ref will throw a yellow flag onto the field and call the penalty against the offending team.

Personal Foul: A type of penalty that includes flagrant offenses such as "roughing the passer" (being very, very mean to the quarterback), "face mask" (intentionally grabbing the opponent's face mask in a particularly vicious way), "late hit" (when a guy is hit, blocked, or tackled after the play is called dead or is out of bounds), and other gratuitous acts of violence.

Punt: A type of kick—a *drop kick* to be specific. The offense punts the ball on fourth down to send the ball (and thus the opposing team) as far back as possible from the goal that the opponent needs to reach. When the offense punts, it has lost possession of the ball (because it didn't get ten yards within four downs).

Quarterback: The big cheese, the head honcho, da man. Football is a team sport, but the quarterback is unequivocally the leader of the team. A team cannot win games without a talented quarterback. The quarterback has to be quick in mind and body; to be cool when tons of human flesh are bearing down on him; to know hundreds of plays backward and forward; and to be the team's psyche. He must exude confidence, a never-say-die attitude, and a winning spirit every second that he's on that field. On top of that, he must have the respect of the entire team. Call the quarterback the "QB" if you want to sound sports-savvy.

Receiver: *Receivers* are part of the offense. They catch the ball (or are supposed to catch the ball) when the quarterback throws it to them. Wide receivers, tight ends, and split ends are all receivers. Generally (although only two types have "end" in their titles), they all have very cute, tight ends.

Roughing the Passer: When the defense gratuitously smashes the quarterback. The quarterback is vulnerable because he starts every play with the ball, and so the other team always wants to hit him (i.e., rush him or sack him, called "the blitz"). On top of that, the QB is usually smaller than the massive linemen because he has to be quick and agile—so everyone is supposed to play fair. The quarterback is paid lots and lots of money and is key to the game, so the owners want to get their money's worth and the coaches want to see the quarterback last more than a play or two. If a quarterback is sacked *before* he releases the ball, it does not count as a penalty, unless the ref decides the hit was illegal (i.e., made with the top of the helmet) or excessively vicious.

Running Back: The *running backs*, which include *halfbacks* and *fullbacks*, are the guys who run with the ball. They stand behind the quarterback, and when the quarterback hands the ball to them, they run, run, run. They are usually somewhat shorter and more compact than their gargantuan teammates, because they need to be quick and shift their body direction really quickly to avoid being blocked or tackled. "Backs" also block. In fact, fullbacks do more blocking than running. Backs also often catch passes. In short, they have a lot to do.

Rush: In football-speak, to *rush* is to *run*. If an offensive player "rushes" for fifty yards, it means he ran fifty yards (with the ball). When the defense "rushes" the quarterback, it means they run toward him.

Sack: A quarterback has been *sacked* when he's been tackled before he's had a chance to release the ball (to hand it off to a running back or pass it to a receiver). Sacks happen behind the line of scrimmage, so they result in a loss of yards for the offense. Sacks are very, very good for the defense, and very, very bad for the offense.

Safeties: Not to be confused with the scoring method that goes by the same name (see next entry). *Safeties* are defensive players. They usually stand behind all the other defenders and form a safety net—they are the last line of defense.

Safety: A rare way for the *defense* to score. Safeties yield two points, and they happen when the defense tackles an offensive player in his own end zone (that is, not the end zone that the offense is trying to get into for a touchdown, but the one at the opposite end of the field), or an offensive player fumbles the ball out of his own end zone. It hardly ever happens, so don't waste too many brain cells dwelling on it.

Snap (or Hike): Each *down* begins when the center *snaps* the ball to the quarterback, whose hands are underneath the center's tush, as previously noted. Sometimes the quarterback will be a few yards back from the center, in a *shotgun* position, so the snap is a slightly longer throw. It has to be a very quick, sharp toss from the center's hands into the quarterback's—it happens in a snap.

Special Teams: In addition to an offense and a defense, each team has *special teams*. These groups come on the field only for kicking situations: kickoffs, field-goal attempts, extra points, and punts.

Split End: A *split end* in football is a kind of wide receiver, but he positions himself farther away from the line than a wide receiver would. (He is *split* away from the line.) Like all receivers, he is counted on to catch the ball.

Tackle: To tackle is to knock the other guy down, usually by wrapping your arms around him and throwing him to the ground. (Note that offensive players cannot *tackle* defensive players; they can only *block* them.) Sometimes you'll see a pileup where a lot of guys have been knocked down on top of one another, and a mountain of hugeness results.

Tackle, Defensive: The *defensive tackles* line up on the defensive line. They are nose to nose with the offensive line, and they try to get past the offensive line to tackle the quarterback or running back. The defensive tackles are really, really big guys—250 pounds seems to be a minimum cutoff.

Tackle, Offensive: The *offensive tackles* line up on the offensive line, directly opposite the defensive line. They try to block the defense so that the quarterback can pass the ball easily (to a receiver or running back), or so the running back can run.

Tight End: Yes, as discussed, *tight ends*' ends are usually tight and cute. They're called *ends*, however, not because of their physique, but because they line up at the *ends* of the offensive line. They are blockers for the running backs and wide receivers who are supposed to catch the ball when the quarterback throws it to them. They also catch passes from the quarterback, like wide receivers.

Time-Out: Each team is allowed three *time-outs* a half. Players use them to stop the clock—to strategize, to regroup, to break the opponent's momentum, and to buy time when the clock is running out. We (the viewer) use them to snack, prepare for tomorrow's big office meeting, begin to panic about the big office meeting, apply nail polish, call a girlfriend, get the kids into bed, or all of the above.

Touchdown: A six-point score that is accomplished when the offense either runs with the ball into their opponent's end zone, or an offensive player catches the ball in the end zone. Of the five ways to score in football (the touchdown, the field goal, the two-point conversion, the extra point, and the safety), a touchdown yields the most points. Thus, the ultimate goal of the offense is to score touchdowns.

Two-Minute Warning: At two minutes before the half, and two minutes before the end of the game, the clock is stopped for a time-out, which is called the *two-minute warning*. This time-out does not use up either of the teams' allotted three time-outs.

Two-Point Conversion: After a touchdown, the offense can go for one or two extra points. It almost always goes for one extra point by kicking the ball through the goalposts. Occasionally, however, when the offense is desperate for more points in order to win or tie the game, it will go for two points. A two-point conversion is much more difficult to execute than the extra point, so it's risky. It's like a mini-touchdown—instead of kicking the ball through the goalposts, the offense must run the ball into the end zone, or throw it to someone in the end zone.

Wide Receiver: *Wide receivers* are not wide at all. They are, however, receivers, and most of them tend to be tall and lean, so they can extend their bodies every which way to reach for a ball, and then run with it once they catch it. They line up away from the line, hence the moniker, "wide."

Zone Defense: A defensive strategy that is the opposite of the "man-to-man" defense—instead of defending each player, each defensive player defends an area, so that no one on the offense can gain yards in that area.

Baseball

THE SOUND: *Thwack.* (A sleek bat making contact with a ball traveling 85+ mph.)

THE LOOK: Fairly fit men in snug-fitting pants and V-neck, button-down, short-sleeved shirts, tucked in and secured with a belt (baseball has a well-developed fashion sense).

THE PLACE: Ballparks. Most are outdoor stadiums, but some are enclosed.

THE ORGANIZATION: Major League Baseball (MLB), which is made up of two leagues, the American League and the National League.

> If a woman has to choose between catching a fly ball and saving an infant's life, she will choose to save the infant's life without even considering if there is a man on base.
> —Dave Barry

It's a bit difficult, even for a bona fide sports diva, to get sassy and irreverent about baseball. It's somehow improper, unpatriotic. With a history that is more than 150 years old, baseball transcends much of the razzle-dazzle hoopla that surrounds other professional sports today.

Baseball is unhurried. It is not bound by the clock—this is what most distinguishes it from the other big spectator sports. Baseball is a game of moments: exhilarating and excruciating, heartwarming and heartbreaking, dazzling and, yes, sometimes even dull. Red Barber, the greatest baseball announcer of all time, said that "baseball is dull only to dull minds," but I respectfully disagree—some games are simply more thrilling than others. Basically, baseball is a lot like life: There are moments of excitement and joy mixed with long stretches of monotony.

In *The Meaning of Sports*, sportswriter Michael Mandelbaum asserts that baseball is "the sport most powerfully associated with the past," the sport that conjures up the strongest feelings of nostalgia. This may be because baseball has a long history, beginning before the Civil War; or it could be, as Mandelbaum purports, that the leisurely and unhurried pace of the game harks back to "the world before the discipline of measured time, deadlines, schedules and wages paid by the hour . . . to the kind of world in which people did not say, 'I haven't got all day.'" More than any other pro sport, baseball brings to mind innocent images of Americana—hot dogs and Cracker Jack, summertime and jaw-dropping home runs.

So by now you can see why it's hard to have a cynical, irreverent attitude toward baseball—even though A-Rod has a $252 million dollar contract; Roger Clemens once threw a broken bat at Mike Piazza; and steroid use is casting a long shadow.

WRITERS AT BAT

Roger Angell, former fiction editor of *The New Yorker* cum baseball writer, calls baseball "the writer's game." Apparently it is the Pulitzer Prize–winning writer's game. Among the winners of this prestigious prize who have written about baseball are John Updike, political writer George Will, historian and journalist David Halberstam, and novelist Philip Roth.

HERE'S HOW IT WORKS

The word "linear" is often used to describe baseball, but I see it as more of a labyrinth, or a giant onion with lots and lots of layers. On one level the game is very simple—all a player has to do is hit the ball and run around the bases and score. *Bim bam boom.* However, if basketball is checkers, baseball is chess—and the endless configurations of its statistics are quantum physics! But have no fear—as with other sports, in baseball, a little bit of knowledge goes a long way. In this case, just the top layer will suffice.

The team *at bat* tries to score *runs* by having its batters hit the ball and then run around the *bases*. The team in the field has one overarching mission: to get *out* of the field and back up at bat so they can score. Thus, those in the field want to get the ball in their glove and then get the batter and/or runners out.

A team is allowed three outs per turn at bat (per *inning*). Once a team makes three outs, they give up their turn at bat and then their opponents (who have been playing the field) come up to bat. Three outs and *that* team is out—and then a new inning begins. Nine innings. Nine players in the batting order. Baseball is obsessed with the number three and its multiples.

Baseball is not a game of constant movement; it is one thing at a time. But that "one thing" (say, an amazing **hit**) can have an impact on the next thing (say, a run), and the next thing (say, a team's winning the game), and so on. The variables in baseball—like how many men are out, how many men are on base and which bases are they on—shift every time the ball is put into play.

THE FIELD

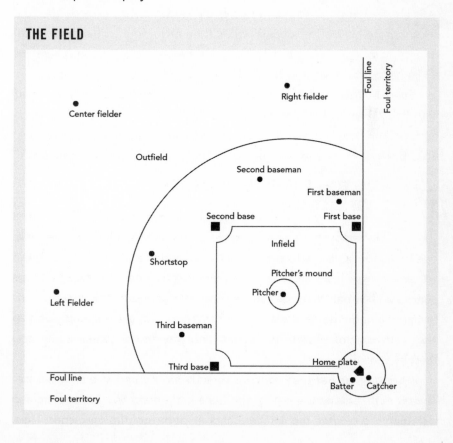

Everyone knows that diamonds are a girl's best friend. Lesser known is what good buddies men are with diamonds too. Not the kind that come with an appraisal and a commitment, but the kind you go to to drink beer and sing the national anthem.

A baseball field is affectionately known as a "diamond" because the *infield* is shaped like a diamond. The *infield* includes the bases and the dirt running paths, and it is *fielded* by the pitcher; catcher; first, second, and third basemen; and the shortstop. The **outfield** is the area beyond the dirt paths farthest from home plate (think large green field) and manned by the right fielder, center fielder, and left fielder.

There are two foul lines, right and left, and each is marked by a white line that extends from **home plate** to the *foul pole* at the edge of the out-field. A ball is considered *fair* when it is hit within fair territory—that is, in-side the foul lines. A *foul ball* is one that a batter hits *outside* the foul lines, before his first or second **strike**. If he hits a foul on his third strike, though, it doesn't count as anything, and he gets to try again. There are no limits to how many foul balls a batter can hit on the third strike.

Every ballpark is different, and each has its own unique character and flair. The distance between bases and the pitcher's mound is the same from park to park, but not the outfield measurements and configurations. (FYI, men get misty-eyed talking about their favorite baseball stadiums.)

THE TIMING

One of baseball's most unique features is that it has no time limit, no clock. The game is divided into periods called *innings*. There are nine innings in a game, and an inning lasts as long as it takes for three players on both teams to get out. A baseball game can't end in a tie. If af-ter nine innings the game *is* tied, it continues into extra innings, and as many innings are played as needed until one team scores a run and thereby wins the game.

During an inning, each team is up at bat once and in the field once. The team that is batting is playing offense; the team that is in the field—including the pitcher, the catcher, the infielders, and the outfielders—are playing defense. Players play both offense and defense (for instance, Derek Jeter, Yankee darling, is both a fab hitter and a very good short-stop). The first half of the inning is called the **"top" of the inning**; the second half is called the **"bottom" of the inning**.

THE LEGEND OF THE SEVENTH-INNING STRETCH

The favored legend about the origin of the *seventh-inning stretch* (the tradition in which everyone stands and stretches in the middle of the seventh inning to the tune of "Take Me Out to the Ball Game") credits President William Howard Taft.

At 300 pounds, Taft was our portliest president ever, and during one game, after seven innings, he was rather uncomfortable in his small wooden chair. So, after the seventh inning, he stood up to stretch his legs. The crowd thought he was leaving, and as a sign of respect, they stood as well. Taft sat down again, and the crowd once more followed suit—thus, the seventh-inning stretch was born.

SCORING

In baseball, a *run* is a score. If the final score of a game is 8–3, one team scored eight runs and the other three. The word "run" is used because, in order to score, a player must *run* around all four bases. He begins at home plate (or "home base," or just "home") then runs to first, second, and third base, and then back to home. Before he can run, however, he must hit the ball, and get on base safely. When a player gets a hit, he will usually make it to first or second base, and then he must wait for a teammate to get a hit and give him a chance to advance to the next base. Occasionally, a player will hit a **home run**, which means that he hit the ball so far (into the stands or out of the ballpark) that he can run around all the bases and score.*

---

*Every now and then, a player will hit an "inside-the-park" home run, which means that the batter got all the way around the bases without hitting the ball into the stands or outside the park.

DIAMONDS ON THE SILVER SCREEN

The Natural (1984): Robert Redford stars in this movie based on the great writer Bernard Malamud's novel about the comeback of a once-promising baseball player and the demons he must fight.

Bull Durham (1988): Kevin Costner, Susan Sarandon, and Tim Robbins star in this combination baseball/love-triangle flick—pure delight for both guys and gals.

Major League (1989): A hilarious movie (starring Tom Berenger and Charlie Sheen) about the worst team in the league becoming the best team in the league, triumphing over the psycho-bitch team owner who wants them to lose.

Field of Dreams (1989): A weird but wonderful movie starring Kevin Costner, who hears a voice that tells him, "If you build it, he will come," and thus builds a baseball field that conjures up the ghosts of Shoeless Joe Jackson and others from the 1919 Chicago Black Sox scandal.

A League of Their Own (1992): Tom Hanks, Geena Davis, Madonna, and Rosie O'Donnell are among the stars of this marvelous must-see movie based on the All-American Girls Professional Baseball League, founded in 1943 to give America baseball in the absence of men, most of whom were off at war.

AT BAT

When a player comes up to **home plate** (also *home base*) to swing at the ball, he is said to be at the plate, or *at bat*. If a player strikes out right away,

you might hear someone say "that was a quick 'at bat.' " Or, if you're talking to a Red Sox fan, you might hear something like, "Johnny Damon's at bat was unbelievable last night."

When a batter is at bat, preparing to hit the ball, he will stand a few inches to the left or the right of the plate, depending on whether he is a righty or a lefty. Some players can hit both left-handed and right-handed, and they are known as **switch-hitters**. Once the batter is in position, the *pitcher* will pitch (throw) the ball to him, sometimes at speeds upward of ninety miles per hour.

Hitting

In life (as in, non-sports life) hitting is usually not a good thing. One does not get excited about getting their car *hit*, nor getting *hit* in the head by a flying object. But in the wacky world of sports, **hit** usually refers to a good thing. This is so in football, for example, where "a good hit" means a good tackle. And in baseball, good hitting is the main event!

As the proverbial "they" say, there's more than one way to skin a cat, and there's more than one way to hit a baseball.

Ways to Hit the Ball

FLY BALLS

A **fly ball**, or simply a *fly*, is a ball that is hit high into the air and usually lands or is caught in the outfield. If it's caught before it touches the ground, the batter is out, and it's known as a *fly-out*.

POP-UPS (OR *POP FLYS*)

A **pop-up** is like a fly ball, only shorter—it is almost always caught by an infielder. Pop-ups are usually pretty easy to catch, so the hitter is usually put out. (Pop-ups are the kind of balls that Charlie Brown—yes, the comic-strip character—should have caught, but never did.)

LINE DRIVES

Line drives are balls that stay in the air, but stay low to the ground. They can be a bit trickier to catch because of how fast they travel.

GROUND BALL

A **ground ball** (or *grounder*) is a batted ball that rolls or bounces along the ground.

BUNT

A *bunt* is a hit that is soft and short. The batter positions the bat horizontally, resulting in a frankly unimpressive weak hit that only goes a short distance. However, the homely bunt plays an important role as a **sacrifice play**—the hitter of the bunt will almost always be forced out at first base, but a runner already on base will usually advance.

Types of Hits

SINGLE, DOUBLE, TRIPLE

Unattached, attached, ménage-à-trois? Hey, that's your business. In baseball, **singles**, **doubles**, and **triples** (all different types of hits) are more comparable to scoops of ice cream than relationship status: three scoops of ice cream are better than two or one, and so it goes in baseball.

In short, a *single* is a base hit that allows the batter to get to first base.* A *double* is a hit that allows the batter to get to second base. And a *triple* is—yep, that's right—a hit that allows the batter to get to third base. Singles, doubles, and triples take on more importance if there are already runners on base, because they increase the chances that the team at bat will send runners home. If a runner is on second base, for example, and a player hits a double, the runner has a very good chance of running home (scoring).

HOME RUNS

Ahhh. The allure, the glamour, the excitement of the *home run*. Simply put, a home run is a superpowerful hit that sends the ball way-way-way out and allows the batter to round all the bases and score. It's a ball that's hit into the stands or out of the park. A home run cannot be defended against.

Nobody doesn't like Sara Lee (except those on the Atkins Diet) and

---

*In order to officially qualify as a single, the batter must actually hit the ball—advancing because of an error or a walk is not considered a single. More on errors and walks follows.

nobody doesn't like a home run (except certain party poopers who point out that, statistically, home-run hitters are not as valuable to the game as other types of hitters). James Kelly, in his book entitled *Baseball*, calls a home run baseball's "signature moment," and he has the following response for those who pooh-pooh home runs: "Purists can argue that home runs are overvalued and that players ruin their swings aiming for the fences instead of the gaps. But here's a guarantee: All of those purists are on their feet yelling along with the rest of us as a record-setting or World Series–winning home run soars through the sky into history." Any home run is exhilarating. It doesn't have to be a record breaker, or a history maker. It's a joyful moment in any baseball game.

HOME RUN, AKA . . .

four-bagger	bomb
homer	dong
Dr. Longball	dinger
home-bagger	smash
money ball	wallop
Babe Ruth	round-tripper
long ball	four play
circuit clout	belt
big fly	big swat

BASES LOADED: ANXIETY LEVEL CODE RED

The phrase *bases loaded* means that there are players on first, second, and third base. Having the bases loaded is anxiety producing (or simply exciting if you're not neurotic) because, with so many runners on base, it's a cryin' shame not to get those boys back home!

When the bases are loaded, even a single can bring a runner home. (But if the opposing team is smart, they will try to get the runner who is at third out while he is trying to run home to score.) If a batter hits a home run while bases are loaded, well, this is a good thing—a very, very good thing known as a *grand slam home run* (usually just referred to as a grand slam). It results in four runs (!) being scored because everyone on base comes home, as does the hitter of the home run himself.

Stealing Bases

In an otherwise honorable game, stealing is allowed. If a player is on base, he can try to advance to the next base—that is, *steal* the base—while the pitcher is pitching. It's a risky, aggressive move. If the pitcher or the catcher sees the runner trying to steal a base, he'll throw the ball to the appropriate fielder who will then try to tag the runner out. Stealing bases is effective not only for advancing on the basepaths, but also for rattling the nerves of the pitcher and catcher by being a distraction.

Striking Out

While at bat, it's three strikes and you're out (as everyone knows, since the metaphor has become an overused, slightly corny part of American vernacular). But what exactly is a strike? In the simplest terms, a *strike* is when the batter is unable to hit the ball. But it's a little more complex than that.

Here's what might happen at a typical at bat: The batter is standing to the side of the plate, ready to receive the pitch. The pitcher throws the ball over the plate. If the ball is in the *strike zone* (between the knees and chest of the batter and directly over the plate), and the batter swings and misses or doesn't swing at all, it's a strike. Once there are *three strikes* against the batter, he's *out*. The player who struck out returns to the *dugout*, the place where the players on the team that's "up" hang out, play practical jokes on one another, and do Pilates (just kidding) while they're waiting for their turn at bat. Then the next hitter on the team is up at bat.

If the pitcher throws the ball and it *misses* the strike zone—if it's too high, too low, too *inside*, or too *outside*—and the batter doesn't swing, it's called a *ball.* If he swings and misses, however, it's a strike. If the pitcher throws four balls, the batter *walks* (advances) to first base.

The umpire determines if a pitch is a ball or a strike. Seems straightforward, but determining a strike is often not clear-cut—it's not as though there are computer-operated lasers that read whether the ball is within the strike zone or not. And what's more, the strike zone is not an absolute—it's determined by the size of the batter. *And* because of the speed of the pitch (from 75 to 100 mph!) it is virtually impossible for an umpire to make the right call 100 percent of the time. Thus, much of the emotional core of the game revolves around the strike zone. Either the pitcher or the batter is unhappy with just about every call, as are the managers, and often the fans. Arguing with the umpire is part of the game, but only a little is tolerated—arguing too much or too often will get a player or manager booted right out of the game. In my opinion, getting apoplectic about a call is part of the fun of it all. No day at the ballpark is complete without at least one rabid fan howling over an ump's decision.

If, on the first or second strike, the batter hits the ball and it goes *foul* (outside the foul lines—see diagram on page 107) it is called a strike. But if, on the *third* strike, the batter hits a foul ball, it doesn't count as a strike—it doesn't count as anything—and he remains up at bat. Sometimes a player will have two strikes against him, and then he'll hit foul after foul and it seems as if he's at bat forever. Thus, an "at bat" can either be very quick—such as when a pitcher makes three pitches and *boom, boom, boom*, the hitter misses all three, or when the batter gets a hit off of the first pitch—or there can be several combinations of strikes, balls, and fouls before the batter is either struck out, walked, or hits the ball.

A PLAYER CAN GET A STRIKE BY

* swinging at a ball and missing it;

* not swinging at a ball when it was in the strike zone; or

* hitting a ball foul on the first or second strike.

The Count

The **count** is the tally of a batter's balls versus strikes while he is at bat. The number of balls is always said first. For instance, a "2-1" count means that the pitcher has thrown two balls and one strike. If the next pitch is a strike, the count will be 2-2. The highest the count can be is 3-2, which is called a *full count*. At this point, the next pitch determines whether the player gets on base by a hit or a walk, or is called out. If the pitcher throws a strike, the player at bat is out. If the pitcher throws a ball, the player at bat walks to first base. And, as you've learned, if the player hits the ball, he runs to first base, or possibly all the way to second or third.

BASEBALL IS BATTY: *QUIRKS ABOUT AMERICA'S PASTIME*

* Baseball is the only sport in which the managers wear the exact same uniform as the players. Imagine a football coach wearing a football uniform with pads and a helmet, or a basketball coach in shorts and a sleeveless jersey!

* To tell players what to do, the manager, first-base coach, third-base coach, and sometimes the bench manager use a series of really weird-looking signals. These involve a rapid series of secret combinations of touching the eyes, the eyebrows, nose, crotch, knees, elbows, and other body parts. The signal communication looks like the coach or manager has a serious malady of uncontrollable tics—or a really itchy rash.

* It is mandated that a player at bat must scratch or otherwise adjust his crotch at least once per at bat. Although this particular rule is not found in the official rules of MLB, empirical evidence suggests that it is so. It also applies to pitchers, infielders, outfielders, coaches, and managers. (On a personal note, this really bugs me. How often do we have to suffer through an underwire bra digging into our flesh, or panties creeping where they shouldn't? And yet, you don't see us adjusting our bosoms or yanking our booties in public.)

Against the Odds

Baseball is a game in which the odds are against the batter. As Michael Mandelbaum points out, "the best batters fail to hit safely in seventy percent of their official times at bat." You might be thinking that this seems awfully high for men who have been training their whole lives and get paid millions of dollars to hit the damn ball, but they're up against the nearly impossible. According to Dan Schlossberg's *Baseball Almanac,* the ball takes only five-tenths of a second to travel from pitcher to hitter—and the hitter has only two-tenths of a second to move his bat from his shoulder to the contact zone. That leaves three-tenths of a second for the batter to:

* visually pick up the ball;

* determine what kind of pitch is coming;

* decide if it will be a ball or a strike; and

* decide whether to swing or "take the pitch" (not swing at it).

Wow. That's why any player with a .300 batting average or higher is considered a great player.

The Batters

When a team is up at bat, each player who stands at the plate tries to do the same thing: hit the ball. If a player is so lucky as to get on base, his job becomes the same as any other player who gets on base—to run to the next base (and the next) as soon as is possible and try to score a run.

BATTING ORDER

Each team has a set *batting order*, which is determined by the manager or coach before the game. The batting order—meaning Johnny is up, followed by Davey, followed by Tommy, and so on—is consistent throughout all nine innings (unless one player is substituted for another, in which case the new player bats in the replaced player's spot in the order). So, if Davey was the last one to bat and the inning ends, Tommy will be up when they are at bat again. The best hitters are usually at "the top of the order"—i.e., they are the first four players to bat in the first inning. The strategy behind this is that (1) these batters end up getting to bat the most, and (2) if the first one or two batters can get on base, then the third and/or fourth, being excellent hitters, have a chance to bring them home. The very first player in the batting order is called the *lead-off hitter*.

Although all the positions in the batting order are essentially equal, there are two "special" at-bat positions that you will occasionally hear about. These positions are called the **pinch hitter** and the **designated hitter**, or **DH**.

PINCH HITTER

A pinch hitter is a player whom the manager substitutes at bat for someone else. The person for whom he substituted is then out of the game. Say it's close to the end of a game, for example, and the bases are loaded, and up next in the batting order is Pete the pitcher, who is a lousy hitter. A manager will remove Pete for a better hitter. But now Pete is out for the rest of the game, and a new pitcher will have to come in and replace him the next time his team is in the field. (Pinch hitters are used to substitute for any lousy hitter, not just pitchers.)

DESIGNATED HITTER (DH)

Before I explain what the designated hitter is, you need to know two things: (1) designated hitters are allowed only in the American League, and (2) the concept of the designated hitter is controversial. Most people are either Republican or Democrat, and you're either for the DH or you're not (not to imply that opinions about the DH are split along party lines).

It seems that the all-around athlete in pro sports is going the way of the general practitioner in medicine—he is disappearing and being replaced by specialists. Yes, the age of specialization has hit sports, and nowhere is it more defined than with the highly controversial designated hitter rule.

The DH is like a pinch hitter, but with a sort of mutation: The DH, who is designated by each manager *before* the game starts, takes the place of his team's pitcher in the batting order, but he doesn't play in the field with the rest of the team—he hits, and then sits. The pitcher, meanwhile, stays in the game but only pitches, because in general, pitchers are poor hitters. So in the American League, pitchers almost never bat, unless the pitcher happens to be an unusually good hitter.

Why are some people vehemently opposed to the DH rule? Purists believe that it diminishes the manager's job of planning strategy for a game. Baseball is a game where every action has consequences that can completely alter the strategy for the following action. A DH, some believe, is a way of cheating, of escaping the natural flow of consequences in the game.

Why are some people vehemently in favor of the DH rule? Pro-DH types believe that DHs make the game more exciting, since there is usually more scoring in games that have DHs.

What happens if an American League team is playing a National League team? you may be wondering. The *home* team's rules are used. So, if the home team is in the American League, both teams are allowed to use a DH. Conversely, if the home team is in the National League, the DH is not allowed to be used by either team.

I'm against the DH rule, because I'm jealous. *I* want a "designated hitter." Say I wake up in a really grouchy mood and it's raining and miserable and cold, and I don't think I would play the role of "Liz at work" very well. Why can't *I* just give a little ring to my "designated hitter" (or worker, whatever) and voilà!, off to work the DH will go in my place? Life doesn't work that way, and neither should sports.

You now know everything you need to know about at bats to be able to hold your own at a sports bar or water cooler. Now let's move on to playing the field.

IN THE FIELD

 The team in the field has one overarching mission: to get out of the field and back up at bat so they can score. Thus, those in the field—infield or outfield—want to get the ball in their gloves and then get the batter and/or runners OUT!

Getting Players Out

You've already learned that a pitcher can *strike out* a player at bat. Other ways for the fielding team to cause outs include:

* A fielder can catch a batted ball before it hits the ground.

* A fielder can "force" a runner out by catching the ball and stepping on the base before the runner arrives at that base. This happens when the runner is *forced* to advance to the next base because another runner is behind him, or when he is running to first (if a batter hits the ball in fair territory, he *has to* run from home to first).

* A fielder can *tag* a runner out, meaning that the fielder actually touches the runner with the ball (or, as is often the case, with a glove that's holding the ball). This often happens when the runner is *not* forced to go to the next base, but when he has the option of advancing to the next base or not. For instance, if a player is on second base and his teammate hits the ball but is going to get only as far as first base, the player at second does not *have* to go to third (he may decide it's too risky and just stay at second). If he does decide to proceed, then the third baseman must tag him out. Sometimes a runner will get trapped between bases while the fielders try to tag him out. This looks like the scene in *The Wizard of Oz* when Dorothy and friends get trapped on the top of the castles between the turrets with the Wicked Witch's army coming from both directions. In baseball, this is called a *rundown*.

Double and Triple Plays

Sometimes baseball players get a lot of play—whoops, Freudian slip. Let me try that again. Sometimes, when the stars are aligned, baseball players (in the field) will execute **double plays** or **triple plays**. A **double play** is when the team in the field makes *two* outs on a single play. The following scenario would be a double play: Joe is at bat, and Mo is on first base. Joe hits the ball, and the opposing team's shortstop gets ahold of it and throws it to second base before Mo gets there, so Mo is out. Then the second baseman throws it to first base before Joe gets there, so Joe is out too. When the team in the field makes *three* outs on a single play, it's called a *triple play*. Triple plays are much rarer than double plays.

Positions

Unlike at bat (or *at the plate*), in the field, there are nine different positions. Four players play near the bases and make up the *infield*: the *first, second,* and *third basemen* and the *shortstop*. The *outfield* has three players: the *right fielder, left fielder,* and *center fielder*. Closer to home plate, there's the *catcher* and the *pitcher*.*

Infielders are more likely to get opposing players out directly (they're the ones who man the bases), while outfielders more often throw the ball to an infielder, who then tags or forces someone out. But anyone in the infield or outfield can catch a fly ball and thus cause an out. And everyone has to think ahead and think fast so they know exactly who to throw the ball to when they get it. If a runner at third is threatening to score, the fielders want to get the ball to the catcher at home plate to prevent the run rather than throwing it to first. The top priority is to prevent runners from scoring. The second priority is to get opposing players out as quickly as possible.

PITCHER

As you've probably picked up by now, the pitcher is the guy who throws—*pitches*—the ball to the batter. To be good, he needs both speed and accuracy (huge biceps and triceps don't hurt either). In baseball, pitching dominates. A pitcher, in some ways, is as important as a football quarterback, in that teams can't win without an outstanding pitcher.

---

*The pitcher pitches from a small mound of dirt known as the *pitcher's mound*.

COMMON TYPES OF PITCHES

Fastball: a pitch that is thrown at a very high speed without much curve.

Curveball: a pitch that curves (the pitcher controls the direction of the curve) on its way to the plate.

Breaking ball: a pitch that starts out straight but then curves as it approaches the plate.

Sinker: a pitch that drops suddenly just as it reaches the plate (it's a kind of breaking ball).

Changeup: a pitch that is thrown the same way as a fastball but is actually a slower pitch—it fools the batter.

Slider: a fast pitch that causes the ball to curve slightly in the opposite direction of the throwing arm.

Knuckleball: a pitch that is thrown with the fingertips or knuckles, which causes the ball to travel slowly, but unpredictably, to the plate.

CATCHER

The catcher wears more equipment than anyone else in baseball, and he needs to. He crouches behind home plate and does a number of jobs (and, I imagine, has thighs of steel). First and foremost, the catcher is in constant communication with the pitcher, telling him, by cryptic hand signals that only his team knows, what kind of pitch to throw (curveball, fastball, etc.). He must also catch any ball that isn't hit or fouled. Pitches travel fast, sometimes ninety miles per hour or more—thus the extra equipment. The catcher always needs to be paying attention to the entire game in front of him.

FIRST BASEMAN

The fielder at first base is pretty busy. Ground balls are often hit to him, and other infielders often throw the ball to him so that he can "force" the batter out at first base. The first baseman must be able to catch and field balls coming from all different angles.

SECOND BASEMAN

The second baseman needs to be a quick thinker and quick with his fielding skills. He sometimes helps make double plays (getting two men out on one play). The second baseman and the shortstop form the middle of the infield and must work well together.

THIRD BASEMAN

The third baseman needs to be quick and be able to react to hard-hit balls. He also must be agile enough to handle bunts (balls that are tapped by batters and travel a short distance). Third base is known as the "hot corner," because the balls hit in its direction are hit harder and faster than those hit to any other position.

SHORTSTOP

The shortstop is positioned between second and third base. This position is considered to be the most difficult in the infield to play, because the shortstop has a lot of ground to cover, and there are endless permutations as to what he needs to do in any given situation. More balls are hit to the shortstop than to anyone else. Also, when a ball is hit so far that an outfielder needs to go all the way to the back wall (which separates the field and the stands, or marks the boundary of the ballpark) to retrieve the ball, he often cannot reach the base he needs to throw it to with one throw. When this happens, the shortstop has to help the outfielders with a "relay throw." In short, he has a lot to do.

LEFT FIELDER

This player covers the left side of the outfield (behind third base, roughly speaking) and is responsible for fielding any balls hit there.

CENTER FIELDER

This player covers the center of the outfield. He must be fast and, like the shortstop, he has a lot of territory to cover.

RIGHT FIELDER

The right fielder covers the right side of the outfield and also helps back up the first baseman.

Errors

An *error* is a goof, a mistake, the equivalent of a fumble in football. It's dropping the ball when any doofus could have caught it. It's throwing to first base when you should have thrown to third base. It's letting the ball roll between your legs. Only the team in the field can make an error.

Errors affect the official stats of players. For example, if a player gets on base because of an error, and he clearly wouldn't have gotten on base if not for the error, he is not credited with a hit. Errors are counted against a fielder's stats as well.

Perfect Games and No-Hitters

PERFECT GAMES

A *perfect game* is the jewel in the crown of a pitcher's accomplishments—in fact, pitching a perfect game is so rare that only seventeen pitchers have ever accomplished it.

A perfect game is when a pitcher retires—gets out—every single player that comes to the plate, zippity-do-dah. It means retiring twenty-seven players in nine innings. No hits, no errors, no walks. Nobody gets on base. The game is a shutout (a game in which the losing team scores no runs). The pitcher has to pitch all nine innings, which in itself doesn't happen very often anymore. So, as you can see, pitching a perfect game is not for mere mortals.

NO-HITTERS

A *"no-hitter"* ain't too shabby either. But it's not as rare or as amazing as a perfect game. Hundreds of pitchers have pitched no-hitters. A no-hitter is a game in which the opposing team gets no hits off the pitcher, but the pitcher (or anyone on his team) has made an error (or errors), or the pitcher has walked a player. In a no-hitter, players do wind up on base from walks or errors, but not from base hits. While a perfect game is always a shutout, in a no-hitter the other team can score (off walks or errors)—although it's rare for this to happen.

THE STATS

Baseball is a statistics-obsessed sport, and baseball fans are statistics-obsessed people. The litany of various stats can make your head spin and often seem to

> You teach me baseball and I'll teach you relativity . . . No we must not. You will learn about relativity faster than I learn baseball.
>
> —*Albert Einstein*

be in direct contrast to the sport itself: Here is this relatively simple-seeming game of hitting a ball, rounding bases, and scratching your crotch, and the stats sound like advanced calculus. But don't be afraid. As with all sports, knowing only the most important stats is enough to gain a foothold in understanding the game, and gain major "props" with whatever sports-obsessed males you are acquainted.

Batting Average

Throughout the history of baseball, the **batting average** has been the big kahuna of baseball benchmarks—any player with a batting average of .300 or higher is an exceptional hitter.

A player's batting average is calculated by dividing his total number of hits by his total number of at bats. (So, if I got 130 hits and had 360 at bats, my batting average would be .361, and I would immediately be drafted by a major-league team.) When calculating a batting average, it doesn't matter whether the batter hit a single (one base), a double (two bases), a triple (three bases), or a home run—all hits are equal.

Runs Batted In (RBI)

This is easiest to explain with an example: Say a player is up at bat, and there are players at second and third base. The batter hits a beauty, and the two men on base are able to score. Regardless of what happens to the batter (i.e., whether he's put out or not), he will be credited with two RBIs because his hit got the other two players home.

Earned Run Average (ERA)

This is an important statistic for pitchers. The lower a pitcher's ERA, the better the pitcher. A low ERA means that the pitcher has allowed few runs to be scored by the opposing team. It's called *earned* run average because, if an opposing player scores because of a fielding error, the run doesn't count in the pitcher's individual statistics. This is a way of acknowledging that the pitcher is not responsible for his teammate's screw-up.

Home Runs

Home-run statistics take on greater glory than perhaps they deserve. Some believe that just because a player hits a lot of home runs, it doesn't make him a great player, nor the most important player on the team. (Yeah, try telling that to a nine-year-old baseball fan.) Home-run stats are easy to calculate—you only need to know how to count. There are two home-run calculations: home runs in a single season and career home runs.

THE GOLD STANDARDS

There are a handful of "gold standards" in baseball. (Two, batting average and career home runs, we've already discussed.) The "gold standards" are as follows:

.300 batting average
300 career pitching victories
3,000 base hits for batters
500 career home runs

If a player achieves these numbers or higher, he's great. Sometimes you'll hear people say that so-and-so is in the "3,000-hit club," or the "500–home run club." These are the standards to which they are referring.

Single-season home-run records are a big deal too. Babe Ruth set the standard in 1927 (with sixty home runs in a single season), and only a handful have broken it since.

THE WORLD SERIES

The **World Series** is the annual Major League Baseball championship. The winners of the American League championship face the winners of the National League championship in a best-of-seven series played in October. The first World Series was played in 1903 and, with the exceptions of 1904, when the Series was prematurely canceled, and 1994, when a labor dispute halted baseball, it has been played every year since. Unlike soccer's World Cup, the World Series isn't very international in nature, since the only non-American team (the Toronto Blue Jays) hails from Canada. People all over the world *watch* it, though, so in that way, it qualifies as a world event.

EAST, WEST, AND IN-BETWEEN: RIVETING RIVALRIES

New York Yankees vs. Boston Red Sox

The Yankees–Red Sox rivalry is not only the greatest rivalry in baseball, but is considered by many to be the most riveting rivalry in all of sports. To be a Yankees fan in Boston is to be a pariah, a traitor. (More on the history of this legendary rivalry below.)

Los Angeles Dodgers vs. San Francisco Giants

On the West Coast, there is the Los Angeles Dodgers–San Francisco Giants rivalry, which originated as an East Coast feud. The Dodgers began life as the Brooklyn Dodgers playing at Ebbets Field; the Giants, then the New York Giants, were their crosstown (well, actually, uptown) rivals, whose home was the Polo Grounds in Manhattan. This is also an old row, dating back to the beginning of the twentieth century. The 450 miles that has separated the teams since they both moved to California in 1958 has taken a bit of the bite out of the feud, but they continue to love to hate each other.

Chicago Cubs vs. Chicago White Sox

In the middle of the country there exists another crosstown (uptown/downtown) thing going on with the Chicago Cubs and the Chicago White Sox. Not surprisingly, Chicagoans think their rivalry is far more fascinating than either the West Coast or East Coast shenanigans. The fact that neither team seems to ever get too close to a championship doesn't seem to lessen the rivalry one bit.

THE RED SOX WIN THE WORLD SERIES

One need only go back to October 27, 2004, at 11:40 EDT, to recall one of the greatest moments in baseball history. After an eighty-six-year drought, the Boston Red Sox, a team that *Sports Illustrated*'s Tom Verducci describes as a "civic religion" in New England, won the World Series for the first time since 1918. And boy did they do it in style, once and for all ending the "Curse of the Bambino."

The myth went like this: In 1918, when Babe Ruth—often referred to as the "bambino" (the Italian word for "babe")—was both pitching and hitting for the Boston Red Sox, his team won the World Series. In 1919, when he hit a then-unprecedented twenty-nine homers, the team was still looking good. But then darkness descended on Boston. That same year, Harry Frazee sold Ruth to the New York Yankees, and for the rest of the century, the Red Sox did not win a World Series. For New Englanders, this became known as the "Curse of the Bambino," and sparked the intense rivalry between the Red Sox and the Yankees. Apparently the Red Sox needed a whole new millennium for a fresh start.

As if made for Hollywood, in October 2004, the Red Sox faced the Yankees in the American League Championship Series (ALCS), and as usual, the Yankees won the first three games. Then, despite the fact that no baseball team had *ever* come back from being down three games in a seven-game series, the Red Sox prevailed in the fourth game . . . and the fifth, sixth, and seventh, winning the **pennant** (championship) and moving on to the World Series where they faced the St. Louis Cardinals, who they *swept* in four games. Red Sox fans all over the nation literally wept with joy. To make it even more wonderful, the winning team was a scraggly bunch of goofy guys who called themselves "the idiots." This was a Series to love no matter where your loyalties lay.

THE STEROID SCANDAL

In the old days, baseball players came in a wide variety of shapes and sizes and, for the most part, didn't sport the super-buff bods of today's players. Babe Ruth, the greatest baseball player of all time, had a notoriously non-hunky body with—let's call it what it was—a beer gut and twiggy legs. Yogi Berra, another baseball great, was only 5'8" with a squat-looking body. Without personal trainers, supplements, sports medicine, and all manner of pampering, the old-timers looked, well, different. Today, we have some serious hunks, but the burning question is: Are they hunks or steroid-using chumps?

Even if one takes into account better nutrition, better training, and better knowledge about how to build a bigger, stronger body, some players look unnaturally beefed up, like overstuffed kielbasas. Thus, it wasn't exactly a bombshell when accusations of the use of illegal supplements hit the headlines in 2004. If the Red Sox hadn't ended their eighty-six-year dry spell to win the World Series in 2004, the entire season would have been tarnished by the steroid (aka "performance enhancing drugs," or simply "supplements") scandal that swept MLB.

As the scandal continues to grow, more and more players have been implicated. One who stands to lose the most, depending on how MLB handles the situation, is Barry Bonds, one of the best players in professional baseball today, who could face having his numerous records stripped and/or being barred from the Baseball Hall of Fame (more on Bonds later). Other record-breakers such as Mark McGwire and Sammy Sosa (who, drugs or not, gave us the most entertaining baseball season in the past few decades with their friendly home-run race in 1998) have both been accused. McGwire has admitted to using supplements that were legal at the time; Sosa denies using anything. The Yankees' Jason Giambi, long under suspicion for being "juiced," *sort of* admitted he used them by apologizing for *something*, but he didn't make it clear what he was apologizing for. And then, in 2005, former Oakland Athletics' star Jose Canseco came forward with his book, *Juiced*, in which he implicated just about everyone who's ever played in the major leagues. His book has been largely discredited by those he indicted, but the scandal hasn't abated. A big part of the problem is that, until the recent scandal, MLB had a very lax drug-testing policy, and supplements that were banned in other sports had not been banned in baseball. All that began to change in early 2005 with a revised policy regarding the use and testing of supplements.

JUST KNOW THIS

A baseball game is made up of nine *innings*. During each inning, each team is up at bat once and in the field once. The team at bat tries to score *runs* by having its batters hit the ball and run around the bases. Three *strikes* and a batter is out. A team is allowed three *outs* per turn at bat (per *inning*). Once a team has three outs, they give up their turn at bat and then their opponents (who have been playing the field) come up to bat. Three outs and *that* team is out—and then a new inning begins. There are nine players in the *batting order*. Baseball is obsessed with the number three and its multiples.

Baseball is both layered and linear—one action (a great hit, for example) determines the next actions, and there are endless permutations. On one level the game is quite simple—hitting, pitching, catching, fielding and, of course, scratching and spitting. On the other hand, it is a sport with multitudes of complexity.

> ### MAJOR LEAGUE BASEBALL TEAMS
>
> | American League | National League |
> | --- | --- |
> | Baltimore Orioles | Arizona |
> | Boston Red Sox | Diamondbacks |
> | Chicago White Sox | Atlanta Braves |
> | Cleveland Indians | Chicago Cubs |
> | Detroit Tigers | Cincinnati Reds |
> | Kansas City Royals | Colorado Rockies |
> | Los Angeles Angels | Florida Marlins |
> | Minnesota Twins | Houston Astros |
> | New York Yankees | Los Angeles |
> | Oakland Athletics | Dodgers |
> | ("A's") | Milwaukee |
> | Seattle Mariners | Brewers |
> | Philadelphia Phillies | New York Mets |
> | Tampa Bay Devil Rays | Pittsburgh Pirates |
> | Texas Rangers | San Diego Padres |
> | Toronto Blue Jays | San Francisco |
> | | Giants |
> | | St. Louis Cardinals |
> | | Washington |
> | | Nationals |
> | | (formerly the |
> | | Montreal Expos) |

Baseball is distinguished from other major spectator sports because it is not bound by the clock—games go on as long as they need to to determine a winner (games never end in a tie).

Baseball is a beloved part of American culture—it's commonly referred to as "America's pastime," or "the national pastime." It has a long and storied history that dates back to the mid-nineteenth century.

Players You Need to Know

The Legends

HANK AARON, 1934–
NICKNAME: "HAMMERIN' HANK"

    1954–65: Milwaukee Braves

    1966–73: Atlanta Braves

    1974–76: Milwaukee Brewers

Hank Aaron holds more major league records than any other player. But the one record with which he is forever linked is hammering 755 career home runs, smashing Babe Ruth's record of 714. Among his other outstanding stats are his:

* 3,771 hits (third all time);

* 2,174 runs scored (tied for second all time);

* and 2,297 RBI (the most ever).

He won two **batting titles** (meaning he had the highest batting average in a particular season), and an MVP award in 1957, the year he helped lead the Braves to a World Series victory.

"Hammerin' Hank" got his nickname solely from the way he hit the ball—his personality was anything but "hammerin'." He was quiet, soft-spoken, and shy—especially compared to some of other players of his day, such as Mickey Mantle and Willie Mays, whose charisma made headlines.

Thirteen years before Hank Aaron broke Ruth's career home-run record, Roger Maris broke Ruth's magical single-season home-run record of sixty. These occasions should have been joyous for Maris and Aaron, but instead they were torturous. Fans did not want to see Babe's records broken, and Maris and Aaron were put through hell—booing crowds, hate mail, and all manner of vicious behavior. Aaron had the added burden of being black, so the onslaught against him came with racial slurs and death threats. And just as Maris was relieved when he finally reached 61, Aaron, after hitting homer number 715 and landing at home plate, said, "Thank God it's over."

Immediately after retiring in 1976, Aaron was hired by the Braves in a management position, making him one of the first blacks to be hired as a professional baseball executive.

YOGI BERRA (LAWRENCE PETER BERRA), 1925–
1946–63: New York Yankees
1965: New York Mets

There's a good chance you've heard of Yogi Berra and his counterintuitive Berra-isms, kernels of wisdom such as:

"Baseball is ninety percent mental, the other half is physical"; *or*

"Slump? I ain't in no slump. I just ain't hittin"; *or*

"Nobody ever goes there anymore; it's too crowded."

What you might not have known is that Yogi was a truly excellent baseball player and is a member of the Baseball Hall of Fame. He played with the Yankees when they were in the process of winning fourteen pennants and ten World Championships. His bio at the Hall of Fame describes him as "the heart of the Yankees for 18 years." He was a quick and agile catcher who could also hit, and he was an American League MVP three times. After his playing career ended in 1965, Berra coached and managed the New York Yankees and the New York Mets at various times.

How did Lawrence Peter Berra become "Yogi"? Well, according to a thorough investigation by Roy Blount Jr., for his 1984 *Sports Illustrated* profile of Berra, no one really knows. Blount reports that it apparently happened in his teens and that at least five different people take credit for bestowing the nickname upon him, for everything from walking like a yogi, or always staying calm in yogi-like fashion, or because he sat around with his legs crossed. The truth shall remain a mystery.

JOE DIMAGGIO, 1914–1999
NICKNAMES: "JOLTIN' JOE," "THE YANKEE CLIPPER"
1936–51: New York Yankees

Joe DiMaggio was the shining star of the Yankees—and of Major League Baseball—during the 1940s. In the thirteen seasons that he played for the "Bronx Bombers,"* the team won ten pennants and nine World Series. DiMaggio's indelible mark on baseball was made in 1941, from May 15 until July 16, when for *fifty-six consecutive games*, he got at least one base hit. This had not happened before and has not happened since.

In a *Newsweek* profile of DiMaggio written shortly after his death, Richard Ben Creamer noted that, as his streak reached into the forties and was climbing to the unthinkable fifty-six, "DiMaggio had almost squeezed Hitler off the front page." Clearly this streak was a big deal. It was like having a good hair day for fifty-six days straight; or fitting into your small-est, tightest skinny-day jeans for fifty-six days straight; or your boss being nice to you for fifty-six days straight. It would have been enough, really, if he had simply been able to hit like this. But he also was a great outfielder. He was a brilliant all-around player.

While the words "elegance," "grace," and "dignity" are always asso-ciated with DiMaggio, he was also known for his reticence and shyness about being in the public eye. And those who knew him personally often described him as being downright cold and aloof. Still, he was grace un-der pressure. As Creamer put it, "He exceeded, withal, the cruelest ex-pectations: He was expected to lead and to win—and he did. He was expected to be the best and he was. He was expected . . . even to look the best. And he looked perfect."

In addition to the fifty-six-game hitting streak, and the ten pennants, and the nine World Series, he also won two batting titles and three league MVPs (tying the all-time MVP record). Then he went and married Marilyn Monroe, who was to stardom and beauty and sex-godliness what he was

---

*The "Bronx Bombers" is an affectionate nickname for the Yankees. The Bronx, New York, is home to Yankee Stadium.

to baseball. The marriage was doomed from the start, although the love and friendship endured. The stories are true—he did in fact ensure that fresh flowers adorn her grave "forever," and he did in fact weep openly at her funeral, even though their nine-month marriage had ended years before.

Everything DiMaggio did, in and out of the ballpark, seemed to reinforce his hero status. As Ted Williams put it, "Joe DiMaggio's career cannot be summed up in numbers and awards. It might sound corny, but he had a profound and lasting impact on the country. How many athletes can make that claim? For many fans [he became] baseball's knight in shining pinstripe armor."

LOU GEHRIG, 1903–1941
NICKNAME: "THE IRON HORSE"
1923–39: New York Yankees

"Today, I consider myself the luckiest man alive."

When you read the background to this famous quote, you will cry. If you don't cry, you need to get yourself to the nearest therapist and start breaking down the impenetrable wall of emotional impassivity you've built around yourself.

But first to why he is one of the greats. Lou Gehrig played alongside Babe Ruth with the Yankees for twelve years, from 1923 to 1934.* While Ruth was busy hitting his monumental sixty home runs in 1927, Gehrig hit forty-seven of his own, as well as a league-leading fifty-two doubles and 175 RBIs, earning him the MVP award that year. And his career batting average was a very impressive .340.

In addition, Gehrig set a record by playing in 2,130 consecutive games (that's *fourteen years* of not calling in sick!), a streak that was not to be broken for another fifty-six years, by Cal Ripken Jr. Another record that still stands today is his hitting twenty-three *grand slams*. He is the

---

*Babe Ruth was with the Yankees from 1920–1934, while Gehrig joined them in 1923 and stayed through 1939.

king of RBIs—in 1931 he had 184 RBIs, an American League record that still stands.

As early as 1934, Gehrig was showing symptoms of his as-yet undiagnosed disease, having difficulty standing up and once nearly doubling over on his way to a base. On May 2, 1939, Gehrig asked to be taken out of the lineup. He had been playing so poorly he thought he was hurting the team.

About six weeks later, the Mayo Clinic in Rochester, Minnesota, gave his condition a name, amyotrophic lateral sclerosis (a hardening of the spinal cord), and diagnosed his condition as incurable. Less than a month later, on July 4, 1939, Yankee Stadium held Lou Gehrig Appreciation Day. Among the crowd of 61,808 who showed up were the members of the 1927 Yankees, who had come to pay tribute to their teammate and friend. Knowing he was doomed to die, Gehrig told the silenced crowd: "You've been reading about my bad break for weeks now. But today I think I'm the luckiest man alive."*

Less than two years later, the luckiest man alive had died, felled by the disease that now carries his name. More than 1,500 telegrams arrived at his home following his death.

SANDY KOUFAX, 1935–

  1955–57: Brooklyn Dodgers
  1958–66: Los Angeles Dodgers

Koufax was one of the best pitchers and also one of the most elusive. He has been called the J.D. Salinger of baseball. In the nearly four decades since his retirement, he has steadfastly refused to claim the spotlight, to cash in on his celebrity, but rather has chosen to live his life in privacy. This has only enhanced his reputation as a living legend of mythic proportions.

Mythic, schmythic. He is, above all, the quintessential nice Jewish boy

---

*I have taken this quote from Drebinger's report in the *New York Times* on July 5, 1955. The wording varies slightly from account to account, one of the versions being that of Gary Cooper playing Gehrig in the Hollywood film *The Pride of the Yankees*. Cooper says: "For the past two weeks you have been reading about the bad break I got. Yet today I consider myself the luckiest man on the face of the earth."

of baseball. In 1965, Sandy Koufax made baseball history and Jewish history. That fall, he pitched a perfect game and secured a revered spot in baseball. On another day that same fall, he became a Jewish hero by refusing to pitch on Yom Kippur (the most holy of the Jewish holidays)—and, mind you, this was no ordinary game, but the first game of the World Series. Koufax was decent, graceful, and honorable—but that's not just the opinion of this nice Jewish girl: In a 1999 *Sports Illustrated* article about Koufax, Tom Verducci described him as "the kind of man boys idolized, men envied, women swooned over and rabbis thanked."

But let's face it—no one would have much cared about Koufax's Yom Kippur decision had he not been a brilliant, record-setting pitcher. During his twelve-year career, he:

* pitched four no-hitters (one of them the perfect game referred to above);

* won the Cy Young Award three times;

* won the pitching **Triple Crown** three times, which means he led the league in wins, ERA (earned run average), and strikeouts;

* won five straight ERA titles (meaning he had the lowest ERA for any pitcher five seasons in a row).

It's no wonder Willie Stargell, a slugger for the Pittsburgh Pirates, once said, "Hitting against him is like eating soup with a fork."

In 1966, at the age of thirty, still appearing to be at the top of his game, Koufax retired. He had been suffering from arthritis in his arm that was becoming increasingly debilitating and painful. Six years later, when he was thirty-six, Koufax became the youngest player ever voted into the Baseball Hall of Fame.

MICKEY MANTLE, 1931–1995
NICKNAMES: "THE COMMERCE COMET," "THE MICK"
1951–68: New York Yankees

In 1951, in the Bronx, New York, along came a naive country boy from Oklahoma to become the heir apparent to none other than Joe DiMaggio. It wasn't easy to fill DiMaggio's shoes, and Mantle faced the boos of a crowd that wasn't ready to let the great Joltin' Joe be replaced on the field or in their hearts. But with his unrelenting talent, "the Mick" won them over. Following Mantle's death in 1995, George Vecsey wrote in the *New York Times*: "Even before the fans grew to like him, and then adore him, they were awed by him." This was due in equal parts to his prodigious talent, his blond good looks, and his cheerful smile. (Vecsey also wrote, "Mickey Mantle was hot. Male baseball fans talked about him the way they might talk about Marilyn Monroe in another context.")

Mantle was a powerful hitter, for whom the term "tape-measure home run" (meaning, a very, very long home run) was coined. He was also a switch hitter, an invaluable commodity in baseball. In addition:

* Mantle's most outstanding achievement was to hit eighteen career home runs during the World Series, a record that still stands.

* He walloped 536 career home runs.

* He won four home-run titles.

* And he was voted MVP three times.

During his first fourteen seasons with the Yankees, Mantle was a major contributor to the team's winning twelve pennants and seven World Series. The great debate in the 1940s was, "Who's better, DiMaggio or Williams?" And in the next decade it became, "Who's better, Mantle or Mays?" (as in, Willie Mays).

Although Mantle's appearance was of the quintessential thick-muscled, broad-shouldered, athletic ideal, he was wracked by physical injuries and psychological demons. Early in his major-league career, he incurred knee and other injuries, and he almost always played with pain. His psychic injuries were rooted in the untimely death of his father at age thirty-nine. And because his spirit was more frail than his body, he turned to the bottle. It was only later in life, long after his baseball career had ended, that he finally faced his alcoholism and got help at the Betty Ford Center. At a news conference about a month before he passed away in 1995, sickly and frail, Mantle said that kids shouldn't look to him as a role model, his honesty and humility at once winning forgiveness.

Mantle's drinking and carousing didn't diminish his status as a sports hero. At Mantle's funeral, sportscaster Bob Costas delivered a moving eulogy that included the following: "He was our symbol of baseball at a time when the game meant something to us that perhaps it no longer does . . . We knew there was something poignant about Mickey Mantle before we knew what poignant meant. We didn't just root for him, we felt for him."

ROGER MARIS, 1934–1985

1957–58: Cleveland Indians
1958–59: Kansas City Athletics
1960–66: New York Yankees
1967–68: St. Louis Cardinals

On October 1, 1961, the last day of the season, Roger Maris broke Babe Ruth's record of sixty home runs in a season, upping the ante to sixty-one.

Ruth's record was a cherished one that had stood for thirty-four years, and many did not want Maris to break it. Some didn't want anyone to break it, and others felt that if someone was going to, it should be the more popular Mickey Mantle. Sportswriters and fans were especially peeved by the fact that Maris didn't even have a .300 batting average—his adversaries felt that it further demeaned Ruth to have a player with a low batting average strip him of his record. What should have been a joyous event for Maris became a harrowing ordeal—so great was the pressure that Maris lost much of his hair in the 1961 season.

For years, until baseball commissioner* Fay Vincent took it away, a controversial asterisk appeared next to Maris's record—Ford C. Frick, the commissioner in 1961, insisted that it be recorded as such in the record books. The asterisk (in reality it was a parenthetical note, not an asterisk) denoted that Ruth hit his sixty homers in a 154-game season, while Maris's sixty-one home runs were accomplished in 162 games. Many believed that the point of the asterisk was simply to diminish Maris's achievement. The asterisk wasn't removed until 1992, seven years after Maris died.

Maris is not in the Baseball Hall of Fame. Some consider him unworthy despite his monumental feat, despite his American League MVP awards in 1961 and 1962, and despite being a part of the great Yankees team with Mickey Mantle that from 1960 to 1964 won five straight pennants.

Looking back on his life, Maris once said, "As a ballplayer, I would be delighted to do it again. As an individual, I doubt if I could possibly go through it again."

WILLIE MAYS, 1931–
NICKNAME: THE "SAY HEY KID"
    1951–57: New York Giants
    1958–72: San Francisco
        Giants
    1972–73: New York Mets

> There have been only two geniuses in the world: Willie Mays and Willie Shakespeare.
> —*Tallulah Bankhead*

Willie Mays was the quintessential all-around player. He was known in baseball as a "five-tool player," the five tools being the ability to hit, hit

---

*The commissioner of Major League Baseball, similar to the commissioner of the NFL, NBA, or NHL, is like the CEO of the corporation. He's head of the business that is baseball, and he thus does the teams' owners' bidding, not necessarily the players'. Ideally, the commissioner wants to do what's best for baseball, but when issues are under dispute between labor (the players) and management (the owners), the commissioner is one of the management.

for power, run, field, and throw. And he displayed his five tools with a sense of joy, exhilaration, and drama. When *The Sporting News* ranked the top 100 players of the twentieth century in 1999, Mays came in at number two, just behind Babe Ruth.

Throughout his brilliant career, Mays:

 * won two MVP awards;

 * became a member of several exclusive clubs—the 3,000-hit club (with 3,283 career hits), and the even more exclusive 600 home runs club, with 660;

 * hit more than fifty homers in two different seasons;

 * is ranked eighth all time in RBIs.

And even more than his abilities at bat, Mays is remembered for his awesome talent (as a center fielder) in the outfield.

Mays is best remembered for a single moment in sports history. It's known as simply "The Catch." It happened during the first game of the 1954 World Series, which pitted the New York Giants against the Cleveland Indians. The game was tied in the eighth inning. The Indians' Vic Wertz hit a deep fly ball that looked uncatchable, but not to Mays, who made a stunning over-the-shoulder catch that robbed Wertz of extra bases. It also helped the Giants win that game, and then the World Series in four games. Baseball was just beginning to be televised at this time, so the grainy footage is considered one of the first magical moments in televised sports.

When DiMaggio was alive, he insisted that he be introduced as "the Greatest Living Ballplayer." No one was really allowed to publicly disagree with this, and DiMaggio made it a prerequisite to his doing any public appearances. When DiMaggio died, though, there didn't have to be a mandate. Willie Mays, in 2005 at age seventy-six, is the Greatest Living Ballplayer. Period.

THE GLORIOUS SUMMER OF 1998
BIG MAC AND SLAMMIN' SAMMY

Warning: I'm about to go all sappy and nostalgic, throwing my stiletto-heeled smart-girl skepticism aside. Unveil the Norman Rockwells, slap on some red, white, and blue, and root-root-root for the home team. The following is why sports sometimes do *rule!*

The summer of 1998 was glorious. The country was united. Everyone was talking about the same thing, and that thing was not war or taxes or political scandals, but baseball! Nineteen ninety-eight was the summer that America was treated to the Great Home Run Race, with Mark McGwire and Sammy Sosa (see the *Legends and Legends in Training* sections) competing against each other to beat Roger Maris's record of sixty-one home runs in a season.

Hollywood could not have cast it better: two great guys. One a redhead as American as apple pie, hailing from a comfortable, middle-class family in California. The other a dark-skinned Dominican who made it out of the streets of grinding poverty to the big leagues. Both full of smiles, dignity, grace, respect for the fans, the media, the game, but most important, for each other.

In the end, Big Mac won the race, breaking Maris's home run record first, and finishing the season with an unheard of seventy home runs. Sosa beat the record too, with sixty-six home runs. I believe that no one, not the fans or the media, and most amazingly, not McGwire or Sosa, cared all that much about who won. It was all about the joy of the race. (And, for both of them, it was a far cry from the nightmarish experience that Maris underwent in his quest for sixty-one. For McGwire and Sosa, the fans were with them, and baseball was with them.)

That same year, in tandem, Sosa and McGwire were selected as Sportsmen of the Year by *The Sporting News* and *Sports Illustrated.* Gary Smith, in the accompanying article, puts it best: "As is our custom late each fall, we at *Sports Illustrated* sat down to discuss nominations for the Sportsman of the Year . . . No, we didn't discuss. We didn't even sit down . . . It was unanimous. . . . It couldn't be one Sportsman of the Year. It had to be two. Mark McGwire and Sammy Sosa. All in favor, say aye. All opposed, report back to your coma."

MARK McGWIRE, 1963–
NICKNAME: "BIG MAC"

1986–96: Oakland Athletics
1997–2001: St. Louis Cardinals

Mark McGwire was reminiscent of all the good things about Babe Ruth, without the detritus. In *Time* magazine, Joel Stein said: "While Ruth drank staggering amounts, slept around to rival Wilt Chamberlain, and smoked his own Babe Ruth brand of cigars, McGwire drinks protein supplements, lifts weights and spends free time with his son." But like the Babe, McGwire was big—a beefy, burly 6'5" and 250 pounds (but without the Babe's twiggy legs). He, too, began his baseball career as a pitcher, and like the Babe, he didn't just hit home runs, he hit them with an awesome power, beyond the stands and out of the park.

In addition to being one of *Sports Illustrated*'s and *The Sporting News*'s Sportsmen of the Year with Sosa, he was the *Associated Press*'s Male Athlete of the Year for 1998. In 1997, he stood alone as *The Sporting News*'s Sportsman of the Year. McGwire hit fifty homers in three consecutive seasons. He might have had fifty homers his rookie year (1986), but he missed a game to be present at the birth of his son. When he announced that he was giving $1 million to a foundation for abused children, he wept. (He has since given millions more.) He is divorced, but he has an amiable relationship with his ex-wife. He loves kids and has provided them with thousands of autographs. And he knew when to retire. In 2001, he was still playing well and was still hugely marketable, but he decided to walk away from it. He had suffered some injuries and was not playing at his peak level. He felt the time was right.

But, alas—while he may be as close to perfect as a professional ballplayer can get, he is still human. During the summer of his home-run race, he admitted to using a supplement called androstenedione, a substance that is banned by the NFL, by the Olympics, and by the NCAA, but when McGwire was using it, it wasn't banned by Major League Baseball. In addition, he was part of the 2005 congressional investigation into steroid use in baseball. It's excruciating to think that Big Mac's lasting legacy could very well be tarnished, but nothing will erase the joy, the thrill, and the wonder that he brought to the summer of 1998.

CAL RIPKEN JR., 1960–

1981–2001: Baltimore Orioles

Cal Ripken Jr. is best known for breaking Lou Gehrig's record of 2,130 consecutive games and going all the way to 2,632. Many conjecture that Ripken might have been better off taking a day off here or there; that he might have been a better player if he had done so. That said, Ripken was twice a league MVP.

The streak, as it went on over the years, was big news and carefully watched. In 1994, after Ripken played his 2,000th consecutive game, and the only person ahead of him in history was Gehrig, a players' strike was announced. There was talk that some owners would use replacement players, but not the Orioles. Owner Peter Angelos said "We have a special problem in Baltimore with the Cal Ripken streak, an extraordinary accomplishment by Cal and one that we certainly will do everything to avoid harming." The strike was settled, and Ripken was able to get back to business.

When, in 1995, he finally matched Gehrig's record at home in Baltimore's ballpark, Camden Yards, the sellout crowd gave him a five-minute standing ovation. The next night, when he surpassed the record, he was treated to a twenty-two-minute ovation, during which he took a victory lap around the field.

If you can judge a person by their retirement remarks (and you probably shouldn't), Ripken is a good guy, more than the sum of his 2,632 games. After announcing his retirement, he said, "One question I've been repeatedly asked these last few weeks is how I want to be remembered. My answer is simple: To be remembered at all is pretty special. I might also add, that if I am remembered, I hope it's because by living my dream I was able to make a difference."

JACKIE ROBINSON, 1919–1972

1947–56: Brooklyn Dodgers

In *Time* magazine, Richard Corliss wrote that April 15, 1947, was the day baseball finally earned the right to be called the national pastime. That was the day Jackie Robinson walked onto the diamond at Ebbets Field in Brooklyn, New York, and broke the color barrier in professional baseball.* It would be seven years until the United States Supreme Court decided *Brown v. Board of Education*; eight years before Rosa Parks took her rightful seat; sixteen years before Bull Conner unleashed his vicious dogs and fire hoses in Birmingham, Alabama.

Robinson, like all professional black baseball players prior to 1947, was playing in the Negro Leagues. Branch Rickey, the president and general manager of the Brooklyn Dodgers, had always been disturbed by the way blacks were treated during his era. But Rickey was also a very savvy businessman who knew what he might gain from bringing in new talent and from all the attention it would attract. Robinson was only one of many great baseball players in the Negro Leagues, but Rickey was smart enough to know that he had to find someone whose poise would match his talent.

Rickey also knew what hardships Robinson would face. The conversation at their very first, widely reported meeting included the following exchange:

Rickey: "I know you're a good ballplayer. What I don't know is whether you have the guts."

Robinson: "Mr. Rickey, are you looking for a Negro who isn't afraid to fight back?"

Rickey: "Robinson, I'm looking for a ballplayer with guts enough not to fight back."

---

*The NFL was integrated a year before, in 1946, when Kenny Washington joined the Los Angeles Rams. But at the time, the NFL was nowhere on America's sports radar screen. It wasn't until the following decade that football became popular, so when Washington joined, it was like the proverbial tree falling in the forest— no one noticed.

With that conversation, a new chapter in the history of race in America was written.

At the end of his first season with the Dodgers, Robinson had led his team to its first pennant in six years and earned himself a much-deserved Rookie of the Year award. Two years later, he won the league's MVP award. Robinson's career batting average was an excellent .311, and in addition to batting, he could do everything else well too—bunt, steal, run, and throw—all with a passion to win.

Robinson's courage, poise, dignity, and his ability to demonstrate excellence in the face of vicious, vile racism is inspirational. He faced death threats; race-baiting from the opposing dugouts; pitchers intentionally throwing at him (instead of to him); and hollering from baseball officials who would yell for him to carry their bags or shine their shoes. All that, and he managed to lead the Dodgers to six pennants.

PETE ROSE, 1941–
NICKNAME: "CHARLIE HUSTLE"
   1963–78: Cincinnati Reds
   1979–83: Philadelphia Phillies
   1984: Cincinnati Reds
   1984: Montreal Expos
   1985: Cincinnati Reds

Pete Rose. Yes, you've heard about him. He's the guy who *isn't* in the Hall of Fame because he gambled on baseball, perhaps on his own team.* He's been banned from baseball for life, and he also spent five months in jail—not for gambling, however, but for tax evasion.

Anyway, Pete Rose is a jerk. There are those—many in fact—who vociferously defend him and say that it's time to forgive him and let him into

---

*The final deal that was struck between Major League Baseball and Pete Rose was that Rose was banned from baseball for life. In exchange for Rose signing this agreement, baseball did not formally declare that Rose had bet on baseball, although there was a 225-page report and seven volumes of additional material offering evidence that this is, in fact, what Rose had done.

the Hall of Fame—even Jimmy Carter (yes, the former president) supports this view. But here's why all smart women should consider him an ass: He once gave one of his mistresses (or girlfriends or whatever) an engraved necklace. Engraved? you say, That's pretty nice. But here's what the inscription said: "To my rookie of the year."

It was Rose who broke Ty Cobb's record for the most career hits when he reached 4,192 on September 11, 1985. Anyhow, he achieved a grand total of 4,256 hits in his career, a record that still stands. In addition:

* His career batting average is .303, which you now know is outstanding.

* He is baseball's career leader in singles (3,215), at-bats (14,053), and games played (3,562).

* He was Rookie of the Year in 1963, and a league MVP, and a World Series MVP, and the list goes on and on.

In 1975, Rose was *Sports Illustrated*'s Sportsman of the Year. (The runner-up was O. J. Simpson . . .) Rose captivated fans and the public with his boundless enthusiasm, and he was a good teammate; he was helpful to rookies. And I will say that he was truly color-blind. He played during the 1960s and 1970s when racism was still rampant, but Rose had a genuine rapport with both black and Latin American players.

I love that Rose's nickname, "Charlie Hustle," has become a big, fat joke on him. Initially, the "hustle" referred to hustling in the good sense— hustling on the field to do whatever it took to win for himself and for his teammates. But in light of what he became, it's pretty funny.

BABE RUTH (GEORGE HERMAN RUTH), 1895–1948
NICKNAMES: "THE BABE," "THE BAMBINO," "THE HOME RUN KING," "THE CIRCUIT SMASHER," "HERMAN THE GREAT," "HOMERIC HERMAN," "THE BULKY MONARCH," "THE KING OF CLOUT," "HIS EMINENCE," "THE SULTAN OF SWAT"

1914–19: Boston Red Sox

1920–34: New York Yankees

1935: Boston Braves

It's not accurate to say that Babe Ruth *was* larger than life; it's closer to the truth to say that he *is* larger than life. Babe Ruth, The Babe, the Sultan of Swat, played his last game more than seventy years ago. His home run record that captivated the nation has been surpassed more than once. But it doesn't really feel that way. He feels as present as A-Rod or Jeter, Jordan or Shaq. It is not a long shadow that he casts, but a continuing burst of sunshine that simply won't be clouded over.

There are numerous top-100 lists for the greatest baseball players of all time. They mostly consist of the same names, but not always in the same order. (A player who's number five on one list, for instance, will appear at number ten on another.) But that doesn't apply to The Babe. He is number one. Always.

Babe Ruth joined the Baltimore Orioles of the International League (a notch below the major leagues) when he was nineteen. Being the baby of the team, he acquired the nickname "Babe," which, you might say, has stuck. He began his major-league career in 1915 as an excellent *pitcher* with the Boston Red Sox, and by 1919 had also set a major-league record with twenty-nine home runs, but the world hadn't seen nuthin' yet. It wasn't until he was sold to the Yankees in 1920 that the full force of Ruthian baseball talent, heart, and personality shook the country. Babe helped define the decade, but the decade defined him as well. Is it only a coincidence that eighteen days after Babe Ruth hit his final homer of the decade the stock market collapsed? As Robert Creamer wrote in *ESPN SportsCentury*, "More than any other athlete, more than any other American, he personified the 1920s—loud, brassy, extroverted, troubled, overachieving, electric, unforgettable."

The Babe accomplished amazing things in his career. In 1919, he hit twenty-nine homers, an unprecedented number for the time. In 1920, he hit fifty-four homers, and in 1921, he hit fifty-nine homers, which was thirty-five more than his closest challenger. But 1927 was his banner year, when he stunned the world with sixty home runs—a record that remained untouched until Roger Maris broke it in 1961—and led the Yankees to a World Series victory. Among Ruth's other feats are:

* For six straight seasons, from 1926 to 1931, he hit *at least* forty-six homers.

* 714 career home runs—a record that stood until 1974, when it was broken by Hank Aaron.

* A slugging percentage of .847 for a season (1920)—a record that stood until Barry Bonds broke it in 2001.

* A career batting average of .342, tied for eighth all-time in baseball's modern era.

And those are just a few of the more obvious stats—and his stats are just part of the story! As Jim Platt says in his book, *Sports Immortals*, "While Ruth's feats on the field were almost beyond belief, it was his personality that had perhaps a greater impact . . . Ruth was perhaps America's first transcendent sports superstar, an athlete so celebrated and talked about that he left the sports pages behind and entered the wider American consciousness." In fact, during his peak years, newspapers across the country featured a column, "What Babe Ruth Did Today."

The Babe was a womanizer and a drinker. He was someone who didn't obey speed limits, on the road or in life. But he didn't have a mean-spirited bone in his body, and he was phenomenally talented. What I especially love about The Babe is that he ate prodigiously, drank heartily, dogged around, looked out of shape (beer belly and all), and yet he was still the greatest athlete of his time. You have to wonder what he would have been able to accomplish if he was as trained and disciplined as today's athletes are—but that wouldn't have been The Babe's style.

Babe Ruth died of cancer on August 16, 1948. Celebrated baseball writer Red Smith wrote: "He was buried on a sweltering day in August 1948. In the pallbearers' pew, Waite Hoyt sat next to Joe Dugan [former teammates]. 'I'd give a hundred dollars for a cold beer,' Dugan whispered. 'So would The Babe,' Hoyt said."

TED WILLIAMS, 1918–2002
NICKNAMES: "THE SPLENDID SPLINTER," "THE THUMPER," "TEDDY BALLGAME," "THE KID"
1939–60*: Boston Red Sox

If you're from New England and have even the slightest interest in baseball and don't think that Ted Williams is the greatest hitter ever, if not the greatest player of all time, I would question your sanity, intelligence, integrity, or all of the above.

Ted Williams is considered to be one of a handful of awesomely gifted ballplayers. He accomplished a remarkable hitting feat in 1941, the same year DiMaggio was working on his equally remarkable fifty-six-game hitting streak: At the end of the 1941 season, Williams's batting average was .406!

Ted Williams also had honor, in spades. With only two games remaining in the 1941 season, Williams's batting average stood at precisely .400, an astonishing achievement that, more than sixty years later, has not been matched. Williams was given the opportunity to skip these last two games, ensuring his .400 would remain intact. He refused, saying "the record's no good unless it's made in all games." He then went out and had six hits in eight times at bat, *increasing* his batting average to .406!

In addition, Williams finished his career with:

---

*Williams's career was interrupted from 1943 to 1945 and in 1952 and 1953, when he was serving in World War II and the Korean War.

* a career average of .344,

* two MVP awards,

* six batting championships,

* 521 home runs,

* and two Triple Crowns (the highest batting average, most home runs, and most RBIs in one season).

Williams worked hard and didn't take his talent for granted. He also served our country, twice—he lost three peak career years in World War II, then returned to service as a heroic fighter pilot in the Korean War. And yet he had a terrible relationship with the fans and the press. He was the opposite of DiMaggio in tone and attitude—unlike the silent, dignified DiMaggio, Williams was cocky, quick-tempered, opinionated, and independent. Even though DiMaggio was the one squiring blondes around the hottest clubs in town while Williams was an early-to-bed outdoorsy type, the press beatified Joltin' Joe and vilified Williams.

Some believe that his attitude with the press cost him the chance to win even more MVP awards, notably in 1941 when he hit .406 but DiMaggio, with his fifty-six-game streak, won the award. Part of the problem for Williams was that the Red Sox weren't winning enough, despite his contributions. (While the Yankees were piling on the pennants and World Series victories, the Red Sox accumulated just one pennant.)

Overshadowing Williams's amazing legacy as a ballplayer is the family feud that ensued after his death in 2002. One of his sons, John Henry, had Williams's body cryogenically frozen. (Yes, I'm being serious.) An uproar erupted within the family (and throughout the country), with some of his children vehemently denying that he wanted to be frozen, insisting that he had wished to be cremated and have his ashes scattered at sea. To make the event more repugnant, his body was decapitated and the head preserved separately. More than two years after his death, the family (and legal) feud remains unresolved.

CY YOUNG (TRUE DENTON YOUNG), 1867–1955

1890–98: Cleveland Spiders
1899–1900: St. Louis Perfectos, St. Louis Cardinals
1901–08: Boston Americans, Boston Somersets, Boston Pilgrims,
Boston Red Sox
1909–11: Cleveland Naps (Indians)
1911: Boston Braves

Even if you haven't heard of Cy Young, you may have heard of the Cy Young Award, which is given annually to the best pitcher in each of the American and National leagues. Cy Young is considered by many to be the greatest pitcher ever. No pitcher has won more games than Young, nor started or completed so many games.* Young won 511 games, *almost one hundred more than other any pitcher in history.* Among his other amazing feats, Young:

 ✷ pitched the first World Series game ever, in 1903;

 ✷ pitched three no-hitters, one of them a perfect game, and one of them when he was forty-one years old;

 ✷ pitched twenty-three consecutive hitless innings over a four-game span (a record that has yet to be broken) in 1904;

 ✷ won more than thirty games in a season five times (which, considering that no one has won thirty games in *one* season since 1968, is truly amazing).

He was born in 1867 and played professional ball from 1890–1911. More than a hundred years later, there still hasn't been anyone as good as Cy. At a muscle-bound, strapping 6'2", 210 pounds ("with shoulders like a barn door," as Arthur Daly of the the *New York Times* described them), Cy "lasted twenty-two seasons and never had a sore arm." Cy once said:

---

*Young also lost more games than anyone, but if you want to keep him as your favorite, simply consider this a function of the fact that he completed more games than any other pitcher.

FUN FACTOID

In 1976 the average major-league salary was $45,000. In 2002, it was $2,389,000.

"Can't understand these modern fellers. I just pitched every third day. 'Twarn't nuthin' to it."

Cy, by the way, whose real name was True Denton Young, does not stand for Cyrus or Cyril, but rather for "cyclone"—as in, he threw with such velocity that it was like a tornado or cyclone. He acquired the nickname right from the start, while he was trying out for the minor leagues in Canton, Ohio. Not having a catcher during tryouts meant that if the batter didn't hit it, his pitches crashed into the stands. "How's that new kid pitcher?" asked the team owner. The manager replied, "Just look at the grandstand." The owner, looking as instructed said, " 'Pears as though a cyclone struck it."

Legends in Training

BARRY BONDS, 1964–
   1986–92: Pittsburgh Pirates
   1993–present: San Francisco Giants

Barry Bonds has spent the new millennium shattering records. Even though he is still playing, he has already reached "legend" status. Among his amazing accomplishments, he:

* broke Mark McGwire's single-season record of seventy home runs, slugging seventy-three;

* has been chosen MVP seven times;

* joined the extremely exclusive club of players (three members only) who have hit more than 700 career home runs (with 703 at the end of

the 2004 season, he's third on the list behind Hank Aaron and Babe Ruth);

* even created his own exclusive club—he's the only player in history to have amassed 500 homers and 500 steals.

It is not surprising that Bonds has also been walked (that is, **intentionally walked**) more than any other player in history.

Bonds has the right genetic code for all this—his father was Bobby Bonds, an outstanding major-leaguer; his godfather is Willie Mays, one of the all-time greats (whom Bonds knocked down to fourth place on the career home runs list); and Reggie Jackson, another Hall of Famer, is a distant cousin. It's difficult to imagine that Barry Bonds could have been anything other than a baseball player.

But in personality, Bonds is more Ted Williams than Babe Ruth. He has an astonishingly bad relationship with the press. He is thought of by many as "the demon of America's pastime," and he is considered a poster boy for sports arrogance. Yet, David Grann, the writer who opened his insightful and revealing profile of Bonds in *The New York Times Magazine* (2002) with the demon reference, more or less debunks the demon myth. As Bonds told Grann, "I'm not a P.R. man. I'm a ballplayer. You know how many words I got to say out on the baseball field? 'I got it!'"

In a July 2004 *Sports Illustrated* article, "10 Reasons Why Baseball Is Back," Barry Bonds is number 8. Tom Verducci admonished that it is our duty to watch this great ballplayer. He writes: "There are grandchildren yet to be born who will look at you aglow with wonder and gasp, *You saw Barry Bonds play?* Only a few who saw Babe Ruth swing a bat still walk the earth, and the legions who caught the prime of Ted Williams dwindle with every sunset. To watch Bonds now is your privilege—nay, your *duty*—as a baseball fan and, in the grand tradition of the game, as an oral historian."

But that was in July. What a difference a day (or a steroid scandal investigation) makes. By the end of that year, news broke that Bonds had testified in front of a grand jury that he had used substances that the authorities claimed were illegal steroids. Bonds claimed that he didn't know that the substances were steroids. The final outcome could mean that all of Bonds's records are a sham and that he may never realize his seemingly guaranteed spot in the Hall of Fame.

ROGER CLEMENS, 1962–
NICKNAME: "ROCKET"

    1984–96: Boston Red Sox
    1997–98: Toronto Blue Jays
    1999–2003: New York Yankees
    2004–present: Houston Astros

Roger Clemens is one of the greatest pitchers of all time. He's also proven himself to be a not-so-nice guy. Of course, unless he murders someone, or joins the Taliban, he will most certainly be a Hall of Famer; although there are rules against gambling, there doesn't seem to be a rule about being an ass.

Anyhow, in his twenty-one-year career, Clemens has:

  ✳ won *six* Cy Young Awards;

  ✳ twice won the pitching Triple Crown award (league leader in wins, ERA, and strikeouts);

  ✳ won two World Series (with the Yankees);

  ✳ been named a league MVP once, and an All-Star Game* MVP once.

In addition, in 2003, he won his 300th game and has been adding to that impressive figure since (he's one of only twenty others in baseball history to have done this). Also that year, he became one of only three pitchers to rack up 4,000 strikeouts.[†] And I *will* say that he works hard. At forty-two, his rigorous workout program keeps him fit and at peak performance.

---

*The All-Star game is an annual event that dates back to 1933. Fans, coaches, managers, and players vote for the best players who then play in an American League versus National League game.
[†]The other two pitchers are Nolan Ryan (5,714) and Steve Carlton (4,136).

Now to his bad behavior. Clemens seems to have anger issues. "A lot of guys go out there and try to be mean," said former Yankees teammate Tino Martinez, "but it doesn't work because it's not their personality. Roger [has] it naturally."

In 1990, Clemens got ejected from Game 4 of the playoffs when he swore at an umpire. Early in the 2000 season, Clemens hit Mike Piazza of the Mets in the head with a fastball. Then, three and a half months later in the 2000 World Series (the Yankees versus their crosstown rival, the Mets), Clemens threw a broken bat at Piazza. (Clemens claimed it was unintentional; Piazza said it wasn't.) Piazza had broken his bat on a pitch from Clemens, and Clemens grabbed the bat and threw it in Piazza's direction while Piazza was running toward first base.

And yet, here is the guy's point of view—Tom Verducci of *Sports Illustrated* to be specific: "Clemens is [simply] . . . an unshaven, unapologetic gunslinger of a power pitcher." What's a smart girl to do?

DEREK JETER, 1974–
NICKNAME: "THE PRINCE OF THE CITY"

1995–present: New York Yankees

Derek Jeter plays shortstop for the Yankees, and he is one of the best ever. He is also a major hottie, a matinee idol who has, along with his DiMaggio-like grace, a bit of Joe Namath in him, due to his reputation for hitting the hippest clubs in New York and staying out until the wee hours. Since joining the Bronx Bombers in 1995, Jeter has won *four* World Series championships. In the 2000 Series, he won the World Series MVP, which followed his All-Star Game MVP award earlier in the season, making him the only player ever to win both awards in one season.

Jeter is polite and humble, and he has a reputation for being a wonderfully decent human being. Whenever his parents are at a game, Jeter finds where they are seated before the game begins, then catches their eye and gives them a wave. And he established the Turn 2 Foundation, which promotes a healthy lifestyle for youths and is designed to prevent and treat drug and alcohol abuse. Jeter's dad, a drug- and alcohol-abuse counselor, gave up his practice to become the foundation's executive director.

In 2003, Jeter was chosen captain of the New York Yankees by their cantankerous owner, George Steinbrenner, who said "I have always been very, very careful about giving such a responsibility to one of my players, but I cannot think of a single player that I have ever had who is more deserving of this honor than Derek Jeter."

The position had been vacant since 1995.

RANDY JOHNSON, 1964–
NICKNAME: "THE BIG UNIT"
1988–89: Montreal Expos
1989–97: Seattle Mariners
1998: Houston Astros
1998: Seattle Mariners
1999–2004: Arizona Diamondbacks
2005–present: New York Yankees

The Big Unit. I think that says it all. Randy Johnson is 6'10", hence the nickname, but I believe I speak for all women in suspecting (hoping) that The Big Unit represents a complete package, in proportion you might say. Regardless, his is the single greatest nickname in sports.

The Big Unit is a big deal. One of the most remarkable feats of his career is that in 2004 he pitched a perfect game, something only sixteen others have done in the history of baseball. And Johnson (I just can't keep referring to him as "The Big Unit"—it makes me giggle) did this at age forty, making him the oldest pitcher ever to do so. He's also the last pitcher to win the pitching Triple Crown (lowest ERA, most wins, and most strikeouts in one league in one season), which he achieved while pitching for Arizona in 2002.

Since pitching a perfect game is such a big deal, the event is always surrounded by a lot of media attention. Johnson taped a "Top Ten" segment for the *Late Show with David Letterman*. The subject was "Top Ten Cool Things About Pitching a Perfect Game." Number six on the list was,

"Can walk up to guys who've thrown no-hitters and whisper, 'Loser.'" (If you're not laughing heartily, go back up to page 119 to review.)

Johnson is a five-time Cy Young Award–winner who most certainly has a place in the Hall of Fame waiting for him.

MARIANO RIVERA, 1969–

1995–present: New York Yankees

The Tale of Me and Mariano: Mariano Rivera, a ***closer*** (a pitcher who usually just pitches the ninth inning and thus "closes" the game) for the Yankees, who was recently awarded a two-year, $21 million contract, needs me. He doesn't know it, and you might be thinking that he's doing just fine without me, but this is not true. The proof lies in an episode that took place a few years ago during the 2000 World Series between the Yankees and the Mets. While the Yankees were on their way to clinching the pennant (winning the American League title so they could compete against the Mets), I dutifully watched Mariano save—close—game after game. Then, during one game, while Mariano was pitching, I was forced to leave the room momentarily (I can't remember what household calamity drew me away, but it must have been serious—the sound of the tub overflowing or something). Anyway, HORROR OF HORRORS, a player got a hit off of Mariano. This happened a couple more times, and then I knew: Mariano needs me.

But enough about me and Mariano—on to just Mariano. The Yankees, like all major-league teams, have several ***relief pitchers*** who come in when the starting pitcher is beginning to falter. Mariano's specialty is coming in at the very end, usually when the team is ahead, to "save" the game. (In other words, if the Yankees are ahead 4-3 in the bottom of the ninth, they'll bring Mariano to the mound because it is almost impossible to hit one of his pitches.) He has won both a league MVP and a World Series MVP. And with more than 300 ***saves*** to his credit, he is arguably the best relief pitcher of all time.

Rivera, who was born in Panama City in 1969 and joined the Yankees in 1995, has twenty-one playoff and nine World Series saves. What this means is that the cool stoicism that he demonstrates (on his adorable boyish face) in the regular season doesn't change one iota in the postseason. In a *New York* magazine profile of Rivera, Buster Olney described Rivera's face as fixed "in the unaffected expression of a customs agent."

ALEX RODRIGUEZ, 1975–
NICKNAME: "A-ROD"
1994–2000: Seattle Mariners
2001–03: Texas Rangers
2004–present: New York Yankees

You would think that one supremely talented, remarkably handsome, genuinely gentlemanly, and well-paid ($189 million contract) star like Derek Jeter would be enough for one team, but for the Yankees, it apparently is not. In 2004, they decided they had a couple of extra dollars on hand and picked up Alex Rodriguez and his $252 million contract from the Texas Rangers.* The only thing that makes A-Rod less desirable than Jeter is that he's happily married. Damn him!

When the Yankees traded for Rodriguez, it caused a big whoop-dee-do in the sports world. With the Rangers, Rodriguez played shortstop, so, since Jeter played shortstop for the Yankees, everyone was waiting to see which player would prevail in holding on to his position. (It was Jeter—A-Rod became the third baseman.) Furthermore, everyone was wondering if one baseball team was big enough for these two *huge* baseball stars. Disappointing sportswriters everywhere, A-Rod and Jeter couldn't be more boring in that they *get along.*

A-Rod, like Jeter, is immensely versatile. He hits homers; he racks up a lot of RBIs; he has a good batting average. He's almost always ranked in the top ten of all the important categories (such as scoring runs, getting on base—all that good stuff). He won the Hank Aaron Award (for the best

---

*A-Rod's ten-year contract, which he signed with the Rangers in 2000, as Michael Mandelbaum notes in *The Meaning of Sports,* is a sum larger than the total cost of building his home field, the Ballpark in Arlington, which opened in 1994.

offensive player in each league) for three consecutive years. "Ask players, ask executives, ask just about anyone in baseball who the best all-around player in the American League is and, usually without hesitation, A-Rod's name pops out," wrote John Donovan in *Sports Illustrated.*

SAMMY SOSA, 1968–
NICKNAME: "SLAMMIN' SAMMY"
        1989: Texas Rangers
        1989–91: Chicago White Sox
        1992–2004: Chicago Cubs
        2005–present: Baltimore Orioles

During the summer of 1998, as Mark McGwire and Sosa were after Maris's home run record, Sammy, with his 24/7 smile, captured the hearts of Americans—all the way to the White House, where he was asked to light the Christmas tree after the 1998 season, and then, the following January, was introduced in President Clinton's State of the Union Address as a hero in two countries.

Sosa works tirelessly as an ambassador for his impoverished homeland. ESPN.com sportswriter Brent Hyland wrote: "His rise to stardom from humble beginnings as a shoe-shine boy in the Dominican Republic coupled with his homage to Roberto Clemente [another Dominican baseball great, who died in a 1972 plane crash while flying relief supplies to Nicaraguan earthquake victims], in both jersey number and humanitarian efforts, evoked the brush strokes of a Caribbean Norman Rockwell."

Among Sosa's many feats, he:

✳ was awarded a National League MVP;

✳ was the first player to slam at least sixty home runs in three seasons;

✳ made the 30/30 club twice—meaning that in two seasons he racked up thirty homers and thirty stolen bases;

✳ belted sixty-six homers in that summer of '98.

Sosa, like McGwire, has had a big oops in his career. On June 3, 2003, Sosa's bat was broken when he hit the ball and it was revealed that it had cork inside—a big no-no. A corked bat will send the ball much farther than a regulation bat, and they are prohibited in the major leagues. The press immediately attacked Sammy, calling him a fraud and a phony. Sammy explained that he had mistakenly taken out one of the bats that he used for entertaining fans in batting practice exhibitions only—not in games. Seventy-six of his other bats were X-rayed and they were all found to be fine—no cork—so he was taken at his word and vindicated. (Many people, however, still don't believe him.)

Sosa began to decline in 2002 following three seasons of hitting more than sixty home runs. In the 2004 season he slumped even further, being demoted from third or fourth in the batting order to fifth and then sixth. In 2005 his slump abated—only to be replaced with another demerit—possible steroid use. Sigh. Like McGwire, Sosa turned out to be human after all. But he'll still have his place on the baseball honor roll in years to come.

BASEBALL RECORDS CHEAT SHEET

*Babe Ruth set an unprecedented season home-run total of sixty.

*Maris broke Ruth's single-season home-run total of sixty with sixty-one.

*McGwire, and then Sosa, broke Maris's record with seventy and sixty-six home runs, respectively.

*Bonds broke McGwire's record with seventy-three single-season home runs.

*Aaron broke Ruth's career home-run total of 714 with 755.

*Ripken broke Gehrig's consecutive games played streak of 2,130 with 2,632.

Glossary

At Bat: When a player comes to the plate for his turn to try to hit the ball, it is called an *at bat*. The number of times a player has been at bat is used to calculate many statistics (batting average, for example, is the total number of hits divided by the total number of at bats). You might hear a sports analyst say, "So and so had a great game last night, with four hits in four at bats." The phrase can also refer to the entire team being up at bat as opposed to in the field, as in, "The Dodgers were at bat when a fan streaked naked across the diamond."

Ball: A pitch that a batter does not swing at and that is *out* of the strike zone. If the pitcher throws four balls, the batter automatically *walks* to first base. (A batter can swing at a lousy pitch, and sometimes hit it quite well and advance to a base; but if he swings at a lousy pitch and misses, it's a strike, not a ball.)

Balk: This is what any decent woman does when she discovers that the perfect little black dress she's been coveting costs more than her month's rent. When talking baseball, a *balk* is when a pitcher tries to fake a runner out—by faking a throw, for example—or not coming to a stop after stretching and before beginning his pitch. When an umpire calls a balk, all runners on base get to advance one base.

Base Hit: Same as a *hit* (see page 164).

Batting Average: A player's batting average is calculated by dividing his total number of hits by his total number of at bats. (For example, if I had 180 hits in 400 at bats, I would have a batting average of .450, which would make me the greatest hitter ever in the entire universe.) A batting average of .300 or higher is excellent. A typical, very good major-league hitter might hit 110 times over 350 at bats, giving him a .314 average.

The Batting Title: The award given by both the American League and the National League to the player with the highest batting average at the end of the season.

Bottom of the Inning: The bottom of the inning refers to the second half of the inning. Each team is up at bat once per inning (while the opposing team is in the field). So, if it's the bottom of the sixth inning and Team Fab Abs has already been up at bat, now Team Beautiful Biceps is up (and Team Fab Abs is in the field). When Team Beautiful Biceps gets three outs, the inning is over, and the game moves forward to the *top* (first half) of the seventh inning, at which point

Team Fab Abs will be at bat again. The home team always bats during the bottom of the inning (see *last licks*).

Bull Pen: The place where pitchers warm up (by practicing with bull-pen catchers) during a game.

Bunt: A type of hit in which a batter, instead of swinging at the ball, simply positions the bat in front of the ball. A bunt results in an unimpressive, rather wussy-looking, slow-rolling ball in the infield. Bunting is strategic, though—it's usually used to advance players already on base.

Closer: A *relief pitcher* (see below) who comes in at the end of the game to "close" it. A closer is an excellent pitcher, but one who is used only for an inning or two per game, and who is usually only brought into the game when his team is ahead, to ensure that his team wins.

Count: The tally of balls and strikes a batter has while at bat. The number of balls is always called first. Therefore, a "2-1 count" means that the batter has two balls and one strike on him.

Designated Hitter: A hitter who is selected before the start of a game to substitute at bat for another, presumably less-skilled hitter, almost always the pitcher. The player for whom the DH is substituting does not have to leave the game (he can still play his defensive position or pitch), but the DH, meanwhile, doesn't play in the field. Designated hitters are allowed only in the American League.

Double: A double is two shots of scotch (or vodka, rye, bourbon, gin, what have you) poured over ice (or not, if you prefer it "neat"). In baseball, *a double* means that the batter hits the ball far enough, fast enough, and/or hard enough to enable him to run to second base without stopping. In both cases, a double is better than a single.

Double Play: When the team in the field gets *two* outs on a single play. The following scenario would be a double play: Joe is at bat, and Mo is at first base. Joe hits the ball, and the shortstop gets ahold of it and throws it to second base before Mo gets there, so Mo is out. Then the second baseman throws it to first base before Joe gets there, so Joe is out too.

Error: A goof, a mistake, a screw-up; it's dropping the ball when any doofus could have caught it (think Charlie Brown from *Peanuts* reaching for the easy ball and missing it). It's throwing the ball into the dirt instead of into your teammate's glove. It's letting the ball roll between your legs. It can result in a batter getting to first, a runner advancing, or a batter having more time at bat. Only the defense (the team in the field) can make an error.

Fair Ball: A fair ball is one that is hit within fair territory—that is, inside the foul lines.

Foul Ball: There are two foul lines on the field—right and left—that are marked by a white line and extend from home plate to the foul pole at the edge of the outfield. A *foul ball* is one that a batter hits *outside* these lines. If a batter hits a foul ball on his third strike, it doesn't count as anything, and he gets to try again. There are no limits as to how many foul balls a batter can hit on the third strike.

Fly Ball: A fly ball is exactly what it sounds like—a ball that is hit up, up, up into the air.

Grand Slam Home Run (or just Grand Slam): A grand slam home run is perhaps one of the most glorious moments in baseball. The bases are loaded (i.e., there's a runner at first, second, and third base), and a player is at bat. Then, suddenly— *thwack!*— he hits a home run, which means that *all four* players score! It doesn't matter if this happens on the Little League field, at the family picnic, at the office outing, or in Yankee Stadium. It's pure happiness, plain and simple.

Ground Ball: A ground ball (also called a *grounder*) is a batted ball that rolls or bounces along the ground.

Hit: When the batter hits the ball and reaches base safely. If it's a fly ball and it's caught, the batter is out, and it's not a hit. Also, if a batter gets on base because of a fielding error, the batter is not credited with a hit.

Hitting for the Cycle: This occurs when a player hits a single, double, triple, and a home run in one game. Hitting for the cycle is as statistically rare as a no-hitter.

Home Plate: Home plate is the beginning and the end, baby. While at bat, the batter stands next to home plate, over which the pitcher throws the ball. Home plate is also the fourth (last) base that must be touched in order for a runner to score.

Home Run: "Home run" qualifies as one of the top ten sports metaphors used ad nauseam in everyday language. In baseball, a home run is a hit that (usually) sends the ball over the outfield fences and into the stands or out of the park, rendering it unretrievable and allowing the batter to circle all the bases and score. While technically the ball doesn't have to be hit out of the park, if it's not, it's unlikely that he'll have time to run around all the bases and get home. If there are other players on base when the batter hits a home run, the home run will be called a two- or three-run homer. Or, if the bases are loaded (men at first, second, and third), then it's a *grand slam home run* (see above), one of life's glorious treats.

Infield: The part of the field that is circumscribed by the bases and the base paths (usually dirt) between them. It is the area inside the "diamond" formed by home plate, first, second, and third base, plus the base paths (see diagram page 107).

Inning: There are nine innings (periods) in a regular baseball game. During an inning, each team is up at bat once and in the field once (except if it's the bottom of the ninth inning, and the team due up at bat is winning—then they don't bother finishing the ninth inning and the game ends after the top half). A baseball game cannot end in a tie; the game goes into extra innings until one team wins.

Intentional Walk: When a pitcher intentionally throws four *balls* (pitches outside the strike zone), allowing the batter to draw a walk. A pitcher might do this if the batter is an excellent hitter who has a good chance of doing more damage than just getting to first base. The thinking behind this is, "Better to get him to first than risking a score (or scores, if there are other men on base)."

 Last Licks: The team that is playing at home always has "last licks," which means that the visiting team always starts the game, batting at the top of the first inning, and the home team is always at bat in the bottom, or second part, of the inning. This way, if it's the ninth inning, and the home team is behind, they have a chance in the bottom of the ninth to win (or tie) the game. If the home team is ahead after the top of the ninth is completed, then they don't bother with the bottom half. The game is over.

Line Drive: A good, solid hit in which the ball stays in the air but low to the ground.

No-Hitter: A no-hitter is a game in which one team gets no hits. The credit for this is almost always given to the pitcher, as in "Joe Schmo pitched a no-hitter." Unlike in a perfect game, though, players can wind up on base from walks or errors, and the opposing team can even score, although it's rare for this to happen. (In this scenario, the opposing team would have to score a run solely off of walks and/or errors.) A no-hitter is usually a shutout.

Outfield: The area outside the "diamond"—that is, the area beyond the infield and the base paths—comprised of right field, center field, and left field (see diagram on page 107).

Pennant Race: Winning a pennant race—or simply, "a pennant"—means that a particular team won its league championship (either the American League Championship or the National League Championship) and will face the other league's pennant winner in the World Series.

Perfect Game: If you want guaranteed coverage in the headlines, pitch a perfect game. There have only been seventeen in all of baseball history! A perfect game is when a pitcher retires (gets out) every single opposing batter. It means retiring twenty-seven players in nine innings. No hits, no walks, no errors by anyone on the winning team. Sounds like it could be as boring as watching paint dry, but actually the suspense is palpable and the (rare) experience of witnessing a perfect game is quite thrilling. On the rare occasions when it looks like a pitcher might pitch a perfect game, the ballpark becomes eerily quiet, almost spooky. Generally, no one will even look at, much less speak to, the pitcher when he returns to the dugout between innings.

Pinch Hitter: A pinch hitter is a player who substitutes at bat for another player. When a pinch hitter is brought in (by the manager), he remains in the same spot in the batting order throughout the remaining innings, and the player for whom he is substituting is out of the game. A pinch hitter is brought in when the player in the regular lineup is not a very good hitter (often the pitcher), and a lot is at stake. But a pinch hitter can substitute for any player. If a hit is desperately needed, and Johnny is more likely to get a hit than Bobby (and assuming that Bobby isn't crucial for the rest of the game), the manager will put in Johnny.

Pinch Runner: A player who is brought into a game (by the manager) to replace a runner who is on base, who is generally a slowpoke or may be injured.

Pop-Up: A ball hit up into the air and easily caught, usually by an *infielder*.

Relief Pitcher: A pitcher who "relieves" the pitcher who started the game. In the old days, pitchers usually pitched a whole game; nowadays, however, it's rare for a pitcher to pitch all nine innings. Once a pitcher starts to show the slightest sign of fatigue, or starts to throw lousy pitches, he's replaced with a relief pitcher. It's common to see several pitchers used in a single game. The starting pitcher will be replaced with a relief pitcher, who himself will probably be replaced with another relief pitcher or "closer" (see above).

Run: A run is a score; each time a player crosses home plate, his team is awarded one run. (A player scores a run by running all the way around the bases and back to home.)

Sacrifice: A *sacrifice* is a play in which the batter hits the ball in a way that results in getting himself out, but that enables a teammate to run to another base or score (in other words, the batter sacrifices himself so that a teammate can advance). Neither a sacrifice bunt nor a sacrifice fly counts as an official at bat for the batter. Sacrifices are only done when there are fewer than two outs (otherwise the sacrifice would end the inning and be pointless).

Save: A situation in which a relief pitcher comes into the game when his team is in the lead and preserves (or "saves") that lead, and records the last out. For example, if it's the ninth inning and the score is Yankees 5, Red Sox 4, and relief pitcher Mariano Rivera comes in to pitch for the Yankees and prevents the Red Sox from scoring, then Rivera is credited with the "save," and the announcer might say something like, "The amazing Mariano Rivera gets his 330th career save and his fiftieth for the season."

Single: To be single is the often maligned, yet ultimately fabulous state of being unattached to a significant other. But that's a lifestyle choice. In baseball, a single is when a batter gets a hit that enables him to run to first base.

Slide: To get to a base safely, a runner will often drop down and slide the last few feet to reach it. Sliding is a speedier way of reaching a base than simply staying on your feet and running to it. When a runner slides, his uniform gets very dirty.

Steal: If a player is on a base, he can try to advance to the next base—that is, *steal* the base—while the pitcher is pitching. If the pitcher or the catcher sees the runner trying to steal a base, he'll throw the ball to the appropriate fielder who will then try to tag the runner out. Stealing bases is very effective for rattling the nerves of the pitcher and catcher by being a distraction. Stealing is risky, but *muy macho*.

Strike: A strike is when a batter swings at a ball and misses; when a batter does *not* swing at a ball that is thrown within the strike zone; and when a batter hits a foul ball on the first or second strike. A player is allowed two strikes; after three strikes, he's out.

Strike Out: A player strikes out by getting three strikes at the plate. Once he strikes out, his time at bat is over, he's out, and the next batter comes up (or if it's the team's third out, the inning ends).

Strike Zone: The strike zone is the area above home plate through which the pitcher must pitch the ball for it to be considered a strike. If the pitcher does *not* pitch the ball within the strike zone, it's called a ball. The strike zone extends from the batter's knees to the midpoint between the top of the batter's uniform pants and the top of his shoulders. In short, knees to chest. If a batter doesn't swing at a ball that was pitched into the strike zone, he gets a strike. The umpire determines if a ball has been pitched into the strike zone.

Switch-Hitter: A batter who can bat either right- or left-handed.

Taking a Pitch: When a batter *doesn't* swing at the pitch, he is said to have *taken the pitch*. If the pitch was inside the strike zone, it's a strike; if it was outside the strike zone, it's a ball.

Top of the Inning: The top of the inning is the first half of the inning. Each team is up at bat once per inning (while the opposing team is in the field). After the team at bat gets three outs, it is the opposing team's turn at bat. (See *Bottom of the Inning*, above, for further explanation.)

Triple: A triple is a hit that allows the batter to get to third base without stopping.

Triple Crown: A player is said to win the Triple Crown when he leads his league in home runs, batting average, *and* runs batted in. This has been accomplished only fourteen times in baseball history. (The last person to win the triple crown was Carl Yastrzemski of the Boston Red Sox, in 1967.) A *pitcher* is said to win the Triple Crown when he leads the league in wins, earned run average, and strikeouts. The last person to do this was Randy Johnson in 2002, when he played for the Arizona Diamondbacks.

Triple Play: A play in which three outs are made. Triple plays are rare.

Walk: After a pitcher has thrown four *balls* (pitches that are outside the strike zone), the batter gets to walk to first base. If a pitcher's having a bad day, he could walk several batters. (Sometimes, though, a pitcher will intentionally walk a batter, to prevent him, for example, from getting an amazing hit.) Note that runs can be scored on walks—if bases are loaded and the batter gets walked, the player who was on third base walks home and scores, and all the other players advance a base.

Hockey

THE SOUND: *Thud.* (Two humans colliding into a wall.)

THE LOOK: Puffy men in Pillsbury Dough boy–style costumes—I mean uniforms—wearing skates, carrying big sticks, and not walking softly. Underneath the puffy suits are lean, mean bodies.

THE PLACE: Ice rinks. (All pro hockey is played in indoor rinks.)

THE ORGANIZATION: National Hockey League (NHL).

Hockey is one long adrenaline rush. It's by far the fastest of the major sports, except for car racing, which probably shouldn't be included in the same category because a 220-pound human cannot compete with a 750-horsepower machine—but we'll save that discussion for later. Anyhow, hockey players skate up to thirty miles an hour and the *puck* (the little round disk that the game revolves around) sometimes travels more than a hundred miles an hour. Which means that, although hockey is a relatively straightforward game, the speed adds *wow* to the sport and demands that its players not just be exceptionally skilled, but be exceptionally skilled *on ice.*

> I went to a fight the other night, and a hockey game broke out.
> —*Rodney Dangerfield*

The speed also means that it is almost impossible for viewers to catch everything that goes on in the rink, even in replay. I'll go out on a limb (a short, sturdy one) and say that no one—not even the commentators—sees every move that's made. It makes sense: The puck is small, the players are big, and the speedcam only skates so fast. As *Sports Illustrated*'s Stephen Canella put it, ". . . the average sports fan is . . . as lost trying to follow [a hockey] game on TV as a third-grader at an astrophysics lecture."

So, *why bother watching?* Well, Canella is exaggerating. After reading this chapter and watching a few games, you will start to see things more clearly; you'll certainly get the gist of what's going on; and you'll hopefully even begin to enjoy it.

THE NEW, IMPROVED NHL

To avoid sounding clueless about hockey, you need to know that there was no pro hockey for the entire 2004–05 season—the NHL canceled the season. In the fall of 2004, players and management could not come to an agreement on a variety of issues, and on September 15 of that year, the players were "locked out" (told not to come to work, essentially) by owners.

But now, hockey is back and better than ever! In July of 2005, the two sides agreed on the business-related issues, and the NHL even instituted some new rules, designed to make the game more entertaining. In a nutshell, the changes in rules benefit the offense and improve the flow and speed of the game, while making it more difficult for the defense—which, ultimately, results in more scoring. The sections below reflect these new rules.

 ## HERE'S HOW IT WORKS

Whichever team gets the most *goals*, which is accomplished by getting the *puck* into the *net* (also known as the *goal*), wins. Hockey is perhaps even more straightforward than basketball: A team earns one **point** for every goal. There is no other way to score. The really great thing about hockey is that, as mentioned earlier, the speed is such that no one sees everything that goes on, so at the water cooler, you are under no pressure to cite details. A simple "Wasn't that a great goal that so-and-so scored?" will suffice.

In order to enjoy a hockey game, there are only a handful of important rules and penalties that you need to know, but in order to do so, you need to know a little bit about the layout of the rink.

THE RINK

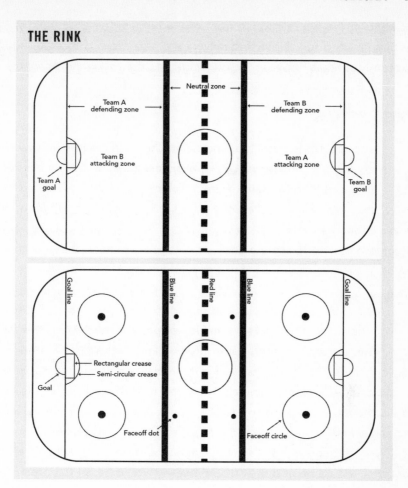

The rink is divided into three major areas: two **defensive/attacking zone**s at either end, and a **neutral zone** in the middle. One team's *attacking zone* is the opposing team's *defensive zone*. Each team's **goaltender*** stays in his team's defensive zone, guarding his team's net.

There are two **blue lines** that separate the defensive zones from the neutral zone, and there is a **red line** through the center of the rink. At

---

*You say toe-may-toe, I say ta-mah-toe; I say goalie, you say goaltender—and Joe Shmo over there says goalkeeper. And Canadians even say "goaler." Although the official rules of the NHL refer to this position as "goalkeeper," all four terms are colloquially correct. I usually say "goalie," but now, the use of the word "goaltender" seems to be what's hip.

each end of the rink, along the front of the *net*, are the *goal lines*, which are also painted red. Note that players are also allowed to skate in the thirteen-foot areas between the goal (*net*) and the walls (*end-boards*).

THE PUCK

A puck is one inch thick and two inches in diameter, and weighs six ounces. Shape-wise, it kind of resembles a slim can of tuna fish, or a Ring Ding. If it were a diamond, I might understand why men are willing to skate their butts (and a few teeth) off for it, but it's *vulcanized hard rubber*. Anyway, it's the round disk that a player needs to get into the net to score a goal.

TIMING

There are three twenty-minute periods in hockey games. Between periods there is a fifteen-minute intermission (two per game). Thus, if sports lived in the real world, the game would last a total of ninety minutes. However, even though hockey is fast-paced, there are still plenty of stoppages—usually due to jabbing, punching, and slamming—that extend the game to two hours or more.

If you put sports on a speed continuum, baseball, where time is a *non*factor, would be at one end, and hockey would be on the other. The game itself is in continuous motion. In other sports, time-outs are often called *in the middle of* a play. (In football, for example, just before the ball is snapped to the quarterback, he might call a time-out.) In hockey, however, **time-outs** are called only during a normal stoppage of play, like when a **penalty** is called, or a goal is scored. Also, each team is allowed only *one* (thirty-second) time-out per game.*

---

*In NBA basketball, six regular time-outs and two twenty-second time-outs (one per half) are allowed per game. In NFL football, three time-outs are allowed per half.

Overtime

Under the new rules instituted in 2005, no hockey game can end in a tie; previously, a regular season game could be tied. If, at the end of the three periods, the score is tied, there is a five-minute *sudden-death overtime*. During sudden-death overtime, whichever team scores first wins, and the game ends (regardless of whether or not the five minutes have been used up). If no one scores during the five-minute overtime period, a *shootout* occurs. During a shootout, three players are selected from each team. Each team then takes three shots, and the team with the most goals after those six shots is the winner.

In the playoffs, a tie has never been allowed to stand. If, after the third period, the score is tied, the game goes into a twenty-minute sudden-death overtime period. There can be as many twenty-minute sudden-death overtime periods as necessary to determine a winner.

SCORING

One point, or *goal*, is scored each time a player shoots the puck into the net. That's it.

When a player scores three goals in one game, it's called a *hat trick*. A commentator might say, "We're here in the locker room to congratulate Mr. Big Shot on scoring a hat trick in a sensational game." This is not an easy thing to do, so if a player achieves a hat trick, he usually walks on water (*frozen* water?) for a while afterward.

Shots on Goal

One term you'll hear in regard to scoring is **shot on goal**, which is a shot that *would have* gone into the goal if the goaltender hadn't deflected, or **saved** it (blocked it from going in the net). A team's shots on goal are kept track of throughout the game, and throughout the season, too. It may seem silly to keep track of all the failed shots, but in hockey, scoring is so difficult that it's a triumph just to get that close to scoring a goal. Shots on goal are also tallied to determine how many saves a goaltender had in relation to the number of goals scored (and to thereby determine how good a game the goaltender had).

TYPES OF SHOTS

There are only so many variations of shots possible with a rigid hockey stick. The most common shots are the **slap shot, wrist shot, backhand shot**, and **flip shot**. The most flamboyant is the *slap shot*, which is also the fastest shot. It looks like a golf swing—the stick is raised high and then brought down—with emphasis—to the puck. In a *wrist shot*, which is slower but more accurate than the slap shot, the stick is not raised off the ice—the puck is propelled by a strong flicking of the wrist. A *backhand shot* is a wrist shot done backhand rather than forehand, and a *flip shot* is when the puck is flicked up off the ice, into the air, toward the goal.

THE POINTS SYSTEM

For the purpose of creating more statistics with which sports fans can become obsessed, players receive **points** for their individual records. A player earns points for goals and assists (goals + assists = points). So, if Bobby scored one goal and three assists in a particular game, he would be awarded four points. (Similar to other sports, in hockey an assist is awarded to a player when he passes the puck to the player who then scores—i.e., when he assists that player in scoring.)

DEFENSIVE TACTICS: CHECKING AND SHOT BLOCKING

Checking

Checking is essentially *the* defensive strategy for the game. It's the way the Team Hottie players will stop the Team Hairy guys, steal the puck, and get on with it toward the goal. Checking (in theory, not necessarily in practice) is permitted only against the player with the puck, or the player who just had the puck. There are two legal types of checking: **stick checks** and **body checks**.

STICK CHECKS

In a stick check, player A uses his stick to poke, sweep, or lift the puck away from player B. It's similar to a basketball player stealing the ball from his opponent, only in hockey, the stick is used.

BODY CHECKS

In a body check, the dermatologist asks you to get naked and then checks your whole body for any suspicious spots. (True, but it means something different in hockey.) In hockey, a body check is when player A bumps or (more commonly) SLAMS his hip or shoulder into player B to block player B's progress or throw him off balance. Checking is usually a full body slam, and it's often done against the **boards** (the walls surrounding the rink). There's *a lot* of checking in hockey, and when you first begin watching the sport, it's pretty tough to get over the idea that checking is legal. Outrageous body slams that involve excessive force or deliberate malice, however, are not allowed—they are considered **penalties** (more on those later).

Shot Blocking

The other defensive tactic used in hockey is shot blocking, which is far less commonly employed. Shot blocking is when a player drops down to one or both knees and uses his body to stop a puck. (Men don't like to drop to their knees. It may involve a commitment.) This is rarely done, because the guy with the puck who Mr. Down-On-His-Knees is trying to block has a relatively good chance of getting around Mr. Knees.

MARSHMALLOW MEN OR HOCKEY HOTTIES?

One thing that distinguishes hockey players from other pro athletes is that they wear these big puffy outfits—I mean, uniforms. Starting from the top down, they wear: a helmet, shoulder pads, elbow pads, a girdle (not the kind that makes the tummy look smaller—these padded "girdles" protect the hips, thighs, and kidneys), gloves, an athletic supporter with protective cup, and shin guards. Those are just the basics—the goaltenders wear even more equipment (about twenty *pounds* more, including large shin pads that can be up to nearly a foot wide).

Hockey players have to wear all this because, without a lot of padding, a puck traveling at, say, 105 miles an hour becomes a lethal weapon. (In fact, there have been a few major mishaps with fans in the stands that have resulted in death, but I'll save that for *The Depressed Girl's Guide to the Dark Side of Everything*.) The real tragedy is that, because of the padding, we can't see who's buff and who's not among the players—although we can safely assume that they are *all* in fantastic shape since they skate at remarkable speeds and take very rough hits continually. (If you're particularly fond of the scarred bad-boy look, hockey players are for you—of course, the scars might be accompanied by toothlessness, which isn't cute past the third grade, but maybe you're into that sort of thing too.)

 ## PENALTIES

As you watch hockey, you'll notice that it looks like pretty much anything goes—especially in comparison to football, in which the strategy for each play is carefully plotted. It's true that hockey is looser than football and even basketball, but this is largely due to the speed of the game, not from a lack of regulations or structure. Hockey has several rules to help impose a sense of order on the game. When you break one of them, it usually results in a *penalty*.

Penalties in hockey can be divided into two categories: *team penalties* and *individual penalties*. (Note, however, that the terms *team penalty* and *individual penalty* are official, rulebook-type terms, not terms generally used in casual conversation. When a team penalty occurs, people will refer to the specific infraction committed, such as **offsides** or **icing** [see below]. Individual penalties are usually just referred to as *penalties*.)

Team Penalties: Offsides and Icing

When a player breaks a rule that results in a *team penalty*, the game is stopped and two players of the teams' choosing* must vie for the puck in a **face-off**. During a face-off, the ref stands between the two players, who are facing each other with their sticks down, and without giving them any warning, he throws the puck onto the ice and the two try to flick the puck back to their teammates, who are standing behind them and to the sides. Two important team penalties in hockey are *offsides* and *icing*. Both deal with where on the rink the puck is heading.

THE OFFSIDES RULE

One rule that forces strategy into the game is the *offsides rule*. Offsides occurs when an attacking player *precedes* the puck across the blue line and into the attacking zone. Here's the scene: Team Hottie is in possession of the puck in its defensive zone and wants to get it across the rink and into Team Hairy's defensive zone (Team Hottie's attacking zone), so that they can shoot it at the net and hopefully score. But Team Hottie cannot send a player into their team's attacking zone to simply wait for the puck—this would make it too easy to score. (And it's all about the chase, isn't it?) The puck must cross the blue line before the player does. Note that with the new rules, the offsides rule is not as strict. If the player who preceeded the puck can *tag up*—go back to the blue line and make contact with it with his skate, before the whistle stops the game—he is not considered offsides.

When an offsides occurs, the ref whistles the game to a stop and two

---

*Teams often choose *centers* (see *Positions*, on page 183) to compete in face-offs, as they are particularly skilled at vying for the puck.

players of the teams' choosing face off all the way back where the offsides pass originated. You might hear an announcer say something like, "Just when Team Hottie was showing signs of taking control, they get called for offsides."

WHY ~~BOYS~~ MEN LOVE HOCKEY

Common practices in the sport include:

* tripping

* shoving

* pushing

* slamming someone into a wall

* going as fast as you can

* propelling an object at a really high speed

* wearing unattractive clothes

* continual engagement of one's stick

It's helpful to note that while you'll see or hear when a ref has called a violation, and you'll see the players in the face-off, it is difficult to see an offsides in motion—it usually happens too fast for the untrained hockey eye to see.

ICING

Sorry, not of the buttercream, chocolate, or vanilla variety. Rather, *icing* (or *icing the puck*) is when the defending team shoots the puck from its half of the rink all the way across the ice, past its opponent's goal line, and an opposing player—other than the goalie—touches the puck first. It is basically the act of *whooshing* the puck from behind the red center line to the end of the rink (*whooshing* is not an official hockey term, but it's rather onomatopoetic, don't you think?). When a player ices the puck, unless it goes in the goal or in the **crease** (the small area immediately in front of the goal), a penalty is called. Icing, like offsides, results in stoppage of play and a face-off. The face-off happens all the way back in the penalized team's defensive zone, meaning that their efforts were completely for naught. (They are sent back to where they initially made contact with the puck.) Icing is often done intentionally when a team feels trapped in its defensive zone; when their opponents are threatening to score; or when a team needs to change strategy or stop the game.

It is also helpful to know that teams are *not* penalized for icing in the following situations: (1) When a team has a player or players in the **penalty box**, meaning it is playing with at least one fewer player than its opponent (discussed more below); (2) when the ref determines that the opposing team could have stopped the puck before it went over the goal line but just didn't feel like it; and (3) if a ref determines that the icing was inadvertent—that is, if a player had attempted to legitimately pass it to his teammate but missed his target. (Number 3 is one of the new rules.)

HOW COME THEY ALL SPEAK CANADIAN, EH?

As you watch a hockey game, you'll notice that the majority of the commentators say "aboot" instead of "about," along with other Canadianisms. The NHL should really be the NAHL (North American Hockey League) because Canada dominates hockey, and I'm sure Mexico would love to get in on the act.

North American hockey originated in Canada in the mid-nineteenth century. Its popularity was a bit slower to develop south of the border (the Canadian border, that is). It's simple: north = cold = ice = skating = hockey. Hockey was born in the rugged outdoors, on the frozen ponds, lakes, backyards, and even the ruts on the side of the road, where hockey legend Gordie Howe honed his skills as a boy. When North American hockey got all dolled up and moved inside, less frigid zones were able to partake of the sport. Now there are teams based in such sunny climes as Florida (the Tampa Bay Lightning and Fort Lauderdale's Florida Panthers), Los Angeles (the Los Angeles Kings), Phoenix (the Phoenix Coyotes), and Dallas (the Dallas Stars).

Like other pro sports today, professional hockey is becoming more diverse, signing players from Europe and beyond, but no one loves to watch or play the sport more than Canadians do. Canada provides about half of the NHL's players and most of its coaches, general managers, and referees.

Individual Penalties

Individual penalties (usually just called *penalties*) are assigned primarily for: illegal contact with a player, endangering a player or actually causing injury, and/or impeding the progress of a player. Specifically, they're called for **boarding, charging, cross-checking, elbowing, fighting, high-sticking, holding, hooking, kneeing, slashing, spearing,** and **tripping** (see the glossary for explanations of each). In plain language: for beating up, smacking, hitting, pushin', and shovin'—basically, for bad playground behavior.

To shed some light on how these routine penalties differ from the hard-core fighting for which hockey is often known, I give you the words of hockey expert Jack Falla, from his book, *Sports Illustrated: Hockey*: "The speed and the physical nature of the game make penalties an almost inescapable part of hockey. Some penalties, such as tripping, are sometimes accidental. Others, like holding and hooking, are almost always deliberate and usually occur when a defender who has been beaten makes one last, desperate attempt to restrain an opponent. Still other penalties, such as high-sticking, slashing, and spearing, are the inexcusable results of undisciplined tempers."

The punishment for an individual penalty in hockey is essentially a *time-out*—not the typical sports time-out in which the game is temporarily stopped, but the kind of time-out used to discipline a tot like Johnny who has just taken the intricately constructed LEGO Ferris wheel that Mikey built and ripped it apart. The grown-up hockey player who has committed a penalty (and is caught by the ref) goes off the ice into the **penalty box*** where he must sit, all by himself, with no toys or juice, for two, four, or five minutes (and in cases of extremely bad behavior—misconduct—ten minutes), depending on the severity of the penalty. I find it amusing that a rough-tough game like hockey has as part of its fundamental framework a disciplinary tactic used by moms the world over.

---

*There is a penalty box for each team, situated on the opposite side of the rink from the team's bench.

MAJOR AND MINOR PENALTIES

Individual penalties are divided into different categories that call for different levels of punishment, meaning different amounts of time spent in the penalty box. The two main categories are **minor penalties** and **major penalties**. A *minor penalty* results in a player being removed from the ice and sent to the penalty box for two minutes. Minor penalties include: boarding, charging, cross-checking, elbowing, high-sticking, holding, hooking, interference, and tripping. A *major penalty* results in a player being removed from the ice and sent to the penalty box for five minutes. Fighting, spearing, and drawing blood (yes, you read correctly, *drawing blood*) are *always* considered major penalties.

Note that minor penalties can be changed to **double-minor** (four minutes) or major penalties by the ref if he decides that a greater degree of violence was used against a player, and some *major penalties* may be deemed *minor penalties* if the penalty seems to have been perpetrated with a minimal degree of malice.

Being Shorthanded Versus Being on a Power Play

When a player is in the penalty box, his team is said to be **shorthanded** (because it is at least one player *short*). As a result, the other team is in a **power play** situation, since it has an advantage (i.e., it has at least one more man than its opponent). Since it is much easier to score a goal in a power play situation, the team that is shorthanded tries to *kill the penalty*—i.e., not allow its opponent to take advantage of its sorry situation. The shorthanded team will bring in **penalty killers**, the players on the team who are most skilled at preventing the team on the power play from scoring. These penalty killers may or may not be on the ice when the penalty is called—if they aren't, the coach will call/substitute them in. Penalty killers stay primarily in their own defensive zone and attempt to get the puck away from their opponent and take time off the clock; they also help the goalie defend the goal.

If the team with the power play scores a goal, the player (or one of the players) in the penalty box gets to reenter the game—even if he has only served a portion of his penalty time. (When the team with the power play scores, it is called a **power-play goal**.) However, if the player or players in the penalty box are serving five-minute or ten-minute major penalties, they are *not* allowed to return to the ice if the opposing team scores. If the shorthanded team scores a goal—which is an impressive feat that only happens every once in a while—it is known as a **shorthanded goal**.

DELAYED PENALTIES

Say Team Hottie has the puck and is moving toward the goal, and Team Hairy commits a penalty. If the penalty were to be called right at that moment and the game were stopped, it could hurt Team Hottie's chance of getting a goal. Team Hottie has the puck and hasn't done anything wrong, so why should its players suffer when it is Team Hairy that committed the penalty? *What to do?* Yep, you guessed it: The official will signal for a **delayed penalty**, which will take effect as soon as Team Hottie scores or loses possession of the puck.

Penalty Shots

A **penalty shot** is a rare and exciting moment in hockey. It's when a player is given the puck at center ice and is allowed to skate alone (all other players except the goalie stand on the side of the rink) toward the goal and have an unimpeded opportunity to score a goal. A penalty shot is usually awarded to a player who was skating toward the goal with a definite chance at a shot, but who was tripped or otherwise im-

HOLLYWOOD HOCKEY

***Miracle* (2004):** Starring Kurt Russell as the late real-life coach Herb Brooks, this film portrays the "miracle" of the U.S. Olympic Hockey Team beating the supposedly invincible Soviet team at the 1980 Olympics in Lake Placid, New York, and thereby moving on to beat Finland and bringing home the gold. It's worth watching just to see Russell in his end-of-the-seventies hairdo and bell-bottoms.

***Slap Shot* (1977):** Hilariously funny, this movie offers a farcical look at a down-and-out team who finds success on the ice through fighting and violence. It stars Paul Newman in his prime as the team's player/coach, which may be enough for you to run and rent it.

peded before he had a chance to shoot. The puck can be taken away or defended, but when the player has a clear shot at scoring, the rules are more stringent regarding proper defense. Since the opportunities to make a goal are not frequent in hockey, it's a kind of "play fair," or "give the guy a break" rule. A penalty shot is also awarded if a defensive player other than the goalie falls on the puck in his own goal crease in an effort to keep the puck from going into the net.

POSITIONS

A hockey team has six players on the ice at a time.* Like basketball, and with the exception of the goaltender, all players on a hockey team have to take on both defensive and offensive roles, depending on who has the puck—if Team Hottie has the puck, everyone on Team Hottie will be offensive-minded; if their opponent, Team Hairy, has the puck, everyone on Team Hottie will be focused on defending their net. That said, there are six different positions in hockey:

* Goaltender

* Center

* Left Wing

* Right Wing

* Right Defense

* Left Defense

The Goaltender

The goaltender is the player who defends the goal. He is positioned in the *goal crease* and spends virtually the entire game there (see diagram). Unlike

---

*Unless a player (or players) has been sent to the penalty box.

the other players, he doesn't get substituted in and out of the game. Goaltending is the opposite of multitasking. It's obsessive single-tasking. For two hours or more, the goalie must keep his eyes on (and deflect) a puck traveling at what might as well be the speed of lightning. A goaltender can, and is expected to, use any means available to him to stop the puck, including using his hands to catch the puck, lying down to use his whole body to deflect or freeze the puck, and all manner of interesting body contortions. Goaltenders, it seems, could have a backup career as breakdancers.

The Defensive Line and the Forward Line

The *defensive line*, whose main job is to play defense, consists of the *right* and *left defensemen*. The defensemen defend their team's goal and try to get the puck away from their opponent. The *forward line*, whose main job is to score, consists of the *wings* and the *center*. The center is often the leader of the forward line, in that he helps to set up and execute plays.

Substitutions

Substitutions (made by the coach) happen often throughout the game—these guys skate so fast without stopping that they have to be taken in and out of the game or else they would spontaneously combust. (Hockey players play only for forty-five seconds to three minutes at a time.) So, although there are only six players on the ice at a time, a hockey team usually has twenty members available to play each game, with various combinations coming and going on and off the ice throughout the game. It's tricky, because you don't want to be left vulnerable with too few players on the ice, but having too many is a penalty, so substitutions have to be executed very quickly. The goalie, however, is rarely substituted.

One thing that greatly distinguishes hockey from other sports is that the players come and go while the action is still happening. Substitutions are said to be made **on the fly** (i.e., a new player can jump over the boards and onto the ice when the player leaving the ice is within five feet of the bench). And usually, a whole line is substituted at once—the whole forward line will come out and a new one will be sent in; the same is true for the defensive pairing. This is called a **line change**. Lines are like mini-teams. The two or three players in a line typically work very well together, so the coach tends to keep them together. If, for example, Team Hottie is in possession of the puck near its own goal or at center ice, the entire offensive line of Team Hairy will speedily make their way to the bench and a new line will hop onto the ice.

THE STANLEY CUP CHAMPIONSHIP

Following the regular season, NHL teams compete in the Stanley Cup playoffs and then two teams advance to the Stanley Cup finals. The NHL is divided into two conferences, the Eastern Conference and the Western Conference. Top teams from these groupings compete for the conference championship, then the two winners face each other in the finals. Like the NBA Finals, the Stanley Cup finals is a best-of-seven series.

The Stanley Cup is an actual cup given to the championship team, all of whose members' names are inscribed on it. The winning team is allowed to keep the trophy for the year they reign as champions, then they must pass it on to the new Stanley Cup winner at year's end (unless, of course, they win it again . . .).

TALES OF THE TALL CUP

* It is the oldest trophy for which professional athletes compete.

* The Cup is a publicity hound, having appeared on numerous talk shows including the *Late Show with David Letterman, The Tonight Show with Jay Leno, Late Night with Conan O'Brien,* and *Meet the Press with Tim Russert.*

* In 1996, Colorado Avalanche defenseman Sylvain Lefebvre christened his child in the bowl of the Stanley Cup after his championship season.

RINKS OF RAGE

As you now know, hockey is a contact sport, and a very physical one. You might even say it's shamelessly violent. According to the official rules of the NHL,* fighting results in a penalty—a major penalty. But the unfortunate reality is that fighting happens very, very frequently in NHL games. (Interestingly, it is much less prevalent—practically nonexistent—in college and European hockey, where players who fight are automatically suspended.) In the NHL, during the regular season, 41 percent of the games are interrupted by fights, as reported by the *New York Times* in April 2004. Or, to put it differently, as of January 2004, there were 1.3 fights per game, a slight rise from the previous season's 1.1.[†] When I say fighting, I mean *fighting*—fisticuffs, brawling, and all sorts of totally uncivilized behavior. And yet, no one in the NHL—not the game officials, league officials, or executives—seems to be able to decide where the line should be drawn.

Many hockey owners, general managers, and even sportswriters think that the NHL would lose its core audience if fighting were eliminated. Meanwhile, according to the *Washington Post* (April 24, 2004) two thirds of NHL teams are losing money—and this was *before* the lock-out and, eventually, the cancellation of the 2004–2005 season.

JUST KNOW THIS

Hockey is a fast paced, low-scoring game. The speed of the game and the skating skills of the players make it mesmerizing (until the players start beating each other up). The point of the game is to get the *puck* (the round disk that all the fuss is about) into the *net* and score a *goal*. Each goal is worth one point, and there are rarely more than seven or eight goals scored in a game, total.

While you can follow and enjoy a hockey game simply by watching

---

*Official NHL rules can be found at http://nhl.com/hockeyu/rulebook/index.html.
[†]According to figures provided by the NHL and reported by Jim Kelley on ESPN.com.

who gets the puck into the net, understanding *penalties* will enhance your understanding of the game. Two key violations that result in *team* penalties—and that add some strategy and order to the game—are *icing* (shooting the puck from one end of the rink to the other) and *off-sides* (when the player precedes the puck over the blue line and into the attacking zone). When a team penalty is called, play is stopped and a player from each team must vie for the puck in a face-off.

Individual penalties result in a player being sent to the *penalty box* for a designated amount of time (two, four, or five minutes), which leaves his team *shorthanded* and gives the opponent a *power play* for the length of time the player remains in the penalty box. Some individual penalties are Freddy Krueger–like (slashing and spearing, for example), while

NHL TEAMS

Anaheim Mighty Ducks	Nashville Predators
Atlanta Thrashers	New Jersey Devils
Boston Bruins	New York Islanders
Buffalo Sabres	New York Rangers
Calgary Flames	Ottawa Senators
Carolina Hurricanes	Philadelphia Flyers
Chicago Blackhawks	Phoenix Coyotes
Colorado Avalanche	Pittsburgh Penguins
Columbus Blue Jackets	San Jose Sharks
Dallas Stars	St. Louis Blues
Detroit Red Wings	Tampa Bay Lightning
Edmonton Oilers	Toronto Maple Leafs
Florida Panthers	
Los Angeles Kings	Vancouver Canucks
Minnesota Wild	
Montreal Canadiens	Washington Capitals

others are only moderately dangerous (tripping, holding, or hooking, for example). The new rules for the 2005–06 season call for more rigid enforcement of these individual penalites (the goal being to make it easier for the offense to score).

Fighting is not supposed to happen, but it does. Hockey is a very physical contact sport, and the lines between legal and illegal contact become blurred and cause tempers and "boys-will-be-boys" behavior to flare.

Players You Need to Know

The Legends

WAYNE GRETZKY, 1961–
NICKNAME: "THE GREAT ONE"

    1979–88: Edmonton Oilers
    1988–95: Los Angeles Kings
    1995–96: St. Louis Blues
    1996–99: New York Rangers

Wayne Gretzky is the greatest hockey player of all time. Truly—there's no dispute. In fact, sportswriters have noted that his numbers are so staggering (he holds sixty-two NHL records) that, statistically, Gretzky is the most dominant athlete ever in North American team sports.

Oh, and besides being the greatest player of all time, he seems to have flawless character. He is always courteous and has always found time to talk to the press, sign autographs, and pat the heads of a few kiddies. This he learned from his own hockey idol when he was growing up, Gordie Howe (see below). Gretzky is handsome, and he has a beautiful wife (the actress Janet Jones) and three kids.

Here are a few key stats about "The Great One" that are sure to dazzle even a hockey neophyte:

* Gretzky won the league MVP award *ten* times (that's more than basketball's Michael Jordan or Kareem Abdul-Jabbar).

* His total career points are 2,856 (goals and assists), which may mean nothing to you, but consider that this total is *1,000* points higher than the second-place scorer. Even if you remove the goals from the figure above and tally assists *only*, Gretzky would *still* be the leading scorer of all time.

While he was never the fastest or the biggest (he is a relatively scrawny six feet, 180 lbs.), Gretzky was far more than the sum of his parts. He was all skill, all finesse, all smarts on the ice. He had such a magical ability to see what was going on during a game that a myth was started, purporting that he had some kind of superhuman peripheral vision, or that his brain could process visual information faster—like a hockey version of Superman's X-ray vision. Hall of Fame coach and G.M. Harry Sinden said, "Gretzky sees a picture out there no one else sees. It's difficult to describe because I've never seen the game he's looking at."

Gretzky began his NHL career with the Edmonton Oilers in Canada in 1979, but in 1988, after winning four Stanley Cup championships, he was sold to the Los Angeles Kings. Canadians became inconsolable, Los Angelinos became rapt. L.A. games were sold out and hockey fever spread south. *San Francisco Chronicle* writer C. V. Nevius explains, ". . . Gretzky['s] popularity also carried the sport to Miami, Tampa, Anaheim, Phoenix, and Nashville. In the simplest terms, Gretzky made hockey cool."

After twenty seasons in the NHL, Gretzky retired in 1999 and was immediately enshrined in the Hockey Hall of Fame, one of very few players who have had the waiting period for induction waived. Then, in August 2005, he began his coaching career as the coach of the struggling Phoenix Coyotes. NHL officials are hoping that, along with the other changes being made within the league, The Great One's presence will help to revitalize hockey.

GORDIE HOWE, 1928–
NICKNAME: "MR. HOCKEY"

    1946–71: Detroit Red Wings
    1973–77: Houston Aeros
    1977–79: New England Whalers
    1979–80: Hartford Whalers

Gordie Howe is nicknamed "Mr. Hockey" for a reason. The man really does embody the sport, for better and for worse. He began his career just after World War II, and he played professionally until he was fifty-two years old. Yes, *fifty-two*. Most athletes have their preschool-aged children in tow when they announce their retirement; Howe had his *grandson* by his side.

While Howe had a reputation for being a sweetheart off the ice, he was one of the toughest hockey players ever. A fellow player once said of him, "[Howe] is everything you expect an ideal athlete to be. He is soft-spoken, self-deprecating, and thoughtful. He is also one of the most vicious, cruel, and mean men I have ever met in a hockey game."

Howe was one of nine children, and he was born in Saskatoon, Saskatchewan, just prior to the stock market crash of 1929. He adored his mother, and it was from her compassion that his hockey career was born. One day, in the depths of the Depression, a woman came by the Howe home hoping to sell her possessions, all stuffed into a sack, so that she could buy food. Although the Howes themselves were in near desperate straits, Kate Howe (Gordie's mother) scrounged a few dollars together to give to the woman. When the contents of the bag were dumped onto the kitchen floor, two skates thudded out and a legendary hockey player was born.

Howe spent most of his extraordinarily long career with the Detroit Red Wings, whom he led to four Stanley Cup victories. Until Gretzky came along in the next generation of players, Howe held most hockey records. He also won the MVP award six times, and was a top scorer six times.

In 1971, after twenty-five years with Detroit, Howe felt it was time to retire. And he did. Briefly. Then, in 1973, he was given an opportunity to skate with his two sons, Mark and Marty, for the Houston Aeros (part of the now-defunct World Hockey Association). He grabbed the chance, playing until 1980. Howe remarked upon his return, "If it wasn't for the kids, I would never have come back. They put fun back in the game."

BOBBY HULL, 1939–

1957–72: Chicago Blackhawks
1972–80: Winnipeg Jets
1979–80: Hartford Whalers

A 1966 *New York Times* headline reads, "Hulls's Success Understandable: Skates Fastest, Shoots Hardest." I guess that pretty much sums it up. Hull shot the puck at close to 120 miles per hour, and he skated at about thirty, striking fear into the hearts of goalies. He was one of the top scorers and the most mesmerizing player of his time.

When Hull scored fifty-one goals in 1966, to break Maurice "Rocket" Richard's and Bernice "Boom Boom" Geoffrion's* record, it was the sporting event of the year. His adoring Chicago fans gave him a seven-minute ovation. Also in his stellar career, Hull:

* won the league MVP award twice;

* was the top scorer three times;

* won the Lady Byng Memorial Trophy for good sportsmanship once;

* was an All-Star ten times.

Along with his Blackhawks teammate, Stan Mikita, Hull also helped to develop the curved hockey stick (the curve allows more whip). And he was the only player to be half of a winning father-son duo—both he and his son, Brett Hull, have won the MVP award.

Hull was also the first player to sign a $1 million contract: After playing thirteen thrilling seasons with the Chicago Blackhawks, the WHA (World Hockey Association) made him an offer he couldn't refuse. In fact, the offer was so grandiose for its day that Hull thought the WHA was joking. As the story goes, the WHA kept bugging him about defecting from Chicago and the NHL, but he wasn't interested and teasingly said that if they offered him a million dollars, he would go. Well, that's exactly what they did, and, in 1972, $1 million had the same jaw-dropping effect that A-Rod's $252 million contract had in 2004. In the end, the joke was on the Blackhawks, who thought Hull was bluffing when he told them what he had been offered by the WHA. They called his bluff, and Hull promptly jumped to the Winnipeg Jets of the WHA,

---

*Geoffrion played alongside Richard and Jean Beliveau in the 1950s and 60s.

paving the way for bigger contracts throughout professional hockey in coming years.

MARIO LEMIEUX, 1965–
NICKNAME: "THE MAGNIFICENT ONE," "LE MAGNIFIQUE," "SUPER MARIO"

1984–present: Pittsburgh Penguins

Let's start with his real appeal—Lemieux is tall, dark, and handsome, and he has one of those devastatingly sexy French accents. He has always been an outstanding player, but only since Gretzky's retirement has he been able to emerge from The Great One's shadow and claim the attention he so richly deserves.

At the age of eighteen, Lemieux joined the Pittsburgh Penguins, and he immediately faced a heavy burden. The team was down and just about out, having finished dead last the previous two seasons. No one was attending the games or watching them on TV, and the team was threatened with extinction. Lemieux was their great hope, their last chance, and he didn't disappoint. He scored a goal on his first shot of his first shift of his first game in the NHL with the Penguins, instantly becoming their savior.

Since then, Lemieux has shone. He's won three MVP trophies; he's a ten-time All-Star; and he's a six-time scoring champion—and he's still playing, so who knows how high the numbers will soar.

In 1993, Lemieux was diagnosed with Hodgkin's disease (a type of cancer) and underwent debilitating radiation treatments. On the last day of his last treatment regimen in March of that year, he finished the radiation, boarded a plane to Philadelphia, and was on the ice that night. He scored a goal and an assist that night and went on to complete the season with a scoring championship. In 1994–95, Lemieux, finally succumbing to the physical and emotional exhaustion of his cancer, in addition to severe back injuries, sat out the entire season, but he returned triumphant the following year, winning the MVP award and another scoring championship.*

---

*Winning a scoring championship means having the most goals in the NHL for the year.

In 1997, Lemieux announced his retirement and was immediately inducted into the Hockey Hall of Fame, making him one of the handful for whom the customary three-year waiting period had been waived and securing his position among the all-time greats. But he wasn't yet finished with hockey. He became a part owner of the Penguins and then in 2000, he announced a comeback, putting him in the unusual position of being both an owner and a player. By that time, his health had improved, he missed playing the game, and he saw an opportunity to have his young son see him play. Announcing his return, Lemieux said: "[I'm] ready to play at a very high level. I'm not coming back to embarrass myself." Not surprisingly, he lived up to his words.

MARK MESSIER, 1961–
NICKNAME: "THE MOOSE"

1979–91: Edmonton Oilers
1991–97: New York Rangers
1997–2000: Vancouver Canucks
2000–2004: New York Rangers

Mark Messier may have grown up on Canada's frozen ponds, and he may have spent thirteen years with the Edmonton Oilers, but he will always belong to New York. It's not easy to become the darling of the big, brash city, but Messier sealed the deal in one shining moment in 1994. What Joe Namath did for the Jets in 1969, Messier did for the New York Rangers—he *publicly* guaranteed the city a win.

The Rangers were competing for the Eastern Conference title against the New Jersey Devils and were down three games to two in a best-of-seven series. To a crowd of reporters (and to all of New York, essentially), Messier promised a Game 6 win, which would thereby prevent his team's elimination. During the third period of the game, Messier made good on his guarantee by scoring a *hat trick* (three goals), an enormously difficult task in hockey. The Rangers went on to clinch the conference title, sending them into the Stanley Cup Finals against the Vancouver Canucks. Drum roll, please: For the first time in *fifty-four* years, the Rangers won the Stanley Cup. It was Messier's sixth Stanley Cup championship, and it made him the first player to captain two Stanley Cup championship teams. More important, it immortalized Messier as the architect of one of the greatest moments in New York sports history.

Messier earned his previous five Stanley Cups with the Edmonton Oilers, where he began his NHL career. Among his teammates (until 1988) was The Great One, Wayne Gretzky, and together they made their team unstoppable. Messier performed best under pressure, particularly in the playoffs. In 1984, while he was still a teammate of Gretzky's on the Oilers, he won the Conn Smythe Trophy as MVP in the playoffs. Messier ranks second in total points in the history of the league (1,887 vs. Gretzky's 2,857).*

On March 31, 2004, Messier most likely played his final NHL game. Although he hasn't officially announced his retirement, he's made it clear that it's probable. His whole family was in attendance at Madison Square Garden that night—always a telltale sign of impending retirement. After the game, Messier pointedly bowed to all four sides of the arena to express his gratitude to his fans. In equally sportsmanlike fashion, his opponents, the Buffalo Sabres, showed their respect for Messier by staying on the ice and tapping their sticks.

BOBBY ORR, 1948–

1966–76: Boston Bruins
1976–79: Chicago Blackhawks

Some people ponder the meaning of life or how to achieve world peace; hockey fans ponder what would have happened if Bobby Orr's knees hadn't given out. According to *ESPN SportsCentury,* "To say [Orr] was the greatest defenseman ever is to miss the point—he changed the position, turned it into one of both defense *and* attack . . . Orr had the creative genius to open the game up in ways previously thought impossible."

---

*Gordie Howe's record of 1,850 career points was surpassed by Messier in 2004.

Unfortunately, though, over twelve seasons, Orr more or less shattered his knees. And it's no wonder—every photo of Orr captures him leaning over, knees bent in positions that even Gumby would find painful. Orr spent most of his career with the Boston Bruins, where, in 1970, he led them to their first Stanley Cup championship in twenty-nine years. He finished up with the Chicago Blackhawks, retiring at a relatively young thirty, unable to overcome his knee problems.

Orr could do everything—skate at the speed of light, handle the puck with remarkable aplomb, and just generally be the best defenseman ever to play the game. As a *defenseman*, he won the *scoring* championship twice. One year, he clinched four of the major awards: the MVP; the Norris Trophy (for best defenseman of the year—which he won a total of eight times); the top scoring award; and the MVP for the playoffs. Once, after a game, a *New York Times* reporter consulted a colleague and said: "I counted six things Orr did tonight that I've never seen in a hockey game. Is that about right?" His colleague replied: "I really couldn't say. We stopped counting about four years ago."

Like fellow hockey great Gordie Howe, Orr was a very good person off the ice—he was once accused by a teammate of spending too much time and money . . . on charity work! Orr was a small-town, baby-faced kid who never lost that small-town goodness. At the opening of the Bobby Orr Hall of Fame in his home town of Parry Sound, Ontario, Orr said: "I've been a very lucky guy . . . I've won some awards and I'm very proud of those accomplishments. But I don't think there's anything greater than to come home and to be recognized at home."

MAURICE RICHARD, 1921–
NICKNAME: "THE ROCKET"
1942–60: Montreal Canadiens

Richard was nicknamed "The Rocket" because of his rocket-like ability to launch the puck into the net—and because of his fiery explosions on the ice. Tough as nails, Richard (that's *ree-shar*, the French pronunciation, *s'il vous plaît*) played during the wild, rough days of hockey in the 1940s and

'50s. He was born and raised in Montreal and spent his entire career with the Canadiens.

In 1955, Richard was the subject of a notorious riot in Montreal. During a game on March 13 of that year, Richard let his temper loose on two players from the Boston Bruins, punching one and viciously slashing (and injuring) another. After an inquiry, the president of the NHL, Clarence Campbell, suspended Richard for the three remaining regular season games and the playoffs to follow. This seems reasonable, but it didn't to the Montreal fans who viewed the action as an affront to French-Canadians. The following week, ignoring Montreal Mayor Jean Drapeau's pleas for him not to attend the home game, Campbell not only showed up, but made a grand, imperious, conspicuous entrance to the Forum, Montreal's hallowed arena. Fans threw eggs and tomatoes at Campbell. Then, with the Canadiens losing, a fan walked up to Campbell, as though he wanted to shake his hand, and instead slapped him across the face. From there, all hell broke loose—tear gas was fired by the police and the mayhem was carried out to the streets, with looting and great damage on Montreal's St. Catherine Street. According to *Sports Illustrated*'s Michael Farber, "the Richard Riot is generally considered the first explosion of French-Canadian nationalism, the beginning of a social and political dynamic that shapes Canada to this day."

Then there was the game against the Boston Bruins where Richard was knocked unconscious during the first period but insisted on returning to the ice late in the third period. Still dazed from his head being conked, Richard literally could not see straight—he had to ask his teammates what the score was and how much time was left. Nevertheless, onto the ice he went—to score the winning goal.

Crazy or just intense, he was a phenomenal player. Among his many accomplishments, Richard:

* was the first player to score fifty goals in a season;

* scored twelve goals in nine games during the 1944 playoffs;

* won eight Stanley Cup trophies;

✳ scored more goals than anybody else for five seasons;

✳ won one MVP award.

Undefeatable, indestructible, undistractable. Those were the qualities that made him a national hero and an unforgettable hockey star.

Legends in Training

MARTIN BRODEUR, 1972–

1991–present: New Jersey Devils

Martin Brodeur is considered the best goalie in the league right now, and could be for many years to come.

Brodeur has won three Stanley Cups with the New Jersey Devils and two Vezina Trophies (the Vezina is awarded annually to the best goalie in the NHL). And those are just the major awards. He's the first NHL goalie to win thirty games in nine consecutive seasons, and the youngest to win 400 games (he's barely into his thirties).

Brodeur is known as much for his puck-handling as for his ability to stop the puck from entering his net. In other words, not only can he react, but he can pass and shoot and make things happen. And Brodeur's endurance is legendary. It's not fun to be his backup goalie.* Sports Illustrated's Stephen Canella put it this way: "On New Year's Eve, New Jersey Devils backup goalie Corey Schwab was placed on injured reserve,† the hockey equivalent of a tree falling in the woods with nobody around to hear it. Who was going to miss a guy who had appeared in only 13 of his 117 games with the team?"

---

*A backup goalie is a player who will substitute for a goalie if he has to come out of the game (for exhaustion or injury or poor play, for example). Unlike the other players who rotate in and out of the game every few minutes, goalies are in for the long haul, each and every game.
†When a player (in any sport) is injured and can't play for a while, he is said to be on "injured reserve."

JEREMY ROENICK, 1970–

1988–96: Chicago Blackhawks
1996–2001: Phoenix Coyotes
2001–present: Philadelphia Flyers

Jeremy Roenick transformed the Philadelphia Flyers. Teammate Brian Boucher described Roenick as "exactly the breath of fresh air [the team] needed," and went on to say: "For years it seemed like everybody on [the Flyers] was the same type of quiet, serious guy . . . Now J.R. comes in, the room's loose, happy. [They're] feeding off it."

Roenick is outspoken, flamboyant, cocky, good-looking, and frankly irresistible. Of course, with such a strong personality, he naturally has his detractors. But Larry Wigge, formerly of *The Sporting News*, describes him as follows: "He's a contradiction. He's fun-loving yet strong-willed. His play is uniquely individualistic, yet he'll go through a wall for his team. He will stand up to his coach when he disagrees, yet he's the first one to jump on the bandwagon when the two are on the same page."

Roenick has earned more than 1,000 points, making him "the fourth-most productive American-born player in league history," as *SI*'s Michael Farber put it. He began his NHL career with the Chicago Blackhawks in 1988, where for eight years he led the team with style and substance. Then he was traded to the Phoenix Coyotes, but talent comes at a high price and eventually, in 2001, they decided they couldn't afford him anymore and traded him to Philadelphia.

Glossary

Attacking Zone: The area between the opponent's blue line and goal. Thus, because Team Hottie wants to score in Team Hairy's goal, the area in front of Team Hairy's goal—between the goal line and the blue line—is Team Hottie's attacking zone (and Team Hairy's defending zone). The reverse is true on the other half of the ice. (See diagram on page 171.)

Backhand Shot: A wrist shot using the backhand instead of the forehand. In a wrist shot, the puck and stick stay on the ice.

Bench Minor Penalty: A penalty that is perpetrated by a player or coach on the bench. It is usually called when a player or coach uses abusive language toward an official, throws something on the ice, or otherwise disrupts the game. It is also called when a team has too many men on the ice. The penalty is assigned to a teammate who is on the ice at the time of the penalty—this player must come out of the game and stay in the penalty box for two minutes (just like with a regular minor penalty). Note that this doesn't happen very often.

Blue Line: There are two blue lines on the rink that divide the rink into three areas: two attacking/defensive zones and the neutral zone. An attacking player cannot cross over the blue line before the puck—this is considered an offsides violation (see diagram on page 171).

Boards: The walls surrounding the rink are known as the *boards*. A lot of activity (banging, slamming, etc.) takes place against the boards, some of it legal (e.g., body checking) and some of it not (e.g., boarding). The boards are usually made of wood or fiberglass.

Boarding: When a player violently slams his opponent into the boards (the walls surrounding the rink) through excessively forceful body checking, elbowing, or tripping.

Body Check: A legal defense tactic used to block an opponent's progress or throw him off balance. It is done by forcefully bumping a hip or shoulder against the opponent. It's a kindler, gentler body slam.

Cage (Goal Cage): The goal cage, usually just called the *cage* or the *goal*, is the term for the net and the frame holding the net. In essence, it's the goal.

Charging: (1) The fundamental reason the United States economy stays afloat. (2) The only way to afford Prada. (3) When a hockey player takes more than two steps and then deliberately, violently checks his opponent. It's a less kind, more mean-spirited body check/slam that results in a penalty.

Checking: The main defensive tactic used for stopping or impeding an opponent in possession of the puck. It involves bumping into an opponent using the stick, shoulders, or hips. When a player uses the stick, it is called a *stick check*. When a player uses a hip or shoulder, it is called a *body check*. Checking (in theory, not necessarily in practice) is permitted only against the player with the puck or the player who just had the puck.

Crease (or Goal Crease): The *crease* (or *goal crease*) is the semicircular area directly in front of the goal (see diagram).

Cross-Checking: Cross-checking is an illegal type of checking that results in a penalty. When a player cross-checks, he uses his stick, instead of his body, to ram another player. Cross-checking is like body checking, but with both hands on the stick, and no part of the stick on the ice. You can also look at it as taking a *stick check* too far.

Defensive Line: The *defensive line* refers to the right and left defensemen who are on the ice at a given time. Coaches will usually substitute both defensive players together, so one defensive line or pairing will come out and another will be sent in. A pair that works well together will continue to be paired together.

Delayed Penalty: If a penalty is called on a player whose team in not in possession of the puck, the official may delay the penalty. This is done because stopping the game could penalize the team that does have the puck. For example, if Team Hottie may have a chance of scoring a goal, but Team Hairy commits a penalty, the official will let the game continue until Team Hottie either scores a goal or loses possession of the puck. Then the penalty is instituted. Also, since teams cannot play with less than four players, if two players are penalized and sent to the penalty box and then a third guy is penalized, the third penalty becomes a *delayed penalty*, and the additional player isn't sent to the penalty box until one of the other penalized players finishes his time and returns to the ice.

Double-Minor Penalty: A *double minor* is not the same thing as being a political science major with a biology/sociology double minor, but rather, in hockey, it's one of two things: (1) When an "accidental" infraction results in an injury. For instance, if a player accidentally high-sticks his opponent when he was really just trying to get the puck. (2) When a player *attempts* to injure another player but fails to actually injure him. When a double-minor penalty is called, the penalized player must stay in the penalty box for four minutes.

Elbowing: Exactly what you may have done on the playground to your third-grade nemesis. It's jabbing your opponent with an elbow.

Empty-Net Goal: A goal that is scored when the net is unguarded by a goaltender. The only time the goal is unguarded is when the goalie has been pulled—see *pulling the goalie*.

Enforcers: Often called *policemen* or *goons*, enforcers are very tough, physical players whose job is to intimidate their opponents and protect their own players. They're like bouncers at a club—you don't want to mess with them. But unlike bouncers, they don't just stand around, they actually skate and play hockey.

Face-off: A face-off is used to restart play after it has been stopped, and to begin each of the three periods. During a face-off, a player from each team faces the other with their sticks on the ice. The official then drops the puck between them and the players vie for the puck, trying to be the first to flick it over to their teammates. This all happens very, very quickly. At the beginning of the game, the beginning of each period, or after a goal, the face-off occurs in the center of the rink. After stoppages, face-offs usually take place in the face-off circle nearest the infraction (see diagram) or where the play was stopped. There are several face-off circles marked on the rink.

Fighting: Fisticuffs, brawling, beating each other up. Hockey differentiates between *roughing* and *fighting*. *Roughing* is a less severe form of fighting—it's your run-of-the-mill pushing, shoving, and typical "boys-will-be-boys" behavior—and it results in a minor penalty. Actual *fighting*—when players drop their sticks, take off their gloves, and really start going at it—results in a major penalty (five minutes in the box for those involved). If the ref decides that one person was the sole instigator of a fight, that player is charged with a *game misconduct* and is banished from the game. How strictly fighting penalties are called varies a lot from game to game.

Flip Shot: In a flip shot, the puck is flicked up off the ice, into the air, toward the goal.

Forward Line: Also called the "attacking line," the forward line is comprised of the *left wing*, the *right wing*, and the *center*. These players, particularly the center, lead the attack and are responsible for most of the scoring.

Full Strength: What your morning cup of joe needs to be when you begin with an 8 A.M. breakfast meeting and end with an 8 P.M. board meeting. It *also* refers to when a team is playing with all six players (goalie included), meaning that none of the team's players are in the penalty box.

Game Misconduct: A game-misconduct penalty is usually called when a player repeatedly attempts to fight another player, or when a third player jumps into a fight already in progress. The ref will determine who the culprits are and assign game-misconduct penalties accordingly. If a player receives a penalty for game misconduct, he is suspended for the remainder of a game. When this occurs, the team is allowed to substitute another player so they don't have to play the rest of the game shorthanded.

Goalie/Goaltender/Goalkeeper: All are correct, but nowadays *goaltender* seems to be in fashion, while goalkeeper is used more often in soccer. The goaltender is the player who defends the goal. He is positioned in the goal, and he spends virtually the entire game there. Unlike the other players, he doesn't get substituted for. Goaltending is the opposite of multitasking. It's obsessive single-tasking. For two hours or more the goalie must keep his eyes on (and deflect) a puck traveling at what might as well be the speed of light.

Goons: The more colorful term for *enforcers* (see page 200), used by commentators and sportswriters fairly frequently.

High-Sticking: High-sticking is not a friendly thing like high-fiving; it's menacing. High-sticking is when a player carries his stick above his shoulder while moving toward an opponent. Note that high-sticking is often not done intentionally. A player might, for example, raise his stick out of reflex if he sees the puck flying toward his head. Regardless, it is not allowed, because it is quite dangerous. If the ref deems it unintentional it is a team penalty resulting in a face-off. If it's intentional, a minor penalty is called. If it causes injury, the ref will call a major penalty.

Holding: In light of all the really evil stuff you can do in hockey and often get away with (slashing, spearing, tripping, and *legally* checking), holding, a minor penalty, seems so lightweight. But just like in football or basketball, one player cannot hold on to another. In hockey, holding is specifically defined as using your hands to grab either your opponent or his stick.

Hooking: Hooking in hockey is a similar act to that of the old vaudeville shows, where, if a performer stunk, he would be yanked off the stage with a giant hook. On the hockey rink, it's when one player hooks the blade of his stick around another player to try to impede his progress or throw him off balance. Hooking is a minor penalty.

Icing: Icing is a violation that results in a face-off. It happens when a player shoots the puck from behind the red line all the way to the other end of the rink, across his opponent's goal line without touching the goal or crease, and it is then touched by an opposing player.

Interference: Impeding the progress of a player who is not in possession of the puck—specifically *checking* a player without the puck—is interference and is a penalty. Sometimes. Interference is one of those penalties that is called by refs as much as it is not called. It depends on how lenient the refs want to be.

Kneeing: Kneeing is a tried-and-true method of stopping unwanted advances. Yes, I am referring to sexual advances, but it works in hockey, too—although in hockey, the knee is not directed to that particular piece of anatomy. In hockey, it's a knee to the opponent's leg, thigh, or lower body. Kneeing is a minor penalty.

Line Change: Hockey players are usually substituted in groups. All three of the forward line (right wing, left wing, and center) will come out, and a new line will come in. The same goes for the defensive line (right defensemen, left defensemen). When a new group comes in, and the old one goes to the bench, it's called a *line change*. This happens very frequently and quickly throughout the game, while play is going on.

Major Penalty: A major penalty sends a player to the penalty box for five minutes. Major penalties are called for fighting, spearing, or drawing blood. (I've always suspected that all men are babies when it comes to blood, and this proves it. Even if the contact wasn't very rough and might have qualified for a minor penalty, if a drop of blood is spilled—*boom*—into the penalty box for a full five minutes.)

Minor Penalty: Minor penalties are the most common types of penalties. They are less deliberate and/or violent than major penalties, and they result in two minutes in the penalty box.

Misconduct: Misconduct is usually called for unsportsmanlike behavior, such as abusive language or gestures (particularly toward an official), failure to follow an official's order, and other idiotic behavior. Misconduct results in a player being removed from the ice to the penalty box for ten minutes. A substitute player is allowed to replace him, however, so the team is not shorthanded. Once the ten minutes are up, the penalized player must wait for the first stoppage of play before he can return to the ice.

Neutral Zone: The neutral zone is the area at mid-ice between the blue lines (on either side of the red center line).

On the Fly: Hockey players play only for forty-five seconds to three minutes at a time. Substitutions are made continuously while the game is in play—in other words, *on the fly*. It's tricky because you don't want to be left vulnerable with too few players on the ice, but having too many is a penalty, so substitutions have to be executed very quickly. A new player can jump over the boards and onto the ice when the player leaving the ice is within five feet of the bench.

Offsides: Offsides is a team violation that results in a face-off. It occurs when an attacking player *precedes* the puck across the blue line and into the attacking zone. This rule prevents a player from hanging out in the attacking zone and waiting for the puck. New rules instituted in 2005 give the player who would be offsides a chance to "tag up"—i.e., get back to the blue line and make contact with it (with his skate). If he gets back before the whistle stops the game, he is not considered offsides.

 Penalty: When a player violates a rule, he is punished with a penalty. Team penalties result in a face-off. Individual penalties result in a player being sent to the penalty box for two to ten minutes, depending on the severity of the infraction. Individual penalties include minor penalties (such as boarding, holding, hooking, etc.), major penalties (such as spearing or drawing blood from any contact), bench minor penalties (when a player or coach on the bench breaks a rule), misconduct (arguing with an official), and game misconduct (fighting), which results in suspension of the player for the rest of the game.

Penalty Box: The penalty box is a little boxed-off area with a bench inside, where a player who committed a penalty has to go sit for his designated time (two, four, five, or ten minutes). There is a penalty box for each team, situated on the opposite side of the rink from the team's bench.

Penalty Killers: Penalty killers are players who the coach calls in when his team is *shorthanded* (i.e., when the opponent is on a *power play*). Penalty killers stay in their own defensive zone and try to get the puck away from the opponent, help the goaltender defend the goal, and kill time off the clock.

Penalty Shot: One of hockey's most exciting moments, a penalty shot occurs when a player gets a free shot at the goal with no one except the goalie defending the shot. It is awarded when an opponent illegally interferes with a player who has a clear scoring opportunity. This includes directly impeding his progress, throwing a stick, or intentionally dislodging the goal cage to stop play and prevent the goal. A penalty shot is also awarded if a defensive player other than the goalie falls on the puck in his own crease to keep the puck from going in the net.

Points: During a game, a team is awarded one point for every goal scored. Hockey games are notoriously low-scoring—it's unusual for a team to score more than four or five goals in a game. Points mean something different for individual players—they're used as a statistic. Players get one point for every assist and goal. So a player will finish a season with a total number of points that equals all his goals plus all his assists.

Power Play: When a team is playing full strength (has all six players on the ice) against an opponent who is *shorthanded*—because one or more of their players are in the penalty box—the team with six players is on a *power play*. This team has a clear advantage over its opponent, and usually employs a very aggressive offensive strategy in order to take advantage of the situation and score.

Power-Play Goal: A goal that is scored when a team is on a power play. Because the team on a power play is in the advantageous position of having more players on the ice than their opponent, it is somewhat easier to score a goal on a power play.

Pulling the Goalie: Near the very end of a game, if a team is behind (especially if they are behind by only one goal) they might pull the goalie out of his net and replace him with an additional *forward* to increase their chances of getting a goal, thereby tying the game and having a chance to win in overtime. If the other team is able to take advantage of their undefended net and score, the team that pulled their goalie hasn't lost anything because they were going to lose anyway. It is a desperation tactic. A goal scored into an unguarded net is called an *empty-net goal*.

Red Line: The red line is, well, a painted red line at the center of the rink, dividing the rink in half.

Roughing: *Roughing* is puerile behavior akin to playground pushing and shoving, and it is a minor penalty. It's wussy fighting. Fighting-lite.

Save: When a goalie prevents a shot from going into the net, it's called a *save*. The shot that would have gone in if the goalie hadn't deflected it is called a *shot on goal*.

Shorthanded: When a team has one or more players in the penalty box, and the other team has their full complement of players (six, including the goalie) they are considered to be shorthanded. This means that their opponent is on a *power play*.

Shorthanded Goal: When a goal is scored by a team that is shorthanded, it is called a shorthanded goal. This is extremely difficult to do, since being shorthanded means being at a disadvantage (the shorthanded team has fewer players on the ice than the opponent).

Shot on Goal: A *shot on goal* is a shot that would have gone into the goal if the goalie hadn't deflected, or saved it. (It's also defined as a shot that does score a goal.) Shots on goal are calculated as part of a player's and team's statistics. Shots on goal are also tallied to determine how many saves a goaltender had in relation to the number of goals scored (and to thereby determine how good a game he had).

Slap Shot: Most important, *Slap Shot* is the name of a hilarious, classic hockey movie starring retro-hottie Paul Newman! A slap shot *also* refers to a type of shot in which a player raises his stick high and then brings it down, with emphasis, into the puck. It almost looks like a golf swing. It's the fastest shot—it can propel the puck to a speed of over a hundred miles per hour—but it's not quite as accurate as a wrist shot.

Slashing: Slashing is a Freddy Krueger–like action, but it's executed with a hockey stick, as opposed to a giant knife. In short, slashing (not to be confused with *spearing* or *high-sticking*) is using the stick to hit or attempt to hit an opponent. As the name suggests, it involves a slashing-type motion against the opponent. Depending on the degree of malice or whether it results in an injury, slashing results in either a major or a minor penalty.

Spearing: Spearing is even more Freddy Krueger–like than slashing—think Freddy Krueger as a fencing champion on skates with a hockey stick. Ridiculous, you say, but not unlike actual *spearing* in hockey, which is when a player literally uses his stick as a spear to stab at an opponent. As with slashing, just the *attempt* to spear qualifies as a penalty. Spearing results in a major penalty.

Stick Check: A stick check is a legal, defensive tactic used to get the puck away from an opponent. There are three varieties of stick checks: the *poke check*, *sweep check*, and *stick-lift check*. They are just what they sound like. In the poke check, Player Hottie pokes Player Hairy's stick in an attempt to get the *puck* away from him. In the sweep check, Player Hottie sweeps the puck away, and in the stick-lift check, Player Hottie lifts up Player Hairy's stick and tries to steal the puck away.

Sudden-Death Overtime: *Sudden-death overtime* is used to end a tie. In regular season games, there is one five-minute overtime period. Whoever scores first during this period wins, and the period is over (even if only a minute was used). (If no one scores during this overtime period, a *shootout* occurs.) In the playoff season, a game will go into as many twenty-minute overtime periods as needed to determine a winner. But again, as soon as a team scores, game over—sayonara, baby—sudden death to the opponent.

Time-Out: Time-outs can only be called during normal stoppage of play (when a player receives a penalty, for example). Each team is allowed only one thirty-second time-out per game.

Tripping: The old-fashioned kind. As in, one player uses his stick or leg or any other body part to trip another player. Tripping is a minor penalty.

Wrist Shot: In a *wrist shot* the stick is not raised off the ice; the puck is propelled by a strong flicking of the wrist. It's slower, but more accurate, than the slap shot.

Zamboni: Not a crime family. A *Zamboni* is the machine that smoothes the ice out before the game and between periods. It was invented by the late Frank Zamboni in 1947. During hockey matches, the ice becomes very scratched, rutted, and pitted—generally beaten up—from a dozen men skating fast and aggressively, so it needs to be smoothed periodically. There is something utterly mesmerizing about watching the Zamboni—it elicits a strong to desire to get on the ice and drive it yourself. Fans will often greet the Zamboni machines with chants of "Zamboni, Zamboni."

FRANK ZAMBONI: FROM SELLING ICE TO SMOOTHING ICE

Frank Zamboni, born at the turn of the century, made his living in the ice business, which was cool until the refrigerator became ubiquitous at mid-century and his trade went the way of the blacksmith. Left with a lot of extra ice in inventory, Zamboni and his brothers opened up an ice rink.

Zamboni soon noticed that it took five men ninety minutes to lay down new ice between skating rounds, and he figured that there had to be a better way. So he tinkered with a war-surplus Jeep, the front ends of two automobiles, pulleys, and a wooden bin to catch the ice shavings—and, in 1947, the first Zamboni machine was born. Shortly after, Sonja Henie, three-time Olympic gold medalist and Hollywood's favorite skating star, visited the Zamboni brothers' skating rink and asked to have one made for her. Then the Chicago Blackhawks ordered one, and the Frank J. Zamboni Company was off and running. Today, more than 4,000 Zambonis resurface rinks all over the world.

Golf

THE SOUND: *Thwack* (a long drive), then *ping* (a putt).

THE LOOK: Players of all shapes, sizes, and fitness levels wearing polo shirts and pleated khaki shorts or slacks.

THE PLACE: A golf course—acres and acres of exquisitely groomed green grass.

THE ORGANIZATION: The PGA Tour, The PGA of America, and the USGA (The United States Golf Association).

> **Golf is a good walk spoiled.**
> —*Mark Twain*

Golf, like The Blob from the 1950s sci-fi classic, is taking over the world, thanks, in part, to Tiger Woods. Both men and women have an interest in golf, both as participants and spectators—yet while women *like* golf, men are *obsessed* with it. And the reason is quite obvious: In golf, the aim is to get the ball in the hole with as little work as possible; with as few strokes as possible, in fact. Need I say more?

Yes, golfmania has swept the nation. James P. Herre, editor of "Golf Plus," *Sports Illustrated*'s section devoted to golf, reports that PGA Tour purses have exploded from $56 million in 1994 to $240 million in 2004. Sportswriter Frank Deford wrote in an article titled "Hooked on Golf" that "golf has become . . . [such] a dominant cultural force that [it] has replaced most sensible, traditional American activities such as reading, the cocktail hour, sunbathing, [and] worship of the Almighty. In the United States today, if you don't play golf, you must explain yourself."

With Deford's comment in mind, there are several reasons why savvy women of the world need to know a thing or two about golf. The first is that, like the other sports in this book, professional golf is always in the headlines, and the champions have mucho celebrity status. (Tiger Woods, by the way, was the highest-paid athlete in the world in 2004, with earnings of $80.3 million,* according to *Forbes*.) Secondly, you might find yourself in a situation where it is strongly to your advantage to participate in golf. Golf has long been a business tool for men. If Mr. Company is deciding between Vendor A and Vendor B, and Vendor B is the one who treated him to a round of golf, Vendor B wins the deal. (Many women have already gotten wise to this and started doing business on the course too.) Golf is also used for all kinds of charity and fund-raising events sponsored by all manner of organizations, from local hospitals to community centers. And finally, if you never plan to spend half a day chasing a little white ball but simply want to endear yourself to the golf-crazed men in your life—boyfriend, husband, son, client, or colleague alike—you'll find it helpful to know the difference between a bogey and a birdie and know that golf is the only sport in which the lowest score wins.

Golf is different from the other major sports in a few important ways. It is the only major sport except baseball that isn't timed. It is an individual sport—the only thing that affects a player's score is the player himself. (A golfer's competitors don't affect his swing, except in the sense of one competitor making another more tense, or more aggressive, perhaps.) And, according to Mike Butler, caddie master and manager of outside operations at North Shore Country Club in Glen Head, New York, golf "is an unconquerable game"—the sport has no undefeated champions. Having the number-one world ranking, for example, doesn't mean a golfer was undefeated, just that he did better overall than all his competitors that particular year. In golf, there is no equivalent to shutting out the other team, pitching a perfect game, or scoring a hat trick.

---

*$70 million of this figure is income from endorsements.

THE END OF THE ALL-WHITE, ALL-MALE ERA IN GOLF

There's a strange paradox in the golf world: More and more women are playing golf—both professionally and for fun—and on May 23, 2003, Annika Sorenstam made history when she became the first woman to compete in a PGA event. And yet, as Mike Butler commented, "golf is [one of] the last bastion[s] of male chauvinism." His theory is supported by the medieval rules that many, many private golf and country clubs have had in place for an eternity that place restrictions on when women can play and even where they can eat. For example, some clubs don't allow women to play on Saturday or Sunday mornings (the most desirable time for anyone *with a job*). And often the "grill room" (what many clubs call their informal dining area) will be off-limits to women.

And then there are some clubs that don't allow women at all. Or blacks, or Jews, or Catholics, or Latinos for that matter. Maybe on paper they do, but clubs have a long, disturbing tradition of bigotry. Fortunately, the last decade has seen a surge in the popularity of golf, and with it a proliferation of courses free of restrictions.

Tiger helped. By becoming the first black to win the Masters at Augusta National,* he incidentally brought to light the fact that the club does not allow female members. Augusta is certainly not the only club to bar women, but because it is one of the citadels of golf and the host of the Masters tournament every year, it became a flashpoint for the issue.

HERE'S HOW IT WORKS

The object of golf is to get the ball into the cup in as few strokes as possible. The game is played on a course of eighteen holes, divided into two nine-hole sections called the *front* nine and the *back* nine. Pros always play eighteen, but regular folk often play nine holes, the perfect solution for husbands who are threatened with murder by their wives

---

*Augusta is not the club next door. Its all-male membership is largely comprised of the rich and powerful—statesmen and politicians, CEOs, captain-of-industry types. In August 2004, *USA Today* published Augusta National's membership list, which included the following, to name just a few: Bill Gates, George P. Schultz (former Sectretary of State), John F. Welch, and Nelson Doubleday.

if they spend the entire day at the golf course instead of finishing the countless household projects still left undone.

An eighteen-hole course covers 150 to 200 acres. And in most professional tournaments, the course is played over four days (once a day), for a total of seventy-two holes. Each set of eighteen holes (or nine holes) played is called a "round." At the end of a round, the player with the lowest score wins.

TIMING

 A typical eighteen-hole round of golf will take about four hours. However, depending on how crowded the course is, and the tempo of the golfers on the course, this can vary. Golf etiquette requires that slower players let faster ones play through—in other words, to simply let them go ahead. This is similar to the sadly not-often-practiced supermarket etiquette rule in which, if your cart is loaded up mountain high, and the person behind you at the check-out has only a loaf of bread and a quart of milk, you should let him or her go first. On busy days, courses will allow only foursomes to play— bigger groups move too slowly, and smaller groups move too fast, throwing off the tempo altogether.

THE HOLE

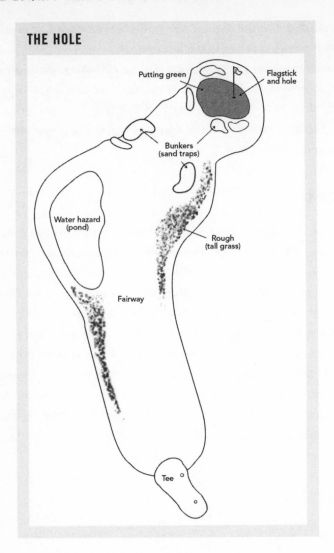

When golfers refer to "the hole," they're usually referring to the parcel of land stretching anywhere from 150 yards to 600 yards from the **tee** (the spot from which they initially hit the ball) to the actual, physical hole, or cup, into which the ball must go. But the whole area is referred to as simply *the hole*, as in, "The 10th hole here at Ultra Snob Country Club is tricky because of its odd shape."

Holes vary in shape and size. When a hole bends to the right or left it is called a **dogleg**. (Depending on which way a hole bends, it is also some-times called a dogleg-left or a dogleg-right.) Holes can go uphill or downhill, and they can have many or few obstacles, known as **hazards** (see below).

The Rough, the Fairway, and the Green

Holes are made up of three different types of surface areas: the **rough**, the **fairway**, and the **green**.

The *rough* is the area that a golfer tries to avoid. It is the unmowed, unkempt grassy area to the sides of the fairway. Rough is what my lawn looks like most of the time, because even if it's mowed, the weeds win—hands down. When a ball lands in the rough, a golfer must swing at his ball wherever it landed. It is difficult to get distance and accuracy from out of the rough.

The fairway and the green are the mowed areas, but calling them "mowed" is like saying Tammy Faye Bakker wears a "touch" of makeup. To walk on a fairway is to walk on carpeting—I'm not talking about the AstroTurf that you throw in the basement and let the Play-Doh get ground in and don't even get upset when the dog barfs on it. I'm talking luxury to bury your toes in. And that's just the fairways. The fairway is lo-cated between the place where the golfers **tee off** (called the *tee*, or *tee box*) and the green. From the fairway, the golfer wants to hit the ball onto the green, which is easier said than done.

The green is so closely mowed (it's the Brazilian-waxed area of the golf hole) that it looks as though it might be hard, but it is dreamily, deliciously soft and smooth on the sole. It has to be, because the green is the **putting area** (more on putting in a minute). The physical hole, marked with a **flag-stick**, is found on the green, and the green's smooth, undulating surface means that, even if the ball is close to the hole, it's not easy to sink it.

Hazards

In and around the fairway are obstacles called *hazards* that make the holes more challenging. A hazard on a golf course is the equivalent of a windmill on a miniature golf course. They are obstacles to hitting the ball exactly the way you want.

There are a few different kinds of hazards: **water hazards** (ponds and streams), **sand traps** (also called **bunkers**), and trees and wooded areas. Hitting your ball into the water is especially bad, because in golf the overriding rule is to "play it as it lies," meaning you can't move the ball from where it has landed without a penalty. Whenever the ball is moved, a **penalty stroke** is added to that player's score. (This is why players try to hit the ball directly out of the *sand traps* and out of the *rough*, rather than move it and get penalized a stroke.) However, when the ball lands in water, it is obviously impossible not only to hit the ball, but often to *find* the ball. Thus, golfers must drop a *different* ball within a designated area (usually within two club-lengths from the hazard—but no closer to the hole), and suffer a penalty stroke.

OUT-OF-BOUNDS

On a golf course, *out-of-bounds* is defined as the area beyond the confines of the golf course. (Everything else is thus considered *inbounds*.) The border between what is inbounds and out-of-bounds is usually marked on the course with a sign that says O.B., or with white stakes—or it can be obvious because of naturally prevailing boundaries (such as a forest or a road that abuts a course).

When a ball is hit out-of-bounds, a penalty stroke is charged to the player. Adding salt to the wound is that the player must then hit the ball from where he originally hit it (you can't just drop the ball near where it went out of bounds and hit it from there)—so a ball hit out-of-bounds costs a player *two* strokes.

SCORING: It's All About Par

In golf, unlike other sports, the lowest score wins. This is one aspect of the sport that flies in the face of typical male tendencies—men usually want everything bigger, stronger, faster. Not so with golf scores, nor with golf **handicaps** (more on handicaps later).

In golf, **par** is the basis for scoring. Par is the number of strokes designated for each golf hole. A hole—depending on the distance from the tee to the cup, the shape, the hazards, etc.—will be designated as a par 3, par 4, or par 5. Par 3 means that it should take three strokes to get the ball in the hole, par 4 means it should take four strokes, and so on. Every course gets an overall par designation, too. Most regulation courses are par 72 for eighteen holes (which is simply the sum of the pars on each of the eighteen holes).

If a golfer uses one less stroke than par to get the ball in the hole, it's called a **birdie.** Two under par is called an **eagle,** which is rare. A **bogey** is a score of one over par, meaning that it took a golfer an extra stroke to get the ball into the hole. A *double bogey* is two over par, a *triple bogey* is three, *quadruple bogey* is four, and after that, most golfers want to throw their clubs in a water hazard. The Holy Grail of golf is the *hole in one*, which means hitting the ball from the tee, onto the green, and into the cup with *one stroke!* A hole in one is just about the rarest of all sports moments, and is very hard to achieve, even for the pros.

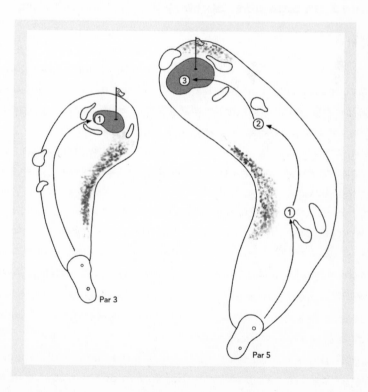

Par 3

Par 5

THE HOLE IN ONE (OR, MIRACLES DO COME TRUE)

Now for a brief personal anecdote.

At the age of seventy-five, my father achieved the unachievable: He got a hole in one. It was the happiest day of his life.

My father has raised three daughters who have jobs, vote, stay out of jail, and have never used heroin (and one of whom has given him a *grandson*); he has been married to the same woman for more than forty years; he has argued (and *won*) a case in front of the United States Supreme Court; he has survived a bout with prostate cancer and angioplasty; and he has walked away scratch-free after falling asleep at the wheel of his car. I repeat: The day he got the hole in one was the happiest day of his life.

Scoring Tournaments: Stroke Play and Match Play

STROKE PLAY

Most golf tournaments use a method of scoring called *stroke play*, also known as *medal play*, in which the total number of strokes per player is tallied, and the golfer with the lowest number wins. So, using stroke play, if Herman shoots a 75 and Trey shoots a 68, Trey wins.

In professional golf tournaments scored using stroke play, a number with a plus or minus in front of it will appear next to each golfer's score, telling the viewers how far below or above par the player is for the total round. For instance, -4 would indicate four under par, and +2 would indicate two over par. (An "E" indicates that the golfer is *even*, or exactly at par.) A -4 on a 72-par course means the golfer recorded a final score of 68. At the end of the tournament, the player with the lowest cumulative score wins.

MATCH PLAY

When a tournament is scored using *match play*, the score is determined by the cumulative number of *holes* won, not the cumulative number of strokes. (Since individual holes are won by having the lowest number of strokes per hole, however, the principle of "fewer strokes wins" is the same in match play—it's just tallied on a hole-by-hole basis.) In match play, a player who is winning is said to be "two up," "three up," and so on, depending on the number of holes he is ahead. A winner is determined when one golfer is ahead by more holes than remain on the course. (If a player is up by three holes and only two remain, it's pointless to continue, and a winner is declared. In this case, the winner is said to have won by a score of *3 and 2*.) The Ryder Cup tournament, one of the major international competitions, uses this system.

When mortal (nonprofessional) men or women go play a round of golf, they almost always use stroke play. This is true for most amateur tournaments as well, although occasionally clubs will have some tournaments that are scored with match play.

The Handicap System

The handicap system allows players of all abilities to play together. It levels the playing field, so to speak. A handicap is a little less than the average number of strokes a player shoots *over par* on an eighteen-hole course. A player who averages eighty strokes on a par-72 course would have a handicap of about seven. The lower the handicap, the better the player. A handicap of six or less is very, very good. (Note that handicap is not a factor in professional golf. Professional golfers are too good to have handicaps. They are all **scratch players**, meaning they have the ability to play at par, no handicap needed.)

The handicap system enables a good player and a bad player to play a competitive match because, at the end of the round, each golfer's final score is adjusted according to his handicap—a golfer's gross score minus his handicap equals his net score. Thus, if someone with a twenty-three handicap shoots a 105, he'll have a final net score of 82. And if someone with a nine handicap shot a 95, his final net score would be 86. You get the picture.

It's All About Trust

Establishing one's handicap is done more or less on an honor system. In the United States, a player will simply give his or her information to a USGA licensed* golf club that will then calculate his or her handicap according to the USGA Handicap System.™ To determine a handicap, a player has to play many rounds of golf before it can be accurately established. Obviously, handicaps can change as a player improves or declines from season to season.

Some people (men) adjust their handicap to their advantage—or foolishness. A player may brag about having a six handicap but then make a fool of himself by playing badly and clearly not living up to his low number. On the other hand, one can claim a twenty-four handicap and make himself look like a hero when he clearly plays better than his handicap implies.[†]

The USGA Handicap System™ has established the Maximum Handicap Index,® which is 36.4 for men and 40.4 for women. The USGA mandates that anything above the maximum must be designated with an "L" which, naturally, I thought stood for "Loser." But it really means for "local Club use only" (i.e., if your handicap is established at Most Snobby Country Club, but then you quit and join Least Snobby Country Club, your handicap could change).

---

*The USGA issues handicaps for the U.S. and Mexico; for everywhere else, the R&A, the international golf governing body similar to the USGA, issues them. (The R&A takes its name from the Royal and Ancient Golf Club of St Andrews, a club in St Andrews, Scotland, that dates back to 1754.)
[†]Men might be particularly inclined to lie about their handicap if there's money on the table. When betting is involved, if a player inflates his handicap, then he increases his chances of winning, a practice commonly referred to as "sandbagging."

THE SCIENCE TO SPORTS

> ## HANDICAP AND PENIS SIZE
>
> A lot of men brag about the size of their handicaps. These are the same men who think that fast cars, big incomes, big desks—you get the point—make women swoon and lead us to think that they've got a lot going on. For these relics of the caveman era, small handicap = big stick. But we smart girls know that it is those who walk softly who carry the big sticks. So, if you're in a situation where a man seems overly excited about his handicap, you know just the type of man you're dealing with. He's a weenie, regardless of his weenie size.

DIFFERENT STROKES

The Long Game

At some clubs, players are given a very specific time (6:03, 7:19, 8:29) to *tee off* (begin playing), which is called a *tee time* (or *tee-off time*). Clubs do this to avoid crowding and waiting at the course. Each hole has a marked tee area (or *tee box*) that varies in distance to the fairway, making it easier or more difficult to hit the ball where you want it (the farther back you start, the more difficult the hole becomes). The tee area is very manicured and smooth, similar to the green.

In the tee area, the golfer puts a wooden tee into the ground and places the golf ball on top of it, then swings at the ball on top of the tee. From the tee, the player wants to **drive** the ball—that is, hit the ball hard and long—and land it in the fairway, and then, in as few shots as possible, advance it to the green, where he'll then try to putt it into the hole. (Note that on par-3 holes, the tee shot is usually made directly from the tee box to the green—because the hole is so short, there's no fairway in between.)

When the ball lands just shy of the green or on the edge of the green, the short shot from the fairway (or the rough) onto the green is called a **chip shot**. The part of the game played from the tee and on the fairway is known as the **long game**, because it usually involves long-distance shots. Most holes have three tees: one for tournament play or for players with very low handicaps; a middle tee for the average male player; and a "forward tee" (which is closer to the green, but not much) for women.

The Short Game

While, for everyday players, the challenge begins at the tee and continues through the rough, the bunkers, the water hazards, and onto the green, professional players are usually far more adept at getting the ball onto the green. Once there, however, they (and eventually recreational players) have to face the music with *putting*. Putting is the frustrating exercise of hitting the ball "just so"—not too hard, not too soft, not too long, not too short—so it will go into the cup. The part of the game played at or near the green is known as the **short game**, because it involves putting or chipping from short distances.

TYPES OF SHOTS

Golfers employ different types of shots to try to get the ball to go exactly where they want it to. The better the golfer, the better he or she is at fine-tuning a particular swing. (Conversely, there are lousy shots that you're far less likely to see a professional fall prey to.) Common types of shots, both good and bad, are outlined here and on page 221.

DESIRABLE SHOTS

Drive	The drive is the first shot from the tee area. It is a long-distance shot, and most men aspire to 250–300 yards.
Fade	A fade is a shot that gently curves to the right (for a right-handed player) or to the left (for a left-handed player).
Draw	A draw is a shot that curves to the left for a right-handed player, or to the right for a left-handed player.

TOOLS OF THE TRADE

Different types of clubs are used for different types of shots. Regulation golf allows players to carry and use up to fourteen clubs. There are two basic types of clubs: **woods** and **irons**, so called because they used to be made of wood or steel. Nowadays, clubs are still made of steel, but they're also made from titanium and graphite and other space-age materials that have enhanced players' ability to hit the ball farther and with more accuracy.

Woods have bigger, rounder clubheads and longer shafts than irons and are used primarily for hitting long distances. *Irons* are used for shorter distances, and where more accuracy is required. Within the two groupings of woods and irons, the clubs are distinguished by number—3-wood, 9-iron, and so on. The higher the number, the greater the *loft*—the degree of angle (slope, pitch, or grade) of the club face from the shaft. Very generally, the higher the number of the club, the shorter the distance the ball will travel.

In addition to woods and irons, there are also specialty clubs such as *drivers*, *putters*, and *sand wedges*. A driver is a wood that is used to hit off the tee for a very long shot (the *drive*); a putter is used to *putt* on the green; and a sand wedge is used to hit the ball out of the sand.

UNDESIRABLE SHOTS

Hook	A hook is a shot that curves dramatically from right to left, ending much more to the left than desired. (The opposite holds true for lefties.)
Slice	A slice is a shot that curves wildly from left to right (for a right-handed player). This is the bane of the beginner's game.
Shank	A shank is a shot in which the ball is hit with, or ricochets off of, the neck of the golf club instead of the head. When this happens, the ball shoots straight off to the right for a right-hander (and vice versa for a lefty).
Thin shot	A thin shot is a lousy shot in which the club strikes the ball too high, without hitting the turf at all, and sends the ball on an undesirably low trajectory, often right along the ground.
Fat shot	A fat shot is a lousy shot in which the club strikes the turf well before it hits the ball, which results in the ball moving about three feet, if you're lucky.

GREENS ON THE BIG SCREENS

***Tin Cup* (1996):** This romantic comedy follows the familiar theme of a mostly down-and-out guy—in this case a golfer played by Kevin Costner—who pulls himself up to woo a beautiful love interest (Rene Russo). Maybe not the most original flick ever, but it's cute and charming and stars Costner who, let's face it, is easy on the eyes.

***Caddyshack* (1980):** A hilariously funny flick about life at a country club, starring Chevy Chase, Rodney Dangerfield, and Bill Murray. This is a movie that men in particular can watch over and over and over again and still find hysterically funny.

THE PGA TOUR

What the National Football League (NFL) is to football, or Major League Baseball (MLB) is to baseball, the PGA Tour is to golf—it is professional touring golf's primary governing body. While there are a lot of golf events that are not run by the PGA Tour, the Tour events are the ones that matter most (to fans and sportswriters) in professional golf. (The other two major golf governing bodies in the United States are the PGA of America, which runs the PGA Championship and many regional professional events, and the United States Golf Association [USGA] which runs the U.S. Open and most amateur championships across the country.)

Each year there are approximately fifty events (both here and abroad) that make up the PGA Tour. Tournaments you may have heard of, such as the "Buick Invitational," or the "Bob Hope Chrysler Classic," or "The Players Championship," are all Tour events.

There is also an international component to the PGA Tour—there's the PGA European Tour, the Southern African PGA Tour, the PGA Tour of Australasia, and the PGA Tour of Japan. A golfer's world ranking comes from his performance in international events. The various tournaments are rated at different levels by the PGA Tour, and winners of the tournaments accumulate points accordingly. More points are allotted for the more important tournaments. (Winning a *major*, for example, yields more points than winning, say, the Buick Classic.)

The Majors

Unlike other sports in which one final event like the Super Bowl or World Series decides the champion, golf has four important annual tournaments. These are the crème de la crème events in which only the most elite professionals compete. The four major tournaments for men's professional golf—often referred to as simply "the majors"—are:

1. The Masters (always played at Augusta National, a private club in Augusta, Georgia).

2. The U.S. Open (rotates among courses here in the United States).

3. The British Open (rotates among courses in England and Scotland).

4. The PGA Championship (rotates among courses in the United States).

The Ryder Cup is another biggie—it's a biennial competition between teams from Europe and the United States that rotates among courses here and abroad. Unlike the "big four" (above), which use stroke-play scoring, the Ryder Cup uses match play.

Finally, the *Senior PGA Tour* (currently known as the "Champions Tour"), is a tour for golfers who are at least fifty years of age. This is a fan favorite because viewers get to watch beloved old-timers compete.

JUST KNOW THIS

The object of golf is to get the ball into the cup in as few strokes as possible. Golf courses have eighteen holes, usually divided into two sections of nine holes, but professional golfers always play eighteen holes. Each hole is assigned a par—par 3, par 4, or par 5. If a golfer uses only three strokes on a par 4 to get the ball in the cup, he or she has made a *birdie* and is one under par. If he or she is lucky enough to shoot two under par on a hole (rare), it's an *eagle*. Going over par on a hole by one stroke more than the number indicates is a *bogey*, while two over par is a *double-bogey*, three over par is a *triple-bogey*, and so on.

Golfers use different kinds of clubs for different types of swings. The two main groups are *woods*, which are used for longer shots called *drives*, and *irons*, which are used for shorter distances. *Putters* are used for *putting*—lightly hitting the ball just so. Putting is done on the green, when the ball is close to the cup.

There are two kinds of scoring in golf. The most commonly used is *stroke play*, in which each player's cumulative number of strokes is tallied, and the one with the lowest number wins. In *match play* scoring, used at the Ryder Cup and other tournaments, the number of holes won is tallied, and play ends when the number of holes a player is ahead of his opponent by exceeds the number of holes remaining on the course. The winner of each hole is determined by who had the fewest strokes on that hole. In either scoring method, the basis of winning is the least number of strokes per hole.

Golfers You Need to Know

The Legends

JACK NICKLAUS, 1940–
NICKNAME: "THE GOLDEN BEAR"

Jack Nicklaus is the Michael Jordan, or the Babe Ruth, or the Wayne Gretzky of golf. *Sports Illustrated*'s Rick Reilly wrote that he is "the best golfer to have ever lived." "At his peak," Reilly wrote, "Nicklaus was so crushing an opponent that most players lost to him just driving into the parking lot."

Here are just a few of Nicklaus's feats:

* He won eighteen major tournaments—more than anyone in history.

* He came in second in nineteen majors (which is equally astounding).

* The first time he played the U.S. Open as a professional, in 1962 at age twenty-two, Nicklaus won, then went on to win three more, making him one of four golfers this century to win the U.S. Open four times (1962, 1967, 1972, and 1980).

* He won every major at least three times—nobody else has won every major twice, and only five golfers have won each major once.

* In all, Nicklaus won seventy-one PGA Tour events.

In the late 1950s and early 1960s, Arnold Palmer (see below) dominated golf, but then Nicklaus came along. In 1962, Nicklaus beat Palmer at the U.S. Open and a rivalry was born. Their styles were completely different: Palmer was emotion and charisma, Nicklaus was pure will and talent. At first, Nicklaus received the usual new-kid-on-the-block treatment by those who didn't want to see their beloved Palmer dethroned, but he prevailed and "won over America with pure unbleached excellence," wrote Reilly. Nicklaus, who was rather stout when he began his reign, went from being known as "Fat Jack" to the "Golden Bear."

"Nicklaus has the remarkable combination of power and finesse, and he is one of the smartest guys ever to walk the fairways," commented golf great Gene Sarazen. "And he has been an extraordinary leader. What more is there to say? Jack Nicklaus is the greatest competitor of them all."*

---

*You might be thinking, *But what about Tiger? Isn't Tiger Woods the greatest golfer ever?* It's a good question. You see, Nicklaus won his last Masters at age forty-six, and Tiger is still very young (born in 1975), so it's well within the realm of possibility for Tiger to break Nicklaus's records. In fact, the Great Golf Debate is whether Tiger will surpass Nicklaus. If Tiger stays the course that he's been on, he surely will, but one never knows—we'll just have to wait and see.

ARNOLD PALMER, 1929–

Palmer is one of the best golfers of all time. And before Tiger Woods's era, he was the most popular. He rose to the top of the golf world in the 1960s by winning seven majors between 1958 and 1964. In 1960 alone, when Palmer was thirty-one, he won eight tournaments, including the Masters and the U.S. Open, and he was named PGA Player of the Year and *Sports Illustrated*'s Sportsman of the Year. He looked more like a football player than a golfer, was known for his boyish enthusiasm, and had the good fortune to rise through the ranks just as golf was emerging on television.

When Palmer won the Masters in 1958, it was only the third time that the tournament had been televised. He was the perfect player for the new TV era—he was "of the masses," rough around the edges with a wild swing and a tousled appearance that included the frequent hitching up of his pants. The gallery of fans who followed Palmer at tournaments was enormous and became known as "Arnie's Army." Palmer started the job that Tiger finished several decades later—he brought the game to the common folk. It was during Palmer's reign that public golf courses began to proliferate and be peopled with not just doctors, lawyers, and accountants, but some truck drivers and plumbers, too.

"The Palmer era," as Palmer's heyday has been called, was eventually eclipsed by the Nicklaus era—it was Nicklaus who ultimately dominated in their great, intense rivalry. Palmer, as Ron Flatter recounted for ESPN.com, once said "At times [Nicklaus and I] became so hyper about beating each other that we let someone else go right by us and win. But our competition was fun and good for the game."

Palmer won a total of sixty-two PGA tournaments and was the PGA Player of the Year twice (1960 and 1962). His biography at the World Golf Hall of Fame says: "For people born in the second half of the twentieth century, it was as if Arnold Palmer invented golf."

TIGER WOODS (ELDRICK "TIGER" WOODS), 1975–

In 1996 a tiger roared across the tees and fairways and greens and then roared across the planet. While he was still at Stanford University (yes, he's really smart in addition to being a golf superstar) and playing in amateur events, Eldrick "Tiger" Woods began to wow the sports world. (Tiger's nickname was given to him at a young age by his father, who had a friend, a Vietnamese soldier, whom he also called by the nickname "Tiger.") Then, immediately upon turning pro at the age of twenty, he won his first professional tournament. He followed with win after win after win, leaving his competitors in the dust, again and again and again.

In the first eight PGA events in which he participated that first year, Tiger won two events and finished in the top ten in three others, and was named *Sports Ilustrated*'s Sportsman of the Year—all this before he could legally drink. In 1997, at the age of twenty-one, he became the youngest person and the first black to win the Masters. (Please note that the Masters is played at Augusta National, a golf club in Augusta, Georgia, where until 1990 blacks were not allowed as members, and were not even allowed as guests until 1974. The founder of the Masters tournament, Clifford Roberts, once said, as *SI*'s Rick Reilly reported, "As long as I'm alive, golfers will be white, and caddies will be black." Let's just say that change is good.)

Tiger, for the record, is part Thai, Chinese, Cherokee, African, and European. I would call that "American"; his mother calls him a "universal child." To the world, he appeared as simply young and black, and that was enough to attract tremendous new interest to golf. Tiger did what other "need-only-one-name" athletes like Babe or Michael or Ali did for their sports—he made people who never before cared stand up and cheer.

After starting with a bang, he went on to do things that no one else had done, most notably winning all four majors (the Masters, the U.S. Open, the British Open, and the PGA) *consecutively*. This feat is known as the "Tiger Slam." Until September 6, 2004, when Vijay Singh dethroned him, Tiger held the number-one world ranking for an unprecedented 264 consecutive weeks (more than five years).

At the time of this writing, Tiger is barely thirty years old, and he's already won forty PGA Tour events. In 2000, he won eleven tournaments. That same year, Tiger was named *Sports Illustrated*'s Sportsman of the Year for a second time, making him the only athlete in the magazine's history to receive the title more than once.

Then suddenly—actually, not suddenly, but starkly—Tiger's star dimmed a bit. What a difference a day makes—or a couple of years, anyway. The year 2004 was not a good year for Tiger—his roar became more of a cat's meow. The press was ready to declare his reign finished. But then, as of May 2005, he reclaimed the number-one spot in the world again, but not quite as firmly as before. Singh continues to nip at his heels.

Whether or not he holds the number-one spot, Tiger is good for golf. He still makes the ratings soar when he plays, even if he's playing poorly and isn't in contention. As Clifton Brown commented in the *New York Times* in June 2004, "Woods remains the dominant personality in golf, even when he is not the most dominant player."

Legends in Training

PHIL MICKELSON, 1970–

Since his professional debut in 1992, Phil Mickelson has proven himself to be an outstanding golfer. And his approachable demeanor, his respect for the fans and press, and his loyalty to his family and friends have made him one of the most beloved contemporary players.

In 2002, Mickelson's world rank reached number two. But until the spring of 2004 he had an albatross around his neck: With all of his success, he had never won a single majors tournament. Even more frustrating, he'd come so close—second or third—eight times, but he never won.*

---

*Mickelson achieved his number-two world ranking by dominating the other less important PGA Tour events.

Then, in 2003, Mickelson had a *really* bad year. For the second time in his career he didn't win *any* tournaments, major or minor. His world ranking plummeted to fifteenth and, most horrible of all, while giving birth to their third child, his wife, Amy—and the baby—both came within minutes of dying. That was in March, and the near-tragedy so rattled him that the remainder of 2003 was a wipeout on the golf course. The turnaround didn't begin until months later when he and Amy, to whom he is totally devoted, regained their footing. Mickelson then got in shape, returned to his golf swing, and began 2004 with a bang—winning once more.

Then came the moment of truth in April 2004, at the Masters. Would he finally free himself of his albatross? In a heartstoppingly dramatic competition that came down to the final hole, Mickelson triumphed at last, beating Ernie Els by one stroke. Mickelson, in a photo flashed round the world, literally jumped for joy.

VIJAY SINGH, 1963–

"If you buy into the premise that golf is entertainment, then James Brown no longer is the hardest-working man in show business. The new title-holder is Vijay Singh . . ." wrote Gary D'Amato in the *Milwaukee Journal Sentinel* in August 2004. A month later, Singh toppled Tiger Woods from his long, long hold on the number-one world ranking by winning the Deutsche Bank Championship. Tiger had hogged the top spot for more than five years—264 consecutive weeks—but now it was Singh's turn on the throne.

While Mickelson was busy commanding everyone's emotional attention after his poignant win at the Masters in 2004, Vijay was busy winning tournaments. His September victory at the Deutsche Bank Championship was his sixth of the year, while no one else had won more than twice. And Singh has no plans to change his rigorous work habits. "The easiest part is getting to the top," Singh said. "The hardest part is staying up there. I'm going to make sure nothing bad creeps in."

Singh has a singular vision backed by an unflappable work ethic. Because he is so driven, he keeps himself at arm's length from the distractions of the media and fans and worries far more about his golf swing than about the public's perception of him. Singh is a native of Fiji, and he is the only person from that country to become a world-class golfer.

Glossary

Ace: See *hole in one.*

Birdie: A birdie is a score of one under par on a golf hole. (For example, when a golfer uses only four strokes to get the ball in the cup on a par-5 hole.)

Bogey: Nickname for one of the greatest actors of the century who delivered one of the greatest lines in one of the greatest movies of all time: "Here's looking at you, kid." In *golf*, a bogey is a score of one over par on a golf hole. Two over par is called a *double-bogey*, three over par is called a *triple-bogey*, and beyond that you'll probably want to throw your clubs into a water hazard.

Bunkers: A golfer does not want to hunker down in a bunker. A bunker is a sand trap—a depression in the ground filled with sand. It is one of several types of hazards on a golf hole that add to the hole's level of difficulty.

Caddie: The primary job of a caddie is to carry golf bags—but he can also act as a shrink, advisor, and motivator. Often—and always, in pro golf—he also suggests what clubs to use and informs the golfer of the distance to the cup.

Casual Water: Casual water is water from rain or sprinklers that has accumulated on a golf course. Unlike a *water hazard*, casual water is not intended to be there. If a ball lands in casual water, the golfer is allowed to place his ball within a club length of the casual water without incurring a penalty stroke.

Chip Shot: A chip shot is a type of short shot used to get the ball from the fairway (or rough) onto the green, when it is just shy of or on the edge of the green.

Divot: A divot is the chunk of earth that comes out of the ground when the ball is struck. Golf etiquette says that divots must be replaced (set back in the ground) by the golfer or caddie.

Doglegs: Golf holes that bend left or right are called doglegs. Depending on which way they bend, they are also called dogleg-lefts or dogleg-rights.

Draw: A draw is a shot that gently curves to the left for a right-handed player, or to the right for a left-handed player.

Drive: The drive is the first shot from the tee area. It is a long-distance shot. Golfers usually use the *driver* for this shot.

Eagle: An eagle is a score of two under par. Eagles are not common, neither in golf nor bird-watching.

Fade: What my attention begins to do when someone starts telling me about their golf game. More technically, it's when a golf shot gently curves to the right for a right-handed player, or to the left for a left-handed player.

Fairway: The fairway is the mowed area between the tee and the green. It's the largest part of the golf hole. To walk on the fairway is to walk on carpeting— luxurious carpeting.

Fat Shot: When a golfer takes a big chunk (too much) out of the earth when swinging at the ball, it is known as a fat shot. Fat shots are a form of deforestation through golf.

Flagstick: The flagstick is the pole with a triangular flag at the top that denotes the number of each hole. It is located in the cup into which the ball must go, and it must be removed before putting and replaced after putting. Sometimes it's called the *pin*.

Fore!: The warning yelled out when someone is about to be conked with a golf ball.

Green: The green is the *putting area* where the cup is located. The grass on this area is mowed to a deliciously smooth (and fast) surface, so that even though the ball may be close to the hole, it's not easy to sink it. It's the Brazilian-waxed area of the hole.

Handicap: Recreational golfers are assigned a *handicap* based on past performance. A golfer's handicap is a little less than the average number of strokes he shoots *over par* on an eighteen-hole course. (A golfer who averages eighty strokes on a par-72 course would have a handicap of seven or so.) The lower the handicap, the better the player. The handicap system allows players of all abilities to play together.

Hazards: Hazards are obstacles on the golf course, including water hazards (ponds or streams), bunkers (sand traps), and wooded areas. Hazards are where you don't want the ball to go.

Hole in One (also called an *ace*): Nirvana. Shangri-La. The Holy Grail. A hole in one is when the ball goes from the tee into the cup with a single stroke. It's one of the rarest of all sports moments.

Hook: An undesirable golf shot that curves sharply from right to left for a right-handed player (or left to right for a left-handed player).

Irons: Irons are the group of golf clubs used primarily for hitting the ball short to medium distances. Irons used to be made of iron and steel, and many are still made of steel, but nowadays there are also clubs made of titanium, graphite, and other space-age materials that have enhanced a player's ability to hit the ball with more accuracy.

Long Game: The long game is the part of the game played from the tee and on the fairway. It's called the *long game* because it refers to using long-distance shots, including *drives*.

Mulligan: A mulligan is golf's version of the do-over—it's when your playing partner(s) allows you to take your shot again. It's not really legal, but it's compassionate. As in, "Sure, take a mulligan." As you may have guessed, it's not part of professional golf.

Net: For nonprofessional golfers who have a handicap, net is the gross score minus the handicap, which equals the final score. You may have heard the amateur golfer in your life say something like, "Hi honey, I had a great day on the golf course. I netted 81, my lowest this year!"

Par: The number of strokes designated for each golf hole, depending on that hole's level of difficulty. Holes range from par 3 to par 5. Par 3 means it should take three strokes to get the ball into the hole; par 4 means it should take four strokes; and so on. Golf courses have an overall par as well, which is simply the sum of the pars of the holes. Most regulation courses are par 72 for eighteen holes.

Penalty Stroke: A stroke that is added to a golfer's score as a penalty for certain situations, such as when a ball goes out of bounds or when a ball is lost.

Pin: Another name for the flagstick.

Putt: A putt is a short, soft stroke used on the putting green to put the ball in the hole. Putting is done with a special type of golf club called a *putter*.

Rough: The unmowed grass on either side of the fairway is known as the rough. The rough, like hazards, is to be avoided.

Sand Trap: See *bunker*.

Scratch Player: A player with a zero handicap is known as a *scratch player*. All professional golfers are scratch players, or better.

Shank: A shank is a lousy shot in which the ball is hit with, or ricochets off of, the neck of the golf club instead of the head. When this happens, the ball goes straight right for a right-handed golfer, and straight left for a lefty.

Short Game: The short game is the part of the game played on the green. It's called the short game because it refers to putting or chipping from short distances.

Slice: Shorthand for pizza, as in, "Wanna get a slice before going to the movies?" In golf, it's a shot that curves wildly from left to right (for a right-handed player). A pizza slice is desirable; a golf slice is not.

Sweet Spot: The "sweet spot" of the golf club is the perfect place on the clubface for striking the ball.

Tee: The tee refers to two things: (1) The wooden peg that is put into the ground, on top of which the ball is placed, and (2) the designated area of a golf hole where play for that hole begins. At the start of each hole, golfers take their initial swing at the ball as it sits on the tee in the tee area, or tee box.

Tee Off: "Tee off" refers to the start of a round of golf, as in, "You better hurry up and finish that cup of coffee because we tee off at 8:02 A.M." (Strangely, most tee times are precise to the minute.) It can also refer to the first shot attempted at a hole. "Tee time" (or "tee-off time") refers to the assigned starting time for golfers. Tee times are used at busy courses because not everyone can be on the course at once.

Thin Shot: A thin shot is a lousy shot—it's the result of the club striking the ball too high, without hitting the turf at all.

Water Hazard: A pond, stream, lake, river, or other body of water that serves as an obstacle for golfers.

Woods: Woods are the clubs that are primarily used for longer-distance shots. They have larger, rounder club heads and longer shafts than irons. Woods used to be made of wood, but today they are made of steel, titanium, graphite, and other materials that have enhanced a player's ability to hit the ball farther.

Boxing

THE SOUND: *Pow!*

THE LOOK: Bare-chested men in amazing shape wearing shorts and oversized gloves.

THE PLACE: Boxing rings (raised, square platforms with ropes around the perimeter) in venues ranging from local gyms to Las Vegas hotels to Madison Square Garden.

THE ORGANIZATION: World Boxing Association (WBA), the World Boxing Council (WBC), the International Boxing Federation (IBF).*

> One plays football, one doesn't play boxing.
>
> —*Joyce Carol Oates*

The first thing you need to know about boxing is that it is the only "sport" in which the goal, the *game* if you will, is to cause injury to your opponent. The target for injury is the head—specifically, the brain—and the ultimate goal is to knock your opponent out. The next thing you should know about boxing is that it is the only major U.S. professional sport without a central regulatory authority. Professional football is governed by the NFL, baseball by MLB, hockey by the NHL, and so on. Even Little League baseball has a governing body—Little League International Baseball and Softball, based in Williamsport, Pennsylvania. But with boxing, we have a sport where the contenders are trying to knock each other out—to beat the bloody crap out of each other, really—and it's not regulated closely. A little creepy, no?

Boxing lives in a netherworld of shady characters and unsavory goings-on. In an article in *USA Today*, Jon Saraceno called boxing "the illegitimate child of professional sports," but then goes on to address

---

*There are others, but these are the three predominant boxing organizations.

readers by saying, "Admit it. You kind of like that boxing walks on the wrong side of the street and hangs out under a lamppost. It's unpredictable, dangerous, sexy. That is part of its enduring appeal—even for highly educated people."

While I must admit that I, personally, have a hard time finding anything sexy about 10,000 pounds of force to the head, about faces pummeled to resemble smashed fruit, and about sleazebag promoters exploiting boxers to their own advantage, many, many people feel differently. The *Dictionary of American History* points out that, "Whereas in other professional sports, athletes merely appearing with gamblers or criminals risk banishment, boxing matches are held in gambling casinos with heavy wagering. . . . [And yet,] despite its many woes, boxing has produced important champions."

This last sentence holds the key. While I have little admiration for the sport, I do admire the champions (most of them, anyway) that it has produced. Their athleticism, courage, dedication to their sport, and competitiveness is impressive, to say the least. Another positive about the sport is that it has provided the many boxers who come from impoverished backgrounds with the means to get off the streets and out of the ghetto. Even small-time boxers can box for money and earn a living. In her seminal book, *On Boxing*,* Joyce Carol Oates said: "Impoverished people prostitute themselves in ways available to them, and boxing on its lowest levels offers an opportunity for men to make a living of a kind. In fact, if a boxer is fortunate and isn't injured, boxing will pay him better wages than most of the jobs available to unskilled and uneducated men in our post-industrial society."

While boxing used to be one of the most popular sports in the country, it has slipped over the last few decades. Michael Mandelbaum, author of *The Meaning of Sports*, attributes this to the rise of team sports at the expense of individual sports. In 2003, professional football was a sought-

---

On Boxing, a collection of three essays, is a must-read. It is a compelling examination of the lure of the sport from the author, who has had a lifelong fascination with boxing. Oates is one of several of our most heralded literati who have been drawn to write about the sport. Others include Ernest Hemingway, Norman Mailer, David Halberstam, David Remnick, and George Plimpton, to name just a few.

after vehicle for advertisers, generating more than $2 billion; boxing, ranking just ahead of bowling and track and field, generated only $5.3 million in ads.

Still, boxing certainly has its fans, and it is a multimillion-dollar business and pay-per-view's biggest attraction.

BOXING'S BUFF BRIGHT SIDE

One great thing about boxing is that boxers have beautiful bodies—they are truly lean, mean, fighting machines. Even better is that boxers conduct their sport in very little clothing—shorts only—so the world can see their gleaming six-packs, their perfect pecs, and their buff biceps.

 ## HERE'S HOW IT WORKS

Two guys with incredibly conditioned bodies get into a "ring," which is essentially a square with ropes around it, and attempt to beat the living daylights out of each other. The person who gets beat up the worst or gets knocked out (or in rare instances, dies) is the loser. Pretty straightforward.

Contrary to how it might seem, there *are* rules in boxing, but because the sport isn't regulated by one single authority, the rules change from state to state, and from country to country. (This means that there can be more than one "heavyweight champion of the world," or "middleweight champion of the world," because each state or national organization goes about its own business independent of the others.) In the *New York Times* in March 2004, Dave Anderson wrote: "It is boxing's first commandment, if not its only commandment: Thou shalt not break the rules, because there aren't any."

Rules or no rules, there is in fact an art to boxing. Even though a boxer's goal is to knock out his opponent, he (or she) must do so with skill and finesse. Street brawling doesn't work in the ring. Boxers use combinations of jabs and punches; their hands must be extremely practiced. On top of that, they need to have quick feet and flawless balance. Finally, in addition to positioning himself to make punches, a boxer must defend himself at all times.

THE RING

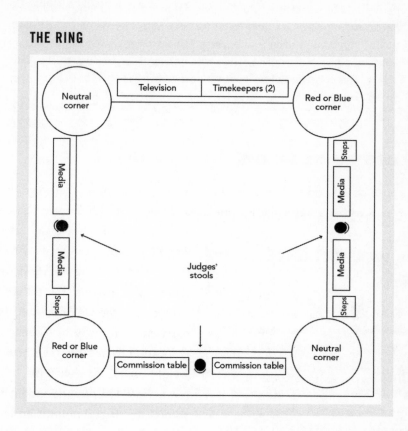

A boxing ring is not a ring at all. It's a raised, square platform with a double rope around the perimeter. Each boxer has one corner that he retreats to between rounds, where his coach, physician, and/or other assistants attend to him. There are also two **neutral corners** to which a ref will send a boxer when the other has been knocked down. (There are chairs or stools in each of the corners.) On the perimeter of the ring, outside the ropes, sit the judges, the press, and representatives from the governing boxing commission.

THE SWEET SCIENCE

Boxing is affectionately known as "The Sweet Science." The phrase comes from an 1824 book titled *Boxiana, or, Sketches of Ancient and Modern Pugilism* ("pugilism" is a fancy name for boxing) by Pierce Egan, who called boxing, "the sweet science of bruising." The shorter version of this phrase was favored by A. J. Liebling, who wrote frequently on boxing for *The New Yorker*. The collection of his classic pieces from 1951 to 1956 is titled *The Sweet Science*.

WEIGHT CLASSES

Because boxers do have the decency to pick on someone their own size, they box within a particular *weight class*. In keeping with the sport's rule-less character, however, even weight classes are not set in stone. Different organizations refer to the classes by different names, and the weights listed for each class can vary from one organization to another. The heavyweight class, for example, can range from 185 pounds and up on some lists, to 200 pounds and up on others.

WEIGHT CLASSES

Heavyweight	over 190 lbs.
Cruiserweight	not over 190 lbs.
Light Heavyweight	not over 175 lbs.
Super Middleweight	not over 168 lbs.
Welterweight	not over 147 lbs.

(Official weight classes go as low as 105 pounds, but the more popular fights tend to be in the heavier weight classes.)

CONTROLLED MADNESS: The Role of the Ref and the Ringside Physicians

In the early twentieth century, fights were practically to the death. Nowadays, however, referees are far more prone to stop fights before they get that far. In some states, the referee is the only person who can stop a fight—if this weren't the case, I'm sure all fights would be stopped by girlfriends, wives, and mothers. (The wife of the champion boxer Sugar Ray

Leonard did in fact faint in her seat once during a particularly brutal match.) In some states, physicians can advise the referee on when a fight should be stopped, and in others, physicians alone can stop a fight. The local commission governing a particular fight determines the number of doctors that are required at ringside.* While it's ultimately the ref who makes the call, it is almost unheard of for a ref not to follow a physician's recommendation.

A referee can (and will) stop a fight if he thinks that a fighter has been severely injured, or if a fighter looks too dazed or out of it to continue. He will also stop a fight if one boxer is so dominant that it becomes obvious that the fight is an unsafe (unfair) mismatch.

TIMING

Boxing matches (also called **bouts**) are divided into periods called *rounds*. The number of rounds per match varies and is decided upon before a match, usually by the boxer's promoter or another one of his representatives. (The promoter in boxing is similar to an agent or manager in other sports, or the producer of a movie. He arranges the fights, procures the financing, and publicizes the fight.) Most professional boxing matches are between four and twelve rounds. Each round is three minutes long, with one minute of rest between rounds. A bell rings at the end of each round, at which point the boxers retreat to their corners to be attended by their assistants, known as **seconds**, and to get relief for cuts and bruises.

It's important to note, however, that a match ends as soon as there is a **knockout** (or **technical knockout**, discussed below). Thus, many of the biggest matches in history have been decided in minutes or less. A fight that is supposed to be a twelve-round match can end in the first round.

There are three timing-related rules in boxing that are important to

---

*There is an ongoing controversy within the medical community regarding physicians and boxing. An organization of boxing physicians, The American Association of Professional Ringside Physicians, was denied endorsement by the AMA (American Medical Association) at their annual meeting in 2002. The long-held position of the AMA is that the sport of boxing should be banned.

understanding how the sport works: the *ten-count*, the **mandatory eight count**, and the **standing eight count**.

Ten-Count

When a boxer is **knocked down** (or, simply, **down**) that is, when any part of his body, except his feet, makes contact with the floor, or when he is hanging helplessly over the ropes as the result of a legal blow—he has ten seconds to get up, or he loses the fight.

Mandatory Eight Count

When a boxer is knocked down and gets back up (within ten seconds), the referee will count eight seconds off to determine if the contender is fit to continue. It doesn't matter when during the ten-count the boxer gets up—the mandatory eight begins once he is back on his feet. Once the boxer gets up, he can't fall down again. He has to remain on his feet for the full eight seconds.

The Standing Eight Count: *He Weebles, He Wobbles, but He Won't Fall Down*

What happens when a fighter is throttled by a punch and looks completely dazed but doesn't actually go down? In this case, the referee stops the fight and gives the dazed dude eight seconds to start fighting again. If the dazed dude doesn't, he loses, and his opponent is the winner by *technical knockout*. You should note, however, that the standing eight count is not employed widely anymore. If a boxer looks that bad, the referee will usually just stop the fight and declare the opponent the winner by technical knockout.

HOW TO WIN

The winner of a boxing match is determined in one of three ways: by *knockout* (KO), *technical knockout* (TKO), or **decision**.

Knockout (KO)

A somewhat dated term for a gorgeous woman, from the days when they were also called "dames" and "broads" and judged on how "stacked" they were. Although champion boxers often have knockouts as "arm-candy," the term means something different in the ring. A knockout is when a boxer has been knocked down and does not get up before the count of ten, at which point his opponent is declared the winner. To win by KO is the most macho way of all to win. A knockout is the home run of boxing.

Technical Knockout (TKO)

PUNCH-DRUNK CINEMA

Million Dollar Baby (2004): This critically acclaimed smash hit, directed by and starring Clint Eastwood (along with Morgan Freeman and Hilary Swank) is just the latest in a surprisingly long list of great movies with boxing as the focus. The film won four Oscars, including Best Picture, Best Director, Best Actress, and Best Actor in a Supporting Role. John Schulman, in a January 2005 *Sports Illustrated* article about the *Million Dollar Baby* frenzy wrote, "It may be the most troubled of sports, but boxing still packs a punch in Hollywood." And it has for a long time. Below are a few more of the most talked about boxing films. Like the grim and gritty nature of the sport, boxing movies are rarely, if ever, comedies.

Raging Bull (1980): A Martin Scorsese film, considered by many film buffs to be a masterpiece, about real-life boxer Jake La Motta, played by Robert De Niro.

Rocky (1976): Well, 1976 was the year the *first Rocky* came out. By *Rocky IV*, the idea was a bit worn, to say the least—but the first one rocked. Sylvester Stallone wrote and starred in all of them.

Ali (2001): Will Smith plays Muhammad Ali in this biographical movie that also stars Jamie Foxx and Jon Voight.

Anytime the ref stops the fight because he decides that one boxer is unable to continue, the boxer's opponent wins by TKO. When the referee stops a fight on a *mandatory eight count*, a *standing eight count*, or because of an injury, it is considered a TKO and the boxer who did the hitting is deemed the winner.

Decision: The Points System

In addition to being regulated by the ref and ringside physicians, boxing matches are *scored* by three boxing judges. During a match, the judges assign *points* to each boxer, based on certain aspects of each boxer's performance; they also deduct points for various reasons as well. If a winner is not declared by knockout or technical knockout, the boxer who has the most points at the end of the final round wins by *decision*. A draw (tie) is also possible.

SCORING POINTS

In order to win a round by decision, the rules (almost always) state that the winner *must* receive ten points, and the loser nine or less. This system is known as the **ten-point must system**. Four criteria—**clean punching**, **effective aggressiveness**, **ring generalship**, and **defense**—are used in scoring. Each counts for twenty-five percent of the boxer's final score.

Note that, in other sports, if a basketball ball goes in the basket or a football is caught in the end zone, there's no equivocating: Points are scored. In boxing, however, it's not so cut-and-dried. As you read the criteria for clean punching, effective aggressiveness, ring generalship, and defense, you'll notice that this is highly subjective territory. That's why there are three judges, who don't necessarily all agree. In other major sports, people may bicker over a particular moment (inbounds or out-of-bounds, strike or ball, etc.), but the overall outcome is conclusive. In boxing, however, when a winner is determined by decision (not knockout), the arguments can go on forever.

CLEAN PUNCHING

Clean punches are sharp, crisp **jabs**; short, tight **hooks**; and **uppercuts** (see below). In essence, clean punching is punching that does the job it's supposed to do: land on a boxer's opponent, firmly and unblocked. In boxing, what counts is not the quantity of punches attempted, but the number that land.

EFFECTIVE AGGRESSIVENESS

The opposite of ineffective aggressiveness, which is like a dog chasing its own tail. In boxing terms, effective aggressiveness means that a boxer is landing punches while moving forward. Just moving forward and not landing punches is clearly not effective.

RING GENERALSHIP

A boxer who is winning in ring generalship is controlling the fight—he is putting his opponent where he wants him, controlling the fight's tempo, and displaying movement around the ring. If Tough-Guy Tom nullifies the aggression of Strong Sam, Tom is the ring general. When a fighter gets his opponent against the ropes, thus taking control of the fight, he is exhibiting ring generalship.

DEFENSE

In boxing, *defense* is the ability to hit the opponent without being hit in return. It can include ducking, dodging, bobbing and weaving, parrying, blocking, slipping, sidestepping, the fox-trot, merengue, tango, and the forbidden dance—the Lambada.

DEDUCTIONS

Points are deducted for **fouls** (see below), for **knockdowns** (when any part of a boxer's body other than his feet makes contact with the floor, or when he is hanging helplessly over the ropes as the result of a legal blow), and for standing eight counts. It is the referee who signals to the judges that points—one, two, or three, at the ref's discretion—should be deducted.

The Judges' Scorecards: Decisions, Decisions, Decisions

At the end of a fight in which neither boxer won by KO or TKO, each judge's points are totaled. The boxer who wins on at least two of the three judges' scorecards is declared the winner.

If all three judges list the same boxer as the winner, that boxer wins by *unanimous decision*. If a boxer is the winner on two of the three cards, he is wins by *split decision*. If two judges list Fighter A as the winner, and the third judge has scored the match a tie, Fighter A wins by *majority decision*. Now it gets a little murkier: Some matches end in a ***draw***. *How can a match end in a draw when there are three judges?* you might ask. Well, in the kooky world of boxing, if two of the three judges score a match a draw, but the third judge gives more points to one boxer, it is still a draw, because the "majority" scored it as such. (I know, I know, it doesn't make any sense, but neither does pummeling for fun, so just go with it.)

FOULS: *You Can Beat Your Opponent to a Pulp, Just Be Sure to Do It Properly*

In a sport where the goal is to harm your opponent, it seems contradictory, to say the least,

---

TYPES OF PUNCHES: ALL PUNCHES ARE NOT CREATED EQUAL

Straight Right: The straight right is a basic and very powerful punch delivered from a straight arm to the opponent's head or body. It often follows a left jab or jabs. It is called a "straight right" because most boxers, like the rest of the world, are right-handed.

Hook: A hook is a type of punch executed with a bent elbow, and with power. The punch curves around to its target (the other guy's head or body), thus forming the shape of a hook.

Jab: A jab is a straight punch that doesn't pack as much power as a hook and that can be used as a setup for a more powerful punch such as a hook or uppercut (see below). It can also be used as a defensive tactic to keep the opponent off balance.

Uppercut: The uppercut is a punch executed in a vertical path. In a right uppercut, the boxer will lower the right side of his body slightly, then straighten up and twist to the left while delivering an upward punch usually aimed at the chin.

that *fouls* would be assigned, but such is the case. Here's what boxers *can't* do:

* hit below the belt (neither in life nor in boxing)

* hit with any part of the body other than the knuckles

* head-butt

* hit while the boxers are in what's known as a *clinch*—when they are either holding each other (it looks like a hug) or leaning on each other

* assault or act aggressively toward the referee

* kidney punch (a punch directed at the kidney area)

* bite your opponent's ear off (à la Mike Tyson vs. Evander Holyfield, 1997)

When a boxer breaks a rule, the referee will issue a minor admonishment called a *caution* to a boxer. Three cautions result in a *warning*. A warning results in a loss of points for the perpetrator or a gain in points for his opponent. Three warnings result in disqualification.

FIGHTS YOU NEED TO KNOW: A CHEAT SHEET

If you only remember the four fights below and not another thing about boxing, that will still be impressive. (More detail on these fights is found in the individual boxers' profiles.)

1938: Joe Louis vs. Max Schmeling. Yankee Stadium, New York. Louis knocks out Schmeling in two minutes, four seconds of the first round.

1971: The Fight of the Century: Muhammad Ali vs. Joe Frazier. Madison Square Garden, New York. Frazier wins in the fifteenth round.

1974: The Rumble in the Jungle: Muhammad Ali vs. George Foreman. Zaire. Ali uses his "rope-a-dope" strategy and knocks out Foreman in the eighth round.

1975: The Thrilla in Manila: Muhammad Ali vs. Joe Frazier. The Philippines. Ali—the winner—called this match the "closest thing to dying [he] knew of."

CRIES FOR REFORM

As a rule, professional sports prefer to regulate themselves, rather than have the government step in and do it for them. For example, during the 2004 steroid scandal in Major League Baseball, when the organization was threatened with government regulation if it didn't clean up its own house, MLB quickly moved to institute new rules for the 2005 season. But the call for government regulation in boxing is growing ever louder with two prominent voices pushing it: Senator John McCain of Arizona and none other than the most celebrated boxer of all time, Muhammad Ali. McCain authored legislation to create a three-person commission, appointed by the president, to license boxers, managers, promoters, and sanctioning organizations, and to set national standards overseeing the activities of the state commissions. (Without a national governing body, it's possible that a boxer could lose his license in one state but go to another state to fight.) The overriding purpose is to protect boxers from unnecessary injury and unsavory promoters. The Senate passed the bill in March 2004, but the House has not yet acted on it.

In September 2004, Muhammad Ali asked Congress to create a U.S. Boxing Commission. In testimony read by his wife before a congressional panel, Ali said that oversight is needed to protect boxers from exploitation and injury. (Ali suffers from Parkinson's disease presumably as a result of boxing injuries, and was thus unable to read his own words.)

DON KING: GENIUS OR DEVIL?

You can't talk about boxing without talking about boxing promoter Don King. It would be like talking about the history of late-night TV and not mentioning Johnny Carson. Don King is the guy whose hair stands straight up like the Bride of Frankenstein, and he is the most successful boxing promoter in history. The list of boxers he's handled is a veritable who's who in the history of the sport, going back to 1974 when he promoted the "Rumble in the Jungle" fight between Muhammad Ali and George Foreman in Zaire. Other luminaries who have been on his roster include: Joe Frazier, Mike Tyson, Sugar Ray Leonard, and Evander Holyfield.

King's hair is illustrative of his larger-than-life personality. To some, King is a genius; to others he is the devil in disguise, or a brash, garish P.T. Barnum huckster. He has been embroiled in numerous investigations, lawsuits, and allegations. In January 2005, he filed a defamation suit against ESPN for a *SportsCentury* television segment that called King "a snake-oil salesman, a shameless huckster and worse."

He has also been entangled with criminal law. He served nearly four years in prison for the 1967 beating death of a man who owed him money. That was the second time he killed a man. The first was in 1954, when he killed a man who was robbing a house, but it was ruled self-defense. He has also beaten federal charges for tax evasion and fraud.

But then there's the other Don King—the one who reporter Gordon Marino called "a marketing genius" in a 2003 *Wall Street Journal* profile and who the *New York Times* called one of the one hundred African Americans who helped shape the country's history during the twentieth century. This Don King has an estimated net worth of $100 million and has made millions for his boxers that they most likely would not have made without him. This Don King was a key figure in establishing the highly lucrative pay-per-view boxing industry. His company, Don King Productions, promoted some of the highest-grossing pay-per-view events ever, and many of the highest-grossing revenues from attendance at live boxing events.

The other Don King also has a little Robin Hood in him as well. Marino also reported that King donated $600,000 and helped raise $5 million to pay off the mortgage on the Dorothy Height Building in Washington, DC, a structure built on the site of a former slave market—the building is now headquarters of the National Council for Negro Women. And the Don King Foundation has, according to a spokesman for Don King Productions, donated millions of dollars to charitable causes.

JUST KNOW THIS

In boxing, two highly trained athletes of approximately the same weight face each other in a ring to fight four to twelve rounds, each three minutes long. A boxer can win by *knockout, technical knockout,* or *decision.* To win by decision, a boxer earns ten *points* per round won (less for rounds lost), and then each boxer's totals are added up. At least two of three boxing judges must declare him the winner.

Boxing is to street brawling as the Mona Lisa is to paint-by-numbers. It is a highly skilled dance of strategy involving various punch combinations and fancy (quick) footwork. Boxers put themselves through rigorous training regimens to develop not only strength, but also defense, hitting strategies, and lightning-quick reflexes.

Boxing suffers from a lack of oversight and regulation, and it is the only sport in which the goal is to harm your opponent. Don King is the sport's most famous and successful promoter. And it has been a source of fascination for writers through the ages, from Ernest Hemingway to Joyce Carol Oates.

Boxers You Need to Know

The Legends

MUHAMMAD ALI (CASSIUS CLAY), 1942–
NICKNAME: "THE GREATEST"
1960–81: 56 wins, 5 losses, 0 draws

Muhammad Ali is a monumental figure of twentieth-century America, and an extraordinary boxer who enraptured not only this country, but the world. As essayist and critic Stanley Crouch wrote in *Time* in December 2001, "Everything [Ali] did was big, when he was right, when he was wrong, when he embarrassed us, when he inspired us. That finally is why he remains a king of the world."

From the start, Ali did not fit the typical boxer profile. He wasn't born into poverty; he wasn't a juvenile delinquent. In 1942, Cassius Marcellus Clay was born to a middle-class family in Louisville, Kentucky. As a mere eighteen-year-old, he won a gold medal at the 1960 Olympics in Rome. The speed of his hands and feet were remarkable for someone who weighed 190 pounds. After winning the gold, Ali went pro. He was a genius at avoiding being hit thanks to his bobbing, weaving, and fancy footwork.

Ali the Legend came into being in 1964, when Ali (still known as Cassius Clay) took the title of heavyweight champion of the world from Sonny Liston, who was favored by 7–1 odds. It was before this fight that Ali intoned his now unforgettable mantra, "Float like a butterfly, sting like a bee." Before the fight, Ali/Clay announced that he would knock Liston out in the eighth round; shocking the boxing world, Liston gave up after only six. In a rematch a year later, Ali retained his title.

Shortly after his fight with Liston, Ali denounced the name Cassius Clay as one given by slave owners. He announced his allegiance to the Nation of Islam, changing his name to Muhammad Ali. If that weren't enough to keep him in the headlines, he then very publicly refused to be drafted into the army and serve in Vietnam with the incendiary words, "I ain't got no quarrel with them Vietcong." As a result, in 1967 he was stripped of his boxing title and license to box in the United States by the New York State Athletic Commission and the World Boxing Association, and he was convicted of "knowingly and unlawfully refusing induction." He was sentenced to five years in prison and a $10,000 fine.

Ali's actions made him both reviled and beloved. He embodied the issues that roiled the sixties: civil rights, black pride, anti-war sentiment. And he did what few others could not or would not do—he would not bow to the white man, and he would not fight a war that he didn't believe in. During the appeals process, Ali did not serve any time in jail, but he lost some of his peak boxing years. After three years, the Supreme Court overturned his conviction and he was free to box again.

In his absence, Joe Frazier (see below) had risen through the ranks to claim the title of heavyweight champion. When Ali returned to the ring in 1971, he fought Frazier in the first of three matches that would be among the most watched, most publicized, and most thrilling of the century. The 1971 fight is known as "The Fight of the Century." It took place in a sold-out Madison Square Garden in New York City, where *both* fighters were guaranteed $2.5 million (just for fighting, not for winning). In the fifteenth round, Frazier landed a left hook that caught Ali on the jaw and knocked him down. Ali rebounded after a four-count, but Frazier won by unanimous decision.

In 1974, Ali and Frazier fought again in New York, and this time Ali triumphed. Then, in 1975, came the fight known as the "Thrilla in Manila," another match between the two, held in the Philippines. After a grueling fourteen rounds, Frazier surrendered and Ali was the victor. But he said of the fight, "It was like death. Closest thing to dying that I know of."

Another one of Ali's legendary fights is the "Rumble in the Jungle," which pitted him against George Foreman (yes, the guy behind the ubiquitous, easy-to-clean, lean, mean grillin' machines) in Zaire. In this fight, Ali employed what would become known as his "rope-a-dope" strategy. He allowed Foreman to get him up against the ropes and go at him in the early rounds, with the intention of tiring Foreman out. The strategy worked, and Ali knocked Foreman out in the eighth round.

Like so many boxers before and after him, Ali stayed too long, fighting for the last time in 1981. By then, the years of punches to his head had taken their toll, and he now suffers from Parkinson's disease. The indelible image of the great Muhammad Ali that we are left with is that of his shaking hand lighting the torch at the 1996 Olympics in Atlanta.

GEORGE FOREMAN, 1949–
NICKNAME: "BIG GEORGE"
1971–97: 76 wins, 5 losses, 0 draws

If you've turned on the television at all during the last few years, it's likely you've seen this adorable, teddy bear of a man selling the must-have appliance of the millennium: the George Foreman Grill, in its many incarnations. *Who is this cute man and why should I buy a grill from him?* you may have asked. George Foreman is one of the legendary heavyweight champions. When he won an Olympic gold medal in Mexico City in 1968, he was a moody and surly young boxer, who later underwent a great public transformation to become a jovial, friendly presence. His charm endeared him to boxing fans and a broader public, while his not-so-nice demeanor in the ring earned him a record of 76 wins and 5 losses—68 of those wins on knockouts.

One of Foreman's most famous fights took place in 1973 in Kingston, Jamaica, against Joe Frazier, who, two years earlier, had defeated Muhammad Ali. Foreman and Frazier entered the ring with impressive records—Frazier was 29–0, and Foreman was 37–0. Both had won gold medals in the Olympics—Frazier in 1964, Foreman in 1968. Frazier, however, was favored. The illustrious sportscaster Howard Cosell was broadcasting the play-by-play commentary of the fight, and when Frazier was knocked down in the first round, Cosell screamed nine words that have gone down in boxing history: "Down goes Frazier! Down goes Frazier! Down goes Frazier!"

Frazier went on to be knocked down twice more in the first round and three times in the second round, prompting the referee to end the match after the second round and declare Foreman the champion.

Foreman retired in 1977 to become an ordained minister, which, you might say, is quite a departure from boxing. A decade later he made a remarkable comeback, the highlight of which was regaining the heavyweight title at the age of forty-five, making him the oldest ever to do so. Today, George Foreman continues to preach at The Church of Lord Jesus Christ in Houston, Texas. He is also a devoted father of ten (!) kids: five boys and five girls. It's easy to remember the boys' names, as they are all George: George Jr., George III, George IV, George V, and George VI. Foreman was tempted to name all his daughters "George" as well, but he decided it might be overkill. "George" is represented among the girls, though—one is actually named George, and another, Georgetta. His wife, by the way, is named Mary, but George affectionately calls her Joan.

JOE FRAZIER, 1944–
NICKNAME: "SMOKIN' JOE"

1965–81: 32 wins, 4 losses, 1 draw

Frazier rose to prominence during the years (1967–70) in which Muhammad Ali was banned from boxing for refusing to be drafted to serve in Vietnam. This son of a South Carolina sharecropper was most known for his relentlessness in the ring. In 1964, he won an Olympic gold medal, and he went on to be named heavyweight champion of the world in 1968 (and he defended that title six times from 1968 to 1970).

You can't talk about Frazier without talking about Ali, his nemesis throughout his career. As you might imagine, Frazier was none too happy with Ali's self-proclaimed "greatest" status and his constant trash talking, which included calling Frazier a gorilla and an "Uncle Tom." And yet, their three fights—of which Frazier lost two—are what forever etched them both in boxing history. As Pulitzer Prize–winning writer David Halberstam put it, "Technically the loser of two of the three fights, [Frazier] seems not to understand that they ennobled him as much as they did Ali . . . that the only way we know of Ali's greatness is because of Frazier's equivalent greatness, that in the end there was no real difference between the two of them as fighters. . . . These are men who, like it or not, have become prisoners of each other and those three nights."

Frazier's style out of the ring couldn't have been more different from Ali's. While Ali was renouncing the war in Vietnam and declaring himself a living legend, Frazier, according to boxing historian Michael Silver, was simply striving to be "a decent, hardworking, law-abiding, church-going family man, who was too busy trying to support his growing family to get involved in any causes."

EVANDER HOLYFIELD, 1962–

1984–present: 38 wins, 8 losses, 2 draws

Holyfield is probably best known for having his ear partially bitten off by Mike Tyson in their infamous 1997 fight. He is also, perhaps more important, a four-time world heavyweight champion, who, as of November 2004, at the age of forty-two, was still fighting. If he's not careful—if he doesn't hang up his gloves soon once and for all—he might be remembered as yet another athlete who wore away his glory by not knowing when to quit gracefully. At his November 2004 fight against Larry Donald, Holyfield performed so poorly (Donald landed three times as many punches as Holyfield) that the chairman of the New York State Athletic Commission, Ron Scott Stevens, took the unusual action of placing Holyfield on indefinite medical suspension for "poor performance."*

Holyfield doesn't have to keep fighting. He has not fallen into the trap of spending his millions as fast as he makes them. He has made an estimated $200 million from boxing and has pursued other investments as well. And he is generous: Every Fourth of July, Holyfield opens up his cozy, 54,000-square-foot house and 235 acres of land in Fayetteville, Georgia, to 5,000 underprivileged children for an annual picnic and fireworks celebration. And, according to a January 2005 New York Times article about the boxer by Ira Berkow, Holyfield also buys $50,000 worth of toys at Christmas and invites hundreds of children to visit, "to see for themselves that a black man can make it . . . To give them hope and something to strive for."

SUGAR RAY LEONARD, 1952–

1977–97: 36 wins, 3 losses, 1 draw

Sugar Ray Leonard was blessed with two cool names. He was born Ray Charles Leonard after the late, great musician Ray Charles (Leonard's mother wanted him to become a singer), and then he decided to take the name of the boxer he admired most, Sugar Ray Robinson, who fought from the 1940s through the 1960s. Sugar Ray Leonard won championships in five different weight classes. He was the first fighter to earn more than $100 million from boxing.

Outside the ring, Leonard displayed a warm charisma punctuated

---

*Normally, medical suspensions are invoked after a boxer is seriously injured or knocked out.

with a winning smile; inside the ring, he was known for his artistry, reminiscent of Ali's style, and for his raw animal instinct, sniffing out his opponent's weakness and pouncing on it. Or, as Leonard himself put it: "In the ring, I can feel that halo over my head turn into those two little horns."

Leonard's most memorable fights were with Roberto Duran, a top fighter in the 1970s, '80s, and '90s who also held championship titles in various weight classes. The two first fought for the welterweight title in 1980, when Leonard wanted to prove to the world (and perhaps to himself) that he was as macho as Duran. During this match he traded in his usual, more genteel style for one that was brutally blow-to-blow. Leonard lost the fight in a fifteen-round decision and commented afterward that "the fight in Montreal was not a boxing match. It was a street brawl . . . I was determined to stand my ground and fight Duran his way. I don't like Duran's way."

In November of that same year, Leonard fought Duran again, this time fighting *his* way, and emerged victorious. In the eighth round, Duran, the symbol of Latin American "machismo," couldn't take it anymore. "*No más, no más,*" he told the ref, and with those words, the title was again Leonard's.

In 1982, after undergoing surgery for a detached retina, Sugar Ray announced his retirement. This turned out to be the first of many retirements. I suppose being offered $12 million for a single fight (as he was in 1987) is a pretty strong incentive to temporarily un-retire.

JOE LOUIS, 1914–1981
NICKNAME: "THE BROWN BOMBER"
1934–51: 68 wins, 3 losses, 0 draws

Joe Louis shone most brightly in the 1930s. He was a champion on many fronts: in the boxing ring, for blacks living in a segregated America, and for all Americans living through the Depression. Outside the ring, Louis was a perfect gentleman; inside the ropes, he became a fierce fighter with a career record of 68 wins (54 of those coming on knockouts) and 3 losses.

Earlier in the twentieth century, another black boxer, Jack Johnson, had been an affront to white America and had, according to Emmett Berg in the journal *Humanities*, "antagonized the white boxing establishment, first by mercilessly pummeling his white opponents, and second, by cavorting with white women and disregarding the racial boundaries of the era." So, for a long time following the Johnson era, black boxers were shut out from the big fights.

But then along came Joe Louis. His managers saw his talent and groomed him carefully—don't be seen with white women, they told him, don't go into nightclubs alone, and always don a poker face. He followed all of society's rules—until he got into the ring, where he refused to throw fights to white boxers, and just won and won and won. African American writer Vernon Jarrett said of Louis, "He was our nonviolent, violent way of expressing ourselves." According to legend, a black man condemned to die in a South Carolina jail uttered these last words: "Save me, Joe Louis. Save me, Joe Louis. Save me, Joe Louis . . ."

And then there was the America vs. Germany scenario that Louis played out for a rapt nation. In the thirties, life was grim, the Depression wore on, and Hitler was on the rise. In 1936, Joe Louis was already a boxing star when he faced Germany's own boxing phenomenon, Max Schmeling, for the first time. Louis lost that fight after twelve rounds, and the next day the *New York Post* declared that "an idol fell, and the crashing was so complete . . . and so totally unexpected that it broke the hearts of the Negroes of the world." Schmeling's victory—emblematic of the white man's dominance over the black man—fueled the fire of Hitler's demonic Aryan supremacy ideology.

By 1938, Hitler had annexed Austria and was marching into Czechoslovakia, and the competition for heavyweight champion of the world had come down to just two fighters: Louis and Schmeling (Louis was the defending champ, having defeated James J. Braddock in 1937 and defended his title three times before his rematch with Schmeling in 1938). That day, 70,000 people filled Yankee Stadium for the fight while seventy *million* more listened on the radio (the U.S. population was only 130 million at the time, so this was more than half the population!). It was worth tuning in to—in a stunning two minutes and four seconds into the first round, Louis knocked out Schmeling. Thousands poured into the streets of Harlem to celebrate. It wasn't only blacks who reveled in this glorious moment. "It was like we had defeated the Nazis then and there," said boxing trainer Steve Acunto.

"Patriotism overcame prejudice that night," wrote Emmett Berg, "and Americans, white and black, cheered together in Louis's corner."

MIKE TYSON, 1966–
NICKNAME: "IRON MIKE"

1985–present: 50 wins, 5 losses, 0 draws

Mike Tyson is insane—perhaps not all the time, but certainly some of the time. He was briefly, in the 1980s, a great boxer—the youngest heavyweight champion in the history of boxing, in fact—and then he morphed into a rapist, and then he morphed into Hannibal Lecter. He was convicted of rape in 1992 and spent a few years in prison as a result; he has been arrested and convicted of various assault charges; and he bit off parts of Evander Holyfield's ear during a boxing match in 1997. And he has made truly frightening comments such as, "I want to eat your children" (to boxer Lennox Lewis).

It is estimated that Tyson has earned more than $300 million in his career. In 1988, he was paid $20 million for a match against Michael Spinks—which he won by KO in ninety-one seconds, meaning his wages were $450,000 per second. Then, in 2003, he declared bankruptcy. By 2004, he was $38 million in the hole, which may have made him regret spending $2 million on a bathtub a few years earlier. Today, way past his prime, reviled by the press and former fans, he is forced to continue fighting, often in humiliating bouts (most recently in June 2005)—all for the IRS.

One of Tyson's biggest fights was in 2002 against the aforementioned Lennox Lewis, a former heavyweight champion. This took place *after* his rape conviction, and *after* snacking on Holyfield's ear, and still, more than 15,000 people came to see the fight, paying as much as $2,400 a ticket, and another *million* paid $54.95 to watch it on pay-per-view. For losing, Tyson was paid $17.5 million.

In 1988, Joyce Carol Oates was inspired enough by Tyson to write "On Mike Tyson," an extended essay that extols the virtue and magic of this boy wonder who went from reform school to world championship. And then, as David Kindred wrote in *The Sporting News*, Tyson became "the saddest, most frightening, most damning evidence of man's capability for bestiality. The fury and the rage that rendered opponents helpless against him in the ring, is the same fury and rage that brought him ruin."

Legend in Training

OSCAR DE LA HOYA, 1971–
NICKNAME: "GOLDEN BOY"

1992–present: 37 wins, 4 losses, 0 draws

Gals, if you're experiencing a moment of boredom at work or elsewhere (or, dare I say, while reading this chapter), I have the remedy: Log on to www.goldenboypromotions.com. Staring at you will be a supreme hottie. All active boxers have beautiful bodies (that may seem like a sweeping generalization, but it's true), but not all boxers have beautifully carved faces to go along with the abs and pecs. Oscar does.

In brief, De La Hoya is a champion boxer. He's also determined to become the next entrepreneurial force in the business of boxing, and to bring boxing back into prominence. He was given the nickname "Golden Boy" in 1992, when he was the only U.S. boxer to take home a gold medal in the Olympics. Since turning pro, he has won titles in *six* different weight classes (and you thought your weight fluctuated!). And over the past few years, he's directed his energy outside the ring as well, with wide-ranging business interests in everything from Spanish newspapers to television production, real estate ventures to, most visibly, Golden Boy Promotions, the company he founded with the aim of restoring respectability and visibility to the boxing profession.

De La Hoya grew up in the ghetto of East Los Angeles, the son of

Mexican immigrants. Both his father and grandfather were boxers in their native Mexico, so when little Oscar started getting beaten up by the neighborhood bullies, his father took him to the gym. There he learned skills that got him off the streets and into the Goodwill Games where, at seventeen, he was the youngest boxer to win the gold medal in his weight class. The thrill of victory was soon tempered, however, by his mother's death from breast cancer at age thirty-eight. De La Hoya vowed to honor her memory by winning the gold at the 1992 Barcelona Olympics, and so he did. Since then, he has earned more than $150 million in his professional career.

Glossary

Bout: A bout (sometimes called a *match*) is a contest between two boxers. (It's interesting that boxing uses a term more commonly associated with illness, as in "I had a bout with the flu," to describe its competitions.) A bout consists of *rounds* that are three minutes long, with a one-minute break between rounds. The number of rounds per bout varies, depending on what state or country the bout is taking placing in.

Break: When two boxers are in a *clinch* (when they're holding on to or leaning on each other without throwing punches), the referee will order the boxers to *break*, meaning to step back and separate.

Caution: A minor admonishment from a referee for a breaking a rule. Three cautions result in a warning. A warning results in a loss of points for the perpetrator or a gain in points for his opponent. Three warnings result in disqualification.

Clean Punching: Clean punching is punching that does the job it's supposed to do: land on your opponent firmly and unblocked. Clean punches are sharp, crisp jabs, short tight hooks, and uppercuts. A punch that lands on an opponent's glove is *not* a clean punch, nor is a punch that is partially blocked. Judges use clean punching as one of four criteria for scoring fights.

Clinch: When a boxer holds his opponent or leans against him, it's called a clinch. It's a defensive tactic in a way, since the opponent cannot punch when being held. The referee is responsible for breaking up clinches.

Cut Man: In addition to a ring physician, each boxer has a "cut man," whose job is to fix the cuts and reduce the swelling that boxers get while being pummeled.

Decision: A decision is one of three ways a boxer can win a fight. (The other two are by knockout or technical knockout.) When determining a winner by decision, three judges use a scoring system called the ten-point must system, which is based on four criteria: clean punching, effective aggressiveness, ring generalship, and defense. A boxer can win by *unanimous decision* (when all three judges list the same boxer as the winner), by *split decision* (when a boxer wins on two of the three judges' cards), or by *majority decision* (when two judges score one boxer the winner, but the third judge scores the bout a draw).

Defense: In boxing, defense is the strategy of not getting hit. Boxers defend themselves by bobbing, weaving, parrying, blocking, sidestepping, using the clinch, and doing the mambo, or better yet, the Lambada. This is one of the four criteria that judges use to score fights.

Down: A boxer is considered *down* if he is knocked down, if any part of his body other than his feet is touching the floor, or if he has taken a serious blow and might as well be down (if he's hanging helpless over the ropes, for example, or if he's dazed, confused, and out of it, but still on his feet). When a boxer is down, the action is stopped by the referee. The ref then begins a count of ten (also called a "ten-count"). If the boxer doesn't get back up within those ten seconds, his opponent wins by knockout.

Draw: A draw is a tie—boxing matches are allowed to end in ties. With three judges, this may seem illogical, but if two of the three judges score a match a draw and the third judge gives more points to one boxer, it is still considered a draw, because the "majority" (of the judges) scored it as such. A boxer's individual record states total number of wins, losses, and draws.

Effective Aggressiveness: The opposite of ineffective aggressiveness, which is like a dog chasing its own tail. In boxing terms, effective aggressiveness means that a boxer is landing punches while moving forward. Just moving forward and not landing punches is clearly not effective. Effective aggressiveness is one of the four criteria judges use to score fights.

Feint: To fake a punch. Boxers will feint to induce an opponent to open up into a vulnerable position (as in, "What a great feint we just saw! Hard-Hitting Harry totally faked that left jab, then came back with a powerful uppercut").

Foul: Any illegal move, including, but not limited to: hitting below the belt; hitting with any part of the body other than the knuckles; head-butting; assaulting or acting aggressively toward the referee; and biting your opponent's ear off (à la Mike Tyson vs. Evander Holyfield). The punishment for a foul can range from reprimand to deduction of points to disqualification.

Heart: A boxer is said to have "heart" when he has the ability, the will, to fight through injury, or to just keep going and going when he's worn down.

Hold: see *clinch*.

Hook: A type of punch executed with a bent elbow, and with power. The punch curves around to its target (the other guy's head or body), thus forming the shape of a hook.

Jab: A straight punch that doesn't pack as much power as a hook and that can be used as a setup for a more powerful punch, such as a hook or uppercut. It can also be used as a defensive tactic to keep the opponent off balance.

Knockdown: A boxer is *down*, or *knocked down*, when any part of his body other than his feet makes contact with the floor, or when he is hanging helplessly over the ropes as the result of a legal blow. A boxer loses points for a knockdown.

Knockout (KO): A knockout is when a boxer has been knocked down and does not get up before the count of ten. In such a case, the boxer who is down is said to have lost by knockout.

Mandatory Eight Count: When a boxer is knocked down and gets back up within ten seconds, the referee will count to eight to determine if he is fit to continue. It doesn't matter when during the ten-count the boxer gets up—the mandatory eight begins once he is back on his feet. Once the boxer gets up, he can't fall down again. He has to remain on his feet for the full eight seconds.

Neutral Corner: During a match, each boxer has his own corner to return to between rounds. There he has his assistants (called *seconds*), coach or trainer, and *cut man*. The other two corners are called *neutral corners*. When a boxer is knocked down, the referee sends the other boxer to the farthest neutral corner.

Ring Generalship: A boxer who is winning in ring generalship is controlling the fight—he is putting his opponent where he wants him, controlling the fight's tempo, and displaying movement around the ring. If Tough-Guy Tom nullifies the aggression of Hard-Hitting Harry, Tom is the ring general. When a fighter gets his opponent against the ropes, thus taking control, he is exhibiting ring generalship. Ring generalship is one of the four criteria that judges use to score fights.

Scoring Blow: In boxing, refers to a specific punch, executed with the knuckles (as indicated by the white stripe of the glove), that lands cleanly on the opponent's head or torso, as in "Tough-Guy Tom just walloped Hard-Hitting Harry with a decisive scoring blow." Boxers can get points for scoring blows.

Second: A boxer's assistant; someone who gives him advice during the match, between rounds. Boxers often have more than one second (but he is still called a second, not a third or a fourth).

Southpaw: A left-handed boxer.

Standing Eight Count: He weebles, he wobbles, but he won't fall down. When a fighter is throttled by a punch and looks completely dazed but doesn't actually go down, the referee stops the fight and gives the boxer eight seconds to start fighting again. If he doesn't, he loses, and his opponent is declared the winner by technical knockout.

Straight Right (or Right Cross): The straight right is a basic and very powerful punch, in which the punch is delivered from a straight arm to the opponent's head or body. It often follows a left jab or jabs. It is called a "straight right" because most boxers, like the rest of the world, are right-handed.

Technical Knockout (TKO): Any time the ref stops the fight because he decides that one boxer is unable to continue, the boxer's opponent wins by TKO. When the referee stops a fight on a mandatory eight count, a standing eight count, or because of an injury, it is considered a TKO.

Ten-Point Must System: The *ten-point must system* is the scoring system used in boxing. The system states that the winner of a round *must* receive ten points, and the loser nine or less.

Third Man in the Ring: The referee. He is the only person allowed in the ring aside from the two boxers.

Uppercut: A punch executed in a vertical path. In a right uppercut, the boxer will lower the right side of his body slightly and then deliver an upward punch, usually aimed at the chin.

Car Racing

THE SOUND: *Vroom, Vroom.*

THE LOOK: Men in jumpsuits plastered with ads—sitting in weird-looking cars plastered with even more ads.

THE PLACE: A racetrack (America has 1,200!).

THE ORGANIZATION: NASCAR—the National Association for Stock Car Automobile Racing—is the one you need to know, although there are other, smaller organizations for different types of auto racing.

> There are only three sports. Bullfighting, mountain climbing and car racing. All the rest are just games.
> —*Ernest Hemingway (or maybe someone else)**

Car racing. The great conundrum regarding the sport is whether it's a sport at all. I mean, there *is* a difference between running the length of a football field with the aid of only cleats, or skating at thirty miles per hour with the aid of only skates, and zooming around a racetrack with the aid of 750 horsepower. According to *The New Oxford American Dictionary*, sport is defined as "an activity involving physical exertion and skill in which an individual or team competes against another or others." Well, car racing most definitely requires physical skill—skill can mean the difference between life and death for a race car driver. And it's fiercely competitive, on both an individual and team level. So the remaining element is physical exertion—and when you look closely at what car racing actually requires of its participants, it's hard to deny that physical

---

*Jim Wright, a professor of sociology at the University of Central Florida and, more importantly, the author of *Fixin' to Git: One Fan's Love Affair with NASCAR's Winston Cup*, tried in vain to confirm that this quote did indeed come from Hemingway, but alas, was unable to do so. Wright went to the Hemingway House in Key West to settle the matter once and for all, but the closest he came was the Hemingway Resource Center saying only that it sounds like something the author would have written.

exertion is a component. The driver must endure temperatures that sometimes climb into the hundreds, for hours; and the crew has to be able to lift and change seventy-pound tires in seconds!

If you're still not convinced that car racing is a sport, how about this: The crème de la crème of race car drivers get paid millions of dollars, plus they get all kinds of endorsement deals, plus they have fan clubs and have celebrity status, and dozens of lovely ladies swoon in their presence. This makes them either athletes or rock stars. But the last rock star to wear a jumpsuit was Elvis and—trust me on this—he's dead.

Regardless of whether it fits the technical definition of a sport or not, in the United States, car racing—particularly NASCAR (National Association for Stock Car Automobile Racing)—is HUGE. Millions and millions of people watch car racing on TV (it's second only to the NFL for television audience size) and millions of people go to the track during the racing season, which runs from February to November, to witness cars (and trucks, in some races) going at speeds of roughly 200 miles per hour. The speed is the core attraction of the sport—everyone loves to go fast, and since we can't do much above seventy miles per hour legally anywhere, we must live vicariously by watching the pros. As Jim Wright, author of *Fixin' to Git: One Fan's Love Affair with NASCAR's Winston Cup* says, "The sheer physical danger of trying to drive a hot rod as fast as it will go, fender-to-fender and bumper-to-bumper with a few dozen other testosterone-crazed wild men, even when experienced vicariously, is what makes automobile racing so addictive. And any fan who says otherwise is lying."

HERE'S HOW IT WORKS

 The object of a car race is to go as fast as you can and beat all the other cars to the finish line, without crashing your car. The cars travel around 200 miles per hour, and a typical race is several hundred miles long and lasts three to four hours. Good drivers take into account that tires wear out, track conditions vary, and accidents help no one—in short, skill, finesse, and a level head count.

While car racing is in fact dangerous, there are many safety precautions that minimize catastrophic crashes and fatalities.

Car racing can be divided into different categories, depending on the type of car that's used. The major categories are **dragsters**, *sports cars*, **open-wheel cars,** and **stock cars**. Within these categories are different **series**, which are similar to "leagues" in other sports—like baseball's American League and National League. The series are then further subdivided into *levels*, which are comparable to baseball's major league versus minor league.

Stock car racing—under the auspices of NASCAR—is the type of car racing that has captivated America, and NASCAR's drivers are the ones making headlines. The car racing tools that you'll need for your water-cooler chat mostly involve NASCAR, so that's what we will focus on in this chapter—but first let's take a quick look at the other categories. (Admit it, secretly you've been yearning to know what a *dragster* really is.)

THE MAJOR TYPES OF RACING CARS

Dragsters

Dragsters look like a cartoon fantasy version of a car. Most have long, pointy fronts with small front tires and bigger rear tires, and they are engineered to travel a short distance (a quarter-mile) in a very short period of time, meaning very, very, very fast. (Dragsters can travel up to 335 miles per hour—and they can go from 0 to 100 miles per hour in less than a second!) And the driver sits in an open cockpit. Think of what that does to one's hairdo!

Sports Cars

These cars are modeled on the expensive sports cars that we've all heard of, like Ferraris or Maseratis, but they are designed specifically for racing, and are not sold in your local Ferrari showroom. They look like a *distant* cousin of an average Ferrari or Maserati (but then again, there's really no such thing as an *average* Ferrari or Maserati).

Open-Wheel Cars

Open-wheel cars look nothing like your ordinary car. They have an open cockpit (no roofs), no fenders, and big wheels—they sort of look like powerful, mutated insects. In the United States, open-wheel racing is the second most popular form of car racing (right after stock car racing). The major *series* for open-wheel car racing are: **Formula One**, **Champ Car World Series**, and the **Indy Racing League (IRL)**.

FORMULA ONE

Not to be confused with a nourishing infant formula, Formula One is the world's most well-known open-wheel series. Formula One racing, also known as Grand Prix racing, takes place all over the globe. Some of the series' most famous races, like the Grand Prix of Monaco, are *road races*, meaning the cars race on actual roads, not on a racetrack. In the United States the most famous name associated with Formula One is Mario Andretti.

INDY RACING LEAGUE (IRL)

This series takes place only in the United States. The Indianapolis 500—or simply the "Indy 500"—one of the most famous of all car races, is part of the IRL. The Indy 500 is a 500-mile, 200-lap race that dates back to 1911—and with the exception of a couple of years during the two World Wars, it has been an annual event. Also very cool is the fact that four women have competed in the Indy 500, lending a whole new meaning to the phrase "fast women."* On May 29, 2005, the IRL became front-page news when Danica Patrick, the fourth woman ever to compete in the Indy 500, proved herself to be a real contender, placing fourth in the race. Before then, the best finish by a woman was ninth place in 1978.

---

*NASCAR, although dominated by men, has also had more than a dozen women compete in top championship series.

CHAMP CAR WORLD SERIES

Champ Car World Series was formerly CART (Championship Auto Racing Teams), which went bankrupt in 2003. CART's assets were purchased by a group of investors who formed this new circuit. Most of this series' races are in the United States, but some are in far-flung places like Korea, Mexico City, and Australia.

Formula One, IRL, and Champ Car (and NASCAR) compete for drivers to some extent. Many great drivers like Mario Andretti and A. J. Foyt have raced with several different kinds of cars in several different series.

Stock Cars

Start with your basic Chevy, Ford, Dodge, or any American-made family sedan. Sprinkle it with millions of dollars' worth of engineering research, special parts, mega-horsepower, and a crew of one hundred to maintain. Then strip it of all the essentials—such as vanity mirrors, beverage holders, headlights, brake lights, and doors—and you've got yourself a stock car. They do look vaguely similar to ordinary cars—certainly more than Formula One cars or dragsters—but they are custom-built from scratch and are designed to travel upward of 200 miles per hour.

Now on to the main event of stock car racing—and of car racing as an American spectator sport.

NASCAR

NASCAR is deeply rooted in the South. It was born from outlaw moonshine runners driving as fast as they could on back-country dirt roads to get out of the sheriff's reach. Over time, it evolved into informal competitions on dirt tracks, and eventually paved raceways. As the tracks evolved, so did the cars, which became highly specialized versions of regular cars. Then, in 1948, Bill France—who had competed in the informal stock car races of the 1930s—founded NASCAR, creating a national, organized association for stock car racing that instituted rules, an insurance plan, and guaranteed purses similar to the NFL or the NBA.

NASCAR has worked hard to bring the sport to a wider national audience and to shed its reputation as a redneck, backwoods sport. Today, racetracks are no longer confined to the Southern states but are sprouting up all over the country, and in the last decade or so, NASCAR has experienced tremendous growth in nationwide popularity.

NASCAR has a very big television audience—much larger, in fact, than the NBA. In 2004, the average audience for the televised weekly *Nextel Cup Series* races was ten million, while for NBA games, the audience was closer to 3.4 million. In fact, NASCAR is second only to the NFL in television sports ratings—perhaps because, in the Nextel Cup Series, NASCAR runs only thirty-seven races a year. So, like the NFL, you get only a weekly dose of your favorite team (as opposed to the NBA and Major League Baseball, which airs several games per week). NASCAR has been marching up the ratings chart ever since 2001, when the organization signed a $2.8 billion deal with Fox and NBC.

In an article in *USA Today* in 2004, Robert Lipsyte discussed how and why NASCAR has captivated the nation: "NASCAR has [won our hearts] for the same reasons baseball once did. It is a uniquely American spectacle that . . . offers friends and families a chance to congregate around a kind of campfire and share the comfort food for the soul. But NASCAR has more. The courage of the star athlete is painfully, sometimes fatally, authentic . . . It is a true team sport of varied everyday skills. More than a hundred hands, from those of accountants to engineers to 'wrenches,' carry the driver. And, of course, almost all of us drive, or can't wait to."

Each race, like each NFL game, is an *event*. More than a quarter million people attend some races—everyone from CEOs to those who have scraped together just enough money to get there. In addition to the grandstands, people, by the thousands, arrive in motor homes and RVs and watch the race from "rooftops." Each weekly race is a several-day affair; it's just one long, raucous party.

In a May 31, 1999, *Time* article, Steve Lopez vividly describes his maiden voyage to a race: ". . . 120,000 fans walk into the stadium wearing roughly half a million racing-related logos. The Winston people are giving away cigarettes.* . . . The noise is obscene . . . The smells of raw horse-power, burned rubber and expectorated snuff are cooked by a wicked sun.

"This is the most unapologetic, politically incorrect, crassly American spectacle I've witnessed since my last trip to Vegas.

"I'm beginning to see the appeal."

NASCAR has one very obvious shortcoming: It suffers from an extreme lack of diversity—it is just about all white. But the organization is actively addressing the problem. In May 2004, Magic Johnson (of NBA fame) signed on to become NASCAR's co-chairman of its new Executive Steering Committee for Diversity.

Johnson, in his unpaid position, will help NASCAR improve diversity within its ranks and market the sport to minorities. Certainly a step in the right direction.

THE SERIES

Within NASCAR, there are three main divisions: the *Nextel Cup Series* (formerly called the Winston Cup Series[†]), the *Busch Series*, and the *Craftsman Truck Series*.[‡] The Nextel and Busch series are very similar, but the Busch series is one notch below the Nextel—the Busch series races are usually shorter and on smaller tracks, and the Busch cars aren't designed to go as fast as the Cup cars. (Drivers will often graduate from the Busch to the Nextel.) The Nextel Cup Series—often referred to simply as the Cup Series—is where you'll find the superstars and big money. Finally, the Craftsman Truck Series is raced with pickup trucks. NASCAR created this series in 1995. Interestingly (and scarily), the horsepower of the pickup trucks used is closer to the Cup cars than the Busch cars:

---

*Until 2004, Winston was the top sponsor of the Cup Series.
[†]Nextel took over title sponsorship in 2004.
[‡]Additionally, NASCAR has several lower profile series, where drivers often hone their skills before moving up to the big leagues.

Nextel Cup cars have 750 horsepower; the Craftsman trucks have 710; and Busch cars have about 550. (Meanwhile your neighbor's passenger pickup has about 160 horsepower; the $14,000 Honda Civic down the road has about 110 horsepower; and the gleaming $118,000 BMW 7 Series tooting around town has about 440. Hey, you get what you pay for.)

SPONSORSHIPS: *Where They Get the Big Money (and All of Those Tacky Decals)*

Within NASCAR are teams, just like teams in the NFL or MLB. The teams have owners and various members. Because it costs millions of dollars to operate a NASCAR team, owners procure *sponsorships* from various companies.* This is why you'll see decals and logos splattered all over every inch of the cars, all over the uniforms, and all over just about everything associated with NASCAR. The sponsorship is so brazen that it becomes a spectacle in and of itself. Kind of like J-Lo's wardrobe.

NASCAR makes no bones about the BIG money associated with it—it's proud that it represents megabucks. To NASCAR fans, the money actually legitimizes the sport.

THE MONEY BEHIND THE MOTORS

To give you an idea why NASCAR teams are so expensive to operate, consider this: Motors alone cost around $40,000 to $50,000, and they must be replaced *after every race*—not to mention the motors used for testing sessions and qualifying races that must also be replaced. (In order to perform at peak performance, much of a race car must be replaced for each race—a little different from your tootin'-around-town car, which often comes with three-year warranties for everything!) Jim Wright tells us that a race team can go through a quarter-million dollars worth of engines *in a single weekend.*† During the racing season, a team might use upward of seventy-five engines.

---

*According to Robert Lipsyte in *USA Today* (October 29, 2003), it takes $12 million to make a top car competitive and millions more to promote the sponsorship.
†Recently, NASCAR instituted a one-motor-per-weekend policy, so teams are less likely to hemorrhage money so quickly.

THE TEAMS

Included in a NASCAR "team" is the car, the driver, and everyone else involved, from the engineers to the mechanics. While the drivers are far and away the big stars of NASCAR, fans are emphatic that it is a team sport. And, when you consider what goes into building, transporting, and maintaining a race car, the driver just might be the *least* important part of the team! Besides the driver, the four most important members of a NASCAR team are the *team owner*, the *team manager*, the **crew chief**, and the *car chief*.

The *owner* of a NASCAR team is like the owner of any other sports team. He has the final say in hiring, and he controls the money. In NASCAR, the owner is also the one who's responsible for procuring the necessary sponsorships for the team. The *manager* of a NASCAR team does the owner's bidding. He oversees everything, from hiring personnel to ordering equipment to the details of the day-to-day operation.

The *crew chief* is like the lead surgeon in a complex operation requiring several hands—and he is key to the success of a driver and a race. In short, his job is to know *everything* about the car. He oversees every aspect of engineering, building, and maintaining the race cars. He may not do the actual hands-on work, but he knows exactly what needs to be done, and he gives directions accordingly. In addition, he is responsible for all racing strategy

THE ENGINEERS AND MECHANICS ON A NASCAR CREW INCLUDE:

*engine specialist

*tire specialist

*engineers

*general mechanics

*truck driver (to transport the car, a backup car, and a portable shop)

*fabricators (responsible for attaching the sheet metal to the frame and making custom parts)

*engine builders

*parts specialists

*manicurist and facialist (Wait, that's not NASCAR; that's my personal dream team.)

decisions. Right below the crew chief in pecking order is the *car chief*. He's the guy who actually executes the work that the crew chief orders. The crew chief will likely spend a lot of time at the computer figuring out how to improve the car according to highly complex engineering specifications, while the car chief will work with the rest of the crew (engineers and mechanics) to physically get the job done.

AT THE TRACK

Before a NASCAR race, several preliminary events take place over the course of about three days. One day (usually a Friday) is allotted for qualifying races (more on qualifying below).* The following day is for practice and making final adjustments to the car. And the next day, usually a Sunday, is race day. A Nextel Cup Series race is typically 400 to 600 miles long and lasts three to four hours.

One interesting thing to note about NASCAR is that there are a lot of variations within the sport—the rules change according to the tracks (which vary in length and shape), the conditions, the drivers, and so on. Unlike, say, football, where the field is always one hundred yards long, or basketball, where the net is always ten feet off the floor, NASCAR rules and specifications vary from race to race.

THE RACETRACK

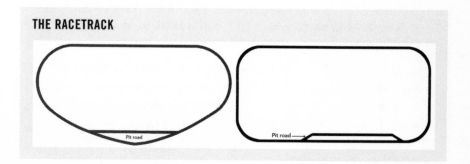

*At the Daytona 500, one of the major annual NASCAR races, qualifying stretches over two days.

NASCAR racetracks vary in shape and length. Above are two typical shapes.* Racetracks have two or more lanes, depending on the track, but for all races, at the beginning of a race, cars line up in two lanes, two by two. *Pit road* is where the cars pull off the racetrack for refueling, tire changes, and other repairs during the race.

Spectator stands are located outside the track, but some racetracks have viewing areas within the track—in the "infield," so to speak. The infield is general-admission madness: It's where people pitch tents; park their motor homes, cars, or pickup trucks; and party it up for a few days.

RACY RACES AND RACETRACKS

Daytona International Speedway: A 2.5-mile *superspeedway,* Daytona International Speedway in Daytona Beach, Florida, hosts the *Daytona 500,* one of the most famous NASCAR races, sometimes called "The Great American Race," and the one that kicks off the NASCAR season in February. Every NASCAR driver dreams of winning the Daytona 500.

Indianapolis Motor Speedway: This Midwestern venue is best known for hosting the *Indianapolis 500* (usually just called the "Indy 500"), an IRL event that has been held there since 1911. It is also home to the *United States Grand Prix* (a Formula One race) and NASCAR's *Brickyard 400.* The Indianapolis Motor Speedway was originally built as a test facility for the Indiana car industry. After a series of races in 1909, it was paved with 3.2 million bricks, of which only a strip marking the start/finish line remains. The rest of the 2.5-mile track has since been paved with a surface more suitable for 200 mph speeds.

Talladega Superspeedway: Located in Talladega, Alabama, Talladega Superspeedway is the biggest and fastest racetrack in the world. It is a 2.66-mile track that can accommodate 143,000 seated spectators, and thousands more in the surrounding area. It is home to the *EA Sports 500* (aka the Talladega), a Nextel Cup Race that takes place in October, and is part of the "Chase for the Championship" series of races (see page 281).

---

*IRL and the Champ Cars often use the same racetracks as NASCAR.

TOP TWO REASONS WHY I COULD NEVER BE A NASCAR DRIVER

1. For me, it's all about the beverage holders. I base my car-purchasing decisions largely on the efficacy and convenience of the beverage holder. Will it hold a large coffee as well as a regular size? How about a Diet Coke? Snapple? The new Vitamin Water? Apparently race car drivers are not concerned with this. How odd.

2. I have a mild-to-medium left-turn phobia—there are certain left turns I just won't make. I plan my errand routes according to left turns. Sometimes this is inconvenient. For example, I have to go to the dry cleaners *before* the bank because the reverse would mean making a life-threatening left turn. But what if I'm out of cash and need to go the bank first? Well, I either just blow off going the dry cleaners that day and go only to the bank, or I drive about three miles out of the way to complete both errands. (Okay, so maybe it's a medium-to-severe left-turn phobia.) The point is, I would probably have some issues making a sharp left at 180 mph. I assume NASCAR aficionado Jim Wright is not afraid of left turns, but he has noted that left-turn phobics are fond of saying, "maybe two wrongs don't make a right, but thank God, three rights do make a left!"

QUALIFYING

In order to compete in a race, a driver must qualify for it. During *qualifying*, as the process is called, a driver is alone on the racetrack and, in simple terms, tries to go as fast as he can around the track. If a driver doesn't go fast enough during *qualifying*, he won't be eligible for the race.

The driver who is the fastest in qualifying is called the **pole winner** (or **pole sitter**). This driver wins the **pole position**—he gets to start the actual race in the most favorable position on the track: on the front row, on the inside of the track. The second fastest winner starts on the *outside pole* (the outside of the front row—the part of the track closest to the grandstand). The other cars line up in twos behind the front row.

The advantage to winning the pole position is obvious—that driver starts off leading the pack on the inside, and so he starts the race as the driver closest to winning. And the pole winner gets money just for winning the pole. Before I learned about car racing, I thought "sitting on the pole" meant something else entirely, something that could result in pregnancy if proper precautions weren't taken.

THE RACE

A typical Nextel Cup Series race has forty-three cars (twenty-one rows of two cars, with the forty-third car alone in the back). Some spots are reserved for *provisional entries,* which basically ensure that the top drivers get in the race even if they completely blew qualifying. The provisional system is complex, but it's based on *points* earned by car owners. Owners get points every time their car is in a race (more on the points system below).

Before the race begins, drivers warm up by following a **pace car** around the track for a few laps. Then, after the laps are completed, the pace car peels off the track, the *flagman* lowers a green flag, and—*zoom, zoom, zoom*—they're off! Once the race begins, it's not quite accurate to say that the drivers go as fast as they can. Good drivers are very skilled—and patient—taking into account that track conditions vary and accidents help no one. So, unlike qualifying, where drivers must go as fast as they can, a good NASCAR driver is *not* all about speed—finesse and stamina count as well. There is also that worrying little issue of passing a car at 180 miles an hour without crashing.

There's an interesting aerodynamic phenomenon that takes place during car races called **drafting**. Drafting is when one car breaks through the air and creates a vacuum or funnel of sorts for the cars directly behind it—allowing them to go faster. Drafting explains why you'll see a bunch of cars nose-to-tail, sticking together, going around and around. A good driver will use the draft, then wait for an opportune moment to pass the car in front of him.

NOT SO FAST, BUDDY . . . RESTRICTOR PLATES: THE GREAT DEBATE

It's no surprise that three of the most celebrated racetracks (Daytona, Indianapolis, and Talladega) are three of the longest: The longer the track, the faster the cars can go. Each of these tracks is at least 2.5 miles in length—long by racetrack standards.

At Daytona and Talladega, NASCAR requires cars to have **restrictor plates.** A restrictor plate is a device that is attached to a car's carburetor to reduce the horsepower, and thus reduce the speed of the car. While it seems contrary to the whole concept of racing cars to reduce a car's speed, the decision to do this was made for one important reason: safety. As technology made it possible for stock cars to go upward of 200 miles per hour, the danger factor increased dramatically—and not just for drivers, but for fans, too. NASCAR realized that an out-of-control, airborne car leaving the track at 200 miles per hour could become a deadly missile in the grandstand.

There is a lot of grumbling and dissent about "to restrict" or "not to restrict," and "how to restrict." Some drivers agree that restrictions are necessary but think that the restrictor plate is not the best solution.

THE PITS

Traveling at tremendous speeds for hundreds of laps and accumulating hundreds of miles simply cannot be done without stopping. Tires need to be changed, fuel needs to be replenished, and other quick repairs need to be made—that's what *pit stops* are for.

When the race car pulls in for a pit stop, a crew of seven snap to and work in unbelievable synchronicity to do whatever needs to be done as fast as possible. Most pit stops last from fifteen to twenty-three seconds. The length of a pit stop can be the difference between winning and losing—every second counts. Thus, drivers often try to make pit stops during a *caution flag* (when the cars are asked to slow down for one reason or another) so they don't lose too much fast racing time.

The main thing that separates real-life driving from race-car driving is that the drivers don't pee at the pit stops. They don't pee for the whole race, in fact (which is another reason I could never be a race car driver). What's the point of a pit stop if you can't pee?

THE FLAGS

If you think that there's simply a green flag for "go" and a checkered flag to announce the winner, you're sadly mistaken. There are almost as many flags employed during a race as there are varieties of khakis sold at the Gap (okay, maybe not *that* many).

Green

As usual, green means go. It signals the start of a race.

Yellow

The yellow flag is a *caution flag*—it's waved when drivers need to slow down because the track is unsafe. (The track can be unsafe due to rain, an accident, debris or oil on the track, and so on.) When the yellow flag is waved, drivers must slow down *immediately* and proceed, in order, to the start/finish line. Once there, they begin a series of caution laps, during which cars cannot pass each other.

Races can end on a caution flag—whichever driver was in the lead when the caution flag was waved becomes the winner. The fans generally don't like it when this happens because it is essentially preempting the last few laps of competition. However, some drivers and fans feel it creates a dangerous situation *not* to end on caution with only a few laps left. In this situation, once the race resumes, since the drivers who aren't in the lead have only a limited time to win, mayhem results in the last few laps, often leading to accidents.

On average, a caution flag comes out three or four times during a race, but it can also come out more than a dozen times. (There is no limit.)

Red

When the red flags come out, cars must immediately stop wherever they are on the track. A pace car will come out and slowly lead the cars to a designated safe place. This flag is used for extremely dangerous situations where it is impossible to continue even under caution. Heavy rain or big wrecks will bring out a red flag, and the race will be suspended until conditions improve.

Black

A black flag is waved to a specific driver when something is obviously wrong with his car, such as oil leaking or smoke billowing out; or if the driver breaks a rule; or if he is so slow that he is a danger to other drivers. When the flag is waved, the driver must get off the track and go to *pit road.**

The driver knows when the flag is for him because his car number will be on the flag. If he ignores the flag, a new, more ominous black flag will come out with an "X" on it. This signifies that his car won't be scored any more, so it behooves a driver to obey the black flag.

Blue with a Diagonal Stripe

This flag is used to signal to a driver that faster, lead-lap cars are about to pass him, and he must yield. Seems unfair, but this is usually only waved at a driver who is a lap down and who is going significantly slower than the cars racing for the win. He could interfere with the real competition among the leading cars.

White

The white flag signals that the driver in the lead is on his final lap. In other words, it means there's one lap to go in the race.

---

*Pit road is a road that is usually located inside the racetrack, parallel to one of the *straightaways* (the longer, straight part of the oval). As you can guess, it is where pit stops are made.

Checkered

This is the flag a driver wants to be the first to see. It's waved when the winner has crossed the finish line.

NASCAR DRIVERS ARE *HOT*

No, I mean *really*. The temperature in the race car can get up to 130 degrees, and drivers wear fire-resistant jumpsuits, fire-retardant long underwear, and space-age, Jetsons-like boots and gloves (which also protect against fire). Whether the drivers are "hotties" is an entirely different discussion. Suffice it to say that NASCAR, like all sports, has its fair share.

RULES

Official NASCAR rules are not made available to the general public. Is it a matter of national security? Evidence of organized crime? No. It's probably just because they are so chock full of technical mumbo-jumbo that they are incomprehensible to anyone without an advanced engineering degree *and* a keen interest in cars. For example, a NASCAR engine must always have between 350 and 358 c.i. (bore × bore × 0.7854 × stroke × 8) and no greater than a 12:1 compression ratio. If you have even an inkling about what that means, *you don't need to be reading this section.* On the other hand, if this stuff revs your engine, you can request the information from NASCAR.

One easier-to-understand NASCAR rule is that the cars must be "American-made steel bodied passenger sedans." Also, there is a rule regarding *rough driving* that speaks to things such as bumping into another car or causing another car to crash when an accident could have been avoided. But this rule is very, very vague, so a bump may mean a penalty or it may not. Ditto for a crash.

When a driver breaks a rule, he is penalized by losing a lap (he must go to his pit box and come to a full stop, often losing a lap as a result);

having *points* deducted (see below for more on the points system); or incurring monetary fines.

A RACING MOVIE THAT'LL REV YOUR ENGINE

Days of Thunder (1990): A stellar cast makes this movie about a hotshot stock car racer (Tom Cruise) who a gets chance to go big-time in NASCAR shine. Other members of the cast include Nicole Kidman, Robert Duvall, and Randy Quaid.

INSPECTIONS

To ensure a level playing field for all drivers, every part of the car must adhere to rigid specifications. Of course, crews spend much of their waking hours trying to get around these rules by doing things like putting a bump in a door that may create turbulence for other cars in the race, or lowering their motor mounts so the car will have a lower center of gravity and handle better. (What's allowed and what isn't in car racing is not unlike the fine line between allowable "supplements" and illegal performance-enhancing drugs in other sports.) The cars are inspected again and again prior to the race, and the winning car (and sometimes the top three cars) gets inspected *after* the race to make sure the car is in compliance.

SAFETY

It does seem somewhat oxymoronic to write about NASCAR and safety in the same sentence. But the reality is that NASCAR drivers are going to walk away from accidents that you or I surely would not. NASCAR race cars, in addition to being built to travel at speeds of 200 miles per hour, are also made to protect the drivers. Below are some of the safety features that these cars have:

* No glass—the cars have no headlights, taillights, or side-windows, which is rather dangerous on the interstate, but, for race cars, means there's no glass to shatter in an accident. The front and rear windshields are made of Lexan, a hard, shatterproof plastic.

✳ The tires have an inner liner, so they don't explode when they run over or into something on the track.

✳ The drivers wear a mega–seat belt, called a *five-point seat belt* because it is formed by five belts that come together in the center.

WHAT NASCAR STOCK CARS *DON'T* HAVE

✳ A vanity mirror

✳ Cup holders

✳ Doors

✳ Windows

✳ Backseats *or* passenger seats

✳ Brake lights *or* headlights

✳ Speedometer (ironically enough . . .)

✳ Gas gauge

✳ Storage space in the trunk

✳ Stereo system *or* speakers

✳ Air conditioning *or* a heating system

✳ Automatic transmission

✳ Antilock brakes

✳ Cruise control

✳ Key ignition (drivers just flip a switch)

✳ Air bags

✳ Locks

✳ A glove compartment

✳ A horn

✳ The gas tanks are rubber so they won't explode, puncture, or burst upon impact.

✳ There are firewalls between the trunk, where gas tank is located, and the driver's compartment, and also between the driver and engine.

✳ Every car is equipped with a fire extinguisher within the driver's reach.

✳ Drivers wear helmets, and their head is also surrounded by head protectors that protrude from the seat and prevent the head from snapping left or right (or off, presumably) during an accident.

THE POINTS SYSTEM

At the end of each racing season, NASCAR declares a champion. This champion is determined by a *point system*.

A driver earns points for each of the first twenty-six races of the season. The winner of a NASCAR race receives 180 points. The second-place finisher receives 170. And from there, the points decline in varying incre-ments. Even the last-place finisher gets some points (34). (I guess it's a feat just to *get* to the finish alive, and with your car still intact.) In addition, bonus points are earned for getting a **lead lap** and for leading the most laps.

The top ten drivers at the end of the twenty-six races earn a spot in the "Chase for the Championship," which is comprised of the final ten races of the season (similar in concept to a playoff series). The top per-former from this final ten is named the champion.

Team owners—who, in effect, own the cars that compete—also earn points. They earn points for just *attempting* to qualify for a race. (Appar-ently NASCAR subscribes to the theory that showing up is the most im-portant part of the job.) For example, say an owner owns two cars; even if one of those drivers fails to qualify, the owner receives points for both. These points help teams obtain *provisional qualifying entries*, discussed above.

JUST KNOW THIS

NASCAR—National Association for Stock Car Automobile Racing—races only stock cars (as the name suggests), and NASCAR races are the most popular car races in the United States today. Stock cars are similar, in certain respects, to the cars and trucks that normal people drive every day. But they are specially built from the ground up, to the tune of hundreds of thousands of dollars, by highly trained engi-neers and car specialists. Other types of racing cars are *dragsters, sports cars,* and *open-wheel cars,* but these are not part of NASCAR.

Within NASCAR there are three main divisions, called *series,* the most popular of which is the *Nextel Cup Series.* Within the series are *teams,* just like teams in the NFL or MLB. Each team consists of the car, the driver, and everyone else involved, from the engineers to the mechanics. While the drivers are, far and away, the big stars of NASCAR, fans strongly feel that it is a team sport. Because it costs millions of dollars to operate NASCAR teams, owners procure *sponsorships*. This accounts for the decals and logos splattered all over every inch of the cars and racing uniforms.

The object of a car race is to drive as fast as you can and beat all the other cars to the finish line, without crashing your car. A Nextel Cup Series race is typically 400 to 600 miles and lasts three to four hours. Good drivers also take into account that tires wear out, track conditions vary, and accidents help no one—in short, finesse and patience count as well. In addition, it requires great skill to go around a track with dozens of other cars all traveling upward of 170 miles per hour.

Car racing is dangerous, but there are many safety precautions that minimize catastrophic crashes and fatalities: If bad weather makes racing dangerous, for example, a yellow caution flag will be waved and the drivers must slow down or get off of the track; also, the cars are devoid of any glass, and drivers wear ample protective gear.

Drivers You Need to Know

RACING IS A FAMILY AFFAIR

Racing runs in families, perhaps because there aren't too many fathers who'll say to their sons: "Sure, son, hop into a car, go as fast as you can, and don't slow down on the curves!" With all of the shared bloodlines, it is often difficult to keep the various drivers straight. Take the Earnhardt family, for example. Ralph Earnhardt raced during the fifties and sixties; his son, the late Dale Earnhardt, was one of the greatest drivers of all time; and *his* son, Dale Earnhardt Jr., is racing today. Another famous racing family is the Petty family. First there was Lee Petty, who begat Richard Petty, who is another all-time NASCAR great. Richard then begat Kyle, and Kyle begat Adam. (Tragically, Adam was killed in a racing accident in 2000.)

The Legends

MARIO ANDRETTI, 1940–
   Racing years: 1964–94

NASCAR may have taken this nation by storm, but Italian-born Mario Andretti is still the first name that rolls off the tongue when considering race-car drivers. During his thirty-six-year career, Andretti drove many different kinds of race cars. He won NASCAR's Daytona 500 in 1967, but he is better known for racing open-wheel cars, in series such as Formula One, Indy, and CART. His reputation as the most versatile driver in auto-racing history remains unchallenged.

   Among Andretti's other notable feats:

* He is the only person ever to be named Driver of the Year in three decades (1967, 1978, and 1984).

* He is the only driver to win the Daytona 500, Indy 500, *and* Formula One world title.

* In 1993, at the age of fifty-three, he set a closed-course speed record during a qualifier at the Michigan International Speedway—his speed (gulp): 234.275 mph!

* He has also raced—and won—on paved tracks, dirt tracks, and road courses.

And talk about living the American Dream! When Italy's Istria Peninsula, where Mario was born, fell under Communist rule, his family was forced to live in a displaced-persons camp for almost seven years. In 1955, they eventually got visas and moved to the United States, where the family of five settled in Nazareth, Pennsylvania, with $125 to their name. Nine years later, in 1964, twenty-four-year-old Mario made his first Indy car appearance. And only a year later, he won the first of his four Indy car national championships. Andretti once said, "You have to show that burning desire. When you do that, nobody faults you."

The Andrettis are a racing family. Mario's twin brother, Aldo, raced too, but injuries didn't allow him the success his brother experienced. In 1991, *four* Andretti family members competed in the Indy Series. Mario, who was then fifty-one, finished seventh in the final standings. His son Michael finished first, winning the championship. Mario's other son, Jeff, also competed, as did a nephew, John (Aldo's son), making it the only time in racing history that four family members have competed in the same series in the same year. John Andretti is currently competing in NASCAR.

Andretti retired after the 1994 season and is enshrined in *three* halls of fame: The Indianapolis 500 Hall of Fame, the Motorsports Hall of Fame, and the Sprint Car Hall of Fame.

DALE EARNHARDT, 1951–2001
NICKNAME: "THE INTIMIDATOR"
Racing years: 1975–2001

Many have said that Dale Earnhardt was to NASCAR what Michael Jordan was to the NBA. Earnhardt won seven NASCAR Winston Cup Series (now called the "Nextel Cup Series") championships. He tied with Richard Petty for the most championships ever. Tragically, on February 18, 2001, he died in a crash at the Daytona 500, NASCAR's signature race.

Earnhardt was known as "the Intimidator" because of his hard-edged driving style. He was not polite and considerate on the track—he was more of a bully. As Mark Martin said, "Take it from me, when an opponent looked in his rearview mirror and saw Dale Earnhardt, it wasn't the most comforting feeling in the world."

U.S. News & World Report called Earnhardt "Elvis on wheels," referring not to his driving style but to the adoration of his fans, which was Presley-like in its magnitude. According to an article in *Time* that appeared shortly after Earnhardt's death, fans "reveled in their hero's orneriness."

Earnhardt's forte was the longer tracks—the *superspeedways*—that allow cars to go even faster. Legend has it that Earnhardt could "see" air coming off the cars around him, and thus navigate through the draft better than anyone. After NASCAR instituted rules to reduce speeds at some of the bigger races by having cars use a *restrictor plate*, Earnhardt said, "If you're not a race driver, stay the hell home. Don't come [out] and grumble about going too fast . . . Put a kerosene rag around your ankles so the ants won't climb up there and eat that candy ass."

Dale Earnhardt's racing legacy came from his father, Ralph, and is currently being carried on by his son, Dale Earnhardt Jr. Earnhardt also established Dale Earnhardt, Inc., a highly successful car-racing company that owns several race cars.

RICHARD PETTY, 1937–
NICKNAME: "THE KING"
Racing years: 1958–92

What the scarecrow is to Dorothy in *The Wizard of Oz*, Richard Petty is to NASCAR—he is the most loved character of all. During his thirty-four seasons on the NASCAR circuit, Petty won 200 races, seven Daytona 500s, and seven driving championships (he is tied with Earnhardt for the record). Petty's father, Lee, was a driver as well. His brother built his engines, and his cousin was his crew chief. When he was asked what accomplishment he was most proud of, he replied, "Still being alive."

Petty's driving style was aggressive but controlled, smooth rather than flashy. He didn't seem to pay much attention to his fame and fortune. He once said, "I don't know anything about greatness. That's for others to decide. My daddy was a race car driver, so I became a race car driver. If he'd been a grocer, I might have been a grocer."

Petty is credited with bringing NASCAR to modern America, lifting it out from its Southern, rural roots by giving all of America a taste of his charm. Handsome and personable with his trademark cowboy hat and dark sunglasses, Petty became a de facto public relations man for NASCAR, signing autographs, schmoozing with fans, and posing for countless pictures. When he won his 200th race, President Reagan was on hand to congratulate him. Petty retired in 1992 at age fifty-four.

Legends in Training

DALE EARNHARDT JR., 1974–
NICKNAME: "JUNIOR"

Racing years: 1992–present

In NASCAR-land, Dale Earnhardt Jr., son of the late great Dale Earnhardt, need only be referred to as "Junior." He may forever live and race in his father's shadow, but it's a pretty good shadow to live in.

In 2004, Earnhardt won the Daytona 500. The Daytona 500—"the Great American Race"—is the granddaddy of NASCAR. Earnhardt the father won it only once, despite being a seven-time Nextel champion. The Daytona 500 was also the place where the elder Earnhardt died, three years after his victory on the same track.

It was three years to the week after Earnhardt's death when Junior faced the very same race on the same pavement. "Every time we come to Daytona . . . it feels like I'm closer to Dad," he said a few days before the race in February 2004. "But at the same time, it's a reminder of losing him. So I wanted to come down here and win." Win he did, in a moment that Lars Anderson in *Sports Illustrated* compared to Babe Ruth's great-grandson hypothetically leading the Yankees to victory in the World Series.

Before moving up to the Nextel Cup Series in 2000, Junior proved his mettle, dominating in the Busch series, a level down from the Nextel, winning thirteen races and two series championships. Earnhardt Jr. is young and likely has a lot more wins ahead of him.

JEFF GORDON, 1971–

Racing years: 1986–present

Jeff Gordon dominated NASCAR in the 1990s, and he remains one of the best today. In February 2005, he opened the season as the winner of the Daytona 500. He's been a NASCAR driver since 1993 and, in just over a decade, has won four series championships. (Petty and Earnhardt Sr. share the record with seven championships apiece, over many more years of driving, so one can only imagine what Gordon will accomplish.) He has also won at the Indianapolis Motor Speedway four times, the only stock car driver to do so.*

Gordon is the hot young driver who some fans love to hate. As Steve Lopez wrote in *Time*, "to the traditional fans, he's too pretty, he's from California (i.e. not a good ol' Southern boy), he's rich, he always wins." Another reason that some fans dislike him is because, when he was a young teenager, his family moved to Indiana for the sole purpose of furthering his racing career. To many, this suggested that Gordon was born with a silver spoon is his mouth. The reality, however, is that when Gordon's family moved to Indiana, they were dependent on his race winnings to help make ends meet. Gordon has *earned* his silver spoon. As Selena Roberts reported in the *New York Times* in 2003, "This is a man relaxed, at peace and not one ounce bitter. This also makes him the uncommon

---

*Indianapolis Motor Speedway hosts both open-wheel races such as the famed "Indy 500" and car races such as the "Brickyard 400."

icon on the crowded landscape of athletes who search out excuses, who lash out under pressure, who retreat from fame's downside, who view women as accessories." It must be this poise, grace, and charm that have made the legions of fans far outnumber his detractors. To these masses, he has rock-star status.

Glossary

Backstretch: The straight section of the track on the opposite side of the start/finish line.

Banking: The *slope* or *pitch* of a racetrack, particularly at the curves or corners. The "degree of banking" refers to the angle of a racetrack's slope. Tracks with steeper banking are generally faster, because steeper banking allows drivers to go around the curves without giving up too much speed.

Champ Car World Series: A series of open-wheel car racing.

Crash Cart: A box that is kept behind the pit wall, next to the pit stall, where equipment and tools are stored.

Crew Chief: The crew chief oversees all the facets of building and maintaining a race car. Crew chiefs are engineers, mechanics, and managers all woven into one, and their role in winning a race cannot be overstated.

Drafting: Drafting is the aerodynamic effect that allows two or more cars traveling nose-to-tail to run faster than a single car. The effect is caused by the first car cutting through the air, reducing the resistance for the cars behind it. The lead car is actually pulling the cars behind it. Good drivers use this draft to their advantage, staying tucked behind a car until an opportune moment to pass that car arises.

Dragsters: For anyone who has spent more than a minute fixin' their hairdo, dragsters are a nightmare. They are a specific kind of race car, engineered to travel a short distance in a very short period of time—up to 335 miles per hour. Dragsters go from 0 to 100 miles per hour in less than a second.

Formula One: The world's best known open-wheel car series. Formula One racing takes place all over the globe. The Grand Prix races, such as the Grand Prix of Monaco and the United States Grand Prix, are part of Formula One.

Frontstretch: The straight section of the racetrack where the start/finish line is.

Groove: The *groove* refers to the quickest or most efficient route around the track. A "high groove" is a route closer to the outside wall, or, if you're a child of the 1960s, probably involves marijuana or hallucinatory substances such as LSD. A "low groove" is a route closer to the apron than the outside, or, if you're a child of the 1960s (or 1970s), would probably involve Quaaludes.

Indy Racing League (IRL): A series of open-wheel car racing. The IRL's showpiece is the annual "Indianapolis 500" (Indy 500).

Lead Lap: A driver who is on the lead lap has completed the same number of laps as the leader.

Open-Wheel Cars: Open-wheel cars are not like ordinary cars—they look kind of like powerful, mutated insects. They have an open cockpit, no fenders, and big wheels. They are specifically designed for racing and are not suitable for a family outing or a trip to the mall. The major series for open-wheel car racing are Formula One, the Champ Car World Series, and the Indy Racing League (IRL).

Over the Wall Crew: In NASCAR racing, only seven crew members are allowed to work on the cars during pit stops. These seven jump over a wall as soon as their car enters the pit box. They are sometimes referred to as the "over the wall crew."

Pace Car: When a yellow flag comes out, a pace car, with flashing lights on top, will slowly lead the race cars around the track. When a red flag comes out, the pace car leads the race cars to a designated safe area. Also, before the race begins, a pace car will lead the cars around the track for a few warm-up laps.

Pit Box or Pit Stall: The pit box (or pit stall) is the area where the car is serviced during a race. Each car and driver has his own pit box. The pit box is a rectangular area marked off with yellow lines. Cars must pull in all the way within the yellow lines or they will be penalized.

Pit Road: Pit road is the road on which the pit stalls are located. It is usually parallel to the front straightaway on the inside of the oval.

Pit Stop: A pit stop is when a driver pulls off the track, onto pit road, and into his pit stall to do everything *but* the one thing mere mortal drivers do when they make a pit stop: pee. Race car drivers have a crew that works at the speed of lightning to change two or four tires, refuel, and make other mechanical adjustments. Most pit stops are between fifteen and twenty-three seconds.

Pit Wall: The pit wall separates the pit road and the pit stalls from the area where the equipment is kept. Behind the wall is a "crash cart," which is a giant box that holds most of the equipment and tools. When a car pulls into its pit stall, seven crew members jump over the wall to service the car.

Pole Position: In NASCAR, cars line up two by two at the beginning of a race, and the first two are said to be in *pole positions*. The pole position is the inside, foremost position. The second pole position is the outside, foremost position.

Pole Winner (or Pole Sitter): The pole winner is the driver who had the fastest time in qualifying. This entitles him to the lead position—the pole position—when the actual race begins.

Restrictor Plate: A restrictor plate is a device that NASCAR requires cars to have on their carburetors during races at superspeedways like Daytona and Talladega. Restrictor plates reduce horsepower and keep the speed down. Races where restrictor plates are mandated are known as "restrictor-plate races."

Series: NASCAR is divided into different series according to speed, types of tracks, and types of cars. The three most prominent series are the Nextel Cup Series, the Busch Series, and the Craftsman Truck Series.

Stock Cars: Start with your basic American-made family sedan. Sprinkle it with millions of dollars in engineering research, special parts, mega-horsepower, and a crew of one hundred to maintain. Then strip it of all the essentials like vanity mirrors, beverage holders, headlights, brake lights, and doors, and you've got yourself a stock car. Stock cars do look vaguely similar to ordinary cars—certainly more than Formula One cars or dragsters—but are built from scratch with the most advanced auto technology and are designed to travel upward of 200 miles per hour.

Superspeedways: While the definition is not precise, the term "superspeedway" usually refers to racetracks that are two miles or longer, like Daytona International Speedway or Indianapolis Motor Speedway. But sometimes it is used more broadly to refer to any track longer than a mile. The longer the track, the faster the cars can travel.

Victory Lane: Victory lane isn't really a lane, but more of a winner's circle (although it's not really shaped like a circle, either). It's the area where the winner parks his car and basks in the glory of victory, and where he's photographed and interviewed after the race. Victory lane has become a primary spot for brazen commercialism, with the driver drawing attention to all of his and NASCAR's sponsors.

Bibliography

GENERAL SPORTS

Books

Bartges, Dan. *Spectator Sports Made Simple*. Chicago: Masters Press, 1999.

Deford, Frank. *The Best of Frank Deford: I'm Just Getting Started*. Chicago: Triumph Books, 2000.

Fleder, Rob, ed. *Fifty Years of Great Writing, Sports Illustrated 1954–2004*. New York: Sports Illustrated Books, 2003.

Garner, Joe. *And the Crowd Goes Wild*. Naperville, Illinois: Sourcebooks, Inc., 1999.

Halberstam, David, ed. *The Best American Sports Writing of the Century*. Boston: Houghton Mifflin Company, 1999.

MacCambridge, Michael, ed. *ESPN SportsCentury*. New York: Hyperion/ESPN Books, 1999.

Mandelbaum, Michael. *The Meaning of Sports*. New York: Public Affairs, 2004.

Platt, Jim. *Sports Immortals*. Chicago: Triumph Books, 2002.

Plimpton, George. *On Sports*. Guilford, Connecticut: The Lyons Press, 2003.

Web Sites

ESPN: www.espn.com

Sports Illustrated magazine: www.si.com

BBC Sport: http://news.bbc.co.uk/sport/default.stm

www.sportsdictionary.com

BASKETBALL

Books

Beard, Butch. *Butch Beard's Basic Basketball*. New York: Michael Kesend Publishing, Ltd., 1995.

Hareas, John. *NBA's GREATEST: The NBA's Best Players, Teams and Games*. New York: DK Publishing, 2003.

Vancil, Mark. *NBA Basketball Basics*. New York: Sterling Publishing Co., Inc., 1995.

Articles

"Alley Oop." Elliott Avedon Museum and Archive of Games. http://gamesmuseum .uwaterloo.ca/Tablegames/AlleyOop/

Araton, Harvey. "Biggest Threat Iverson Poses Is on the Court." *The New York Times*, 18 Dec. 2002.

———. "Allen Iverson Highs and Lows." *The Commercial Appeal*, 17 Jul. 2002.

———. "In Latest Lakers Drama, Bryant Says Malone Made Pass at Wife." *The New York Times*, 13 Dec. 2004.

————. "Magic, Petrovic, Globetrotters Get Their Day." ESPN.com, 28 Sept. 2002.

The Associated Press. "O'Neal Scores 40, as Promised." *The New York Times*, 14 Dec. 2004.

————. "Yao Leads Early All-Star Voting." *The New York Times*, 17 Dec. 2004.

Beck, Howard. "The Collapse of Kobe." *The New York Times*, 17 Dec. 2004.

Berkow, Ira. "Magic Johnson's Legacy." *The New York Times*, 8 Nov. 1991.

Berrios, Jerry. "Shaq Leads Winterfest Parade." *The Miami Herald*, 19 Dec. 2004.

Brown, Clifton. "Leaving on His Terms, Johnson Retires Again." *The New York Times*, 15 May 1996.

Bunn, Curtis. "Generation Gap: Karl Malone Is Last Link to an NBA Old Guard of Players Who Defined Professionalism." *The Atlanta Journal-Constitution*, 11 Feb. 2001: 1D.

Chaplin, Julia. "A Night Out With: Yao Ming." *The New York Times*, 10 Oct. 2004.

Cialini, Joe. "NBA: Erving Had Winning Touch." *United Press International*, 18 Apr. 1987.

Colbert, Ron. "Is Jason Kidd(ing)?" *United Press International*, 11 Jul. 2003.

Deitsch, Robert. "Q & A with Magic Johnson." *Sports Illustrated*, 4 Nov. 2002.

Denlinger, Ken. "Erving's Talent Soars, His Ego Is Earthbound." *The Washington Post*, 20 Apr. 1987.

Deveney, Sean. "Immovable Object." *The Sporting News*, 3 Mar. 2003.

————. "No One Is Hungry Like the Wolves." *The Sporting News*, 3 May 2004.

Dupree, David. "The Book on . . . Dirk Nowitzki." *USA Today*, 25 Feb. 2000.

————. "The Book on . . . Karl Malone." *USA Today*, 23 Dec. 1999: 15C.

Greenfeld, Karl Taro. "Kobe's Two Worlds." *Sports Illustrated*, 22 March 2004.

Halberstam, David. "In the Satellite Age, Michael Jordan Has Become the Global Star of a Global Show." *Sports Illustrated*, 23 Dec. 1991: 76.

Hilton, Lisette. "Auerbach's Celtics Played as a Team." ESPN.com, 26 Apr. 2004.

Holder, Stephen F. "O'Neal Tops East All-Star Voting." *The Miami Herald*, 17 Dec. 2004.

Kirkpatrick, Curry. "For All His Fame and Fortune, Jordan Is, at Heart, Just a Carolina Kid Called Mike." *Sports Illustrated*, 23 Dec. 1991: 70.

Klein, José. "Phil Jackson." Salon.com, 29 May 2001.

Kornheiser, Tony. "In Praise of 'The Doc,' an Aviator for the Ages." *The Washington Post*, 19 Apr. 1987.

Lipper, Bob. "Growth Spurt: Allen Iverson Has Matured a Lot in a Year." *Richmond Times-Dispatch*, 13 Jun. 2001.

Lipsyte, Robert. "Bigger Than Life, Yet Buffeted by Life." *The New York Times*, 29 Dec. 1991.

Maaddi, Rob. "Same Old Allen Iverson? Look Again." *The Associated Press*, 10 Nov. 2000.

————. "Basketball's Best." *Sports Illustrated*, SI.com, 12 Nov. 2003.

————. "It's Shaq's World." *Sports Illustrated*, 26 Jun. 2002: 20.

McCallum, Jack. "Michael Jordan, a Singular Sportsman and Athlete, Stands at the Pinnacle of His Game." *Sports Illustrated*, 23 Dec. 1991: 66.

————. "The Dark Side of a Star." *Sports Illustrated*, 28 Jul. 2003.

————. "The Importance of Being LeBron." *Sports Illustrated*, 27 Oct. 2003.

————. "Twice Blessed." *Sports Illustrated*, 15 Dec. 2003: 58.

————. "When Great Isn't Good Enough." *Sports Illustrated*, 29 Dec. 2003: 92.

————. "Who's Going to Stop Tim Duncan?" *Sports Illustrated*, 9 Jun. 2003.

Mead, Rebecca. "A Man-Child in Lotusland." *The New Yorker*, 20 May 2002.

"Nothing But Garnett." *Newsweek*, 14 Feb. 2000: 56.

"O'Neal Scores 40, as Promised." *The Associated Press*, 14 Dec. 2004.

Pellegrini, Frank. "Person of the Week: Dirk Nowitzki." *Time*, 3 May 2002.

Price, S. L. "A Clean Start." *Sports Illustrated*, 28 Jan. 2002.

————. "The Quiet Man." *Sports Illustrated*, 15 Dec. 2003: 66.

Reilly, Rick. "The Appeal of O'Neal." *Sports Illustrated*, 5 Jun. 2000: 112.

Robbins, Liz. "At Last, Abdul-Jabbar Could Join the Knicks." *The New York Times*, 20 Feb. 2004.

————. "From Any Position on the Floor, Jason Kidd Can See Tomorrow." *The New York Times*, 8 Feb. 2002.

Roberts, Selena. "How Did Kobe's M.J. Imitation Go Wrong?" *The New York Times*, 26 Dec. 2004.

Rovell, Darren. "Can Jordan Be Like the Mike of Old?" ESPN.com, 23 Sep. 2001.

————. "Magic's Kingdom." ESPN.com, 24 Mar. 2004.

————. "Sources: LeBron, Nike Agree to Seven-Year Deal." ESPN.com, 26 May 2003.

Samuels, Allison and Mark Starr. "Kobe Goes It Alone." *Newsweek*, 31 May 1999.

Schaller, Tom. "Don't Be Like Mike." Salon.com, 5 Dec. 2001.

————. "Magic Made Showtime a Show." ESPN.com, 24 Mar. 2004.

————. "Michael Jordan Transcends Hoops." ESPN.com, 2004.

Schwartz, Larry. "Plain and Simple, Bird One of the Best." ESPN.com, 2004.

————. "Wilt Battled 'Loser' Label." ESPN.com, 2004.

Shapiro, Ouisie. "Zen of Championships." ESPN.com, 4 May 2004.

Siegel, Stephen. "Payton Is Good, but Kidd Is Mr. Point Guard." *The Sporting News*, 3 Jan. 2000: 51.

Smith, Gary. "Now, More Than Ever, a Winner." *Sports Illustrated*, 23 Dec. 1985: 78.

Stein, Joel. "Grownup Kidd." *Time*, 10 Jun. 2002: 56.

Stein, Marc. "Magic His Old Self at Hall of Fame Induction." ESPN.com, 27 Sep. 2002.

Stevenson, Richard W. "Magic Johnson Ends His Career, Saying He Has AIDS Infection." *The New York Times*, 8 Nov. 1991.

Tafur, Vittorio. "Malone Has Starring Role in 'As the Lakers' World Turns.'" *The New York Times*, 21 Apr. 2004.

Thomsen, Ian. "Kevin Up." *Sports Illustrated*, 5 Jul. 2004: 94.

Vitale, Dick. "Cavs Get No. 1, Can Keep LeBron Close to Home." ESPN.com, 9 June 2003.

Wilbon, Michael. "The Evolution of Allen Iverson." *The Washington Post*, 8 Jun. 2001.

Wise, Mike. "It's All Image, Except with Karl Malone." *The New York Times*, 6 March 2000: D5.

————. "The Americanization of Dirk Nowitzki." *The New York Times*, 7 Feb. 2001.

Web Sites
Basketball Hall of Fame: www.hoophall.com
NBA (National Basketball Association) www.nba.com

FOOTBALL

Books
DeLuca, Sam. *Football Made Easy*. Middle Village, New York: Jonathan David Publishers, Inc., 1983.

Madden, John. *One Knee Equals Two Feet*. New York: Villard Books, 1986.

Articles
Adande, J. A. "Congratulations, Mrs. Barber, It's Twins." *The Los Angeles Times*, 24 Jan. 2003.

Attner, Paul. "Hearts and Smarts." *The Sporting News*, 4 November 2002: 44.

Bradley, Mark. "Wise Investment in Rare Commodity." *The Atlanta Journal-Constitution*, 24 Dec. 2004.

Brown, Clifton. "Elway Leads Class of '04 in Canton." *The New York Times*, 9 Aug. 2004.

Crossman, Matt. "Back on Top." *The Sporting News*, 8 Dec. 2003: 20.

Freeman, Mike. "Football Remembers Payton, the Ultimate Player." *The New York Times*, 2 Nov. 1999.

Hiestand, Michael. "Bradshaw Keeps Fans Entertained." *USA Today*, 4 Feb. 2005: E10.

Kindred, Dave. "Marino's Moment Come and Gone." *The Sporting News*, 13 Mar. 2000.

———. "S'Warnerful." *The Sporting News*, 7 Feb. 2000.

King, Peter. "The Real Deal." *Sports Illustrated*, 11 Sep. 2000.

Kriegel, Mark. "Where Have You Gone, Joe Namath?" *Sports Illustrated*, 9 Aug. 2004.

Litsky, Frank. "Walter Payton, Extraordinary Running Back for Chicago Bears, Dies at 45." *The New York Times*, 2 Nov. 1999.

Longman, Jere. "In McNabb and Vick, Quarterbacks Who Do It All." *The New York Times*, 11 Jan. 2003.

McClain, John. "McNabb Proving He Has What It Takes to Be Super." *Houston Chronicle*, 3 Oct. 2004: 1.

Murphy, Austin. "Where Are They Now?" *Sports Illustrated*, 31 Jul. 2000: 84–90.

Myers, Gary. "Out of Nowhere Kurt Warner and His Family Take the NFL by Storm." www.rollanet.org/ramfan/warner.html.

O'Donnell, Chuck. "Immortality Awaits." *Football Digest*, Aug. 2000: 48.

Ostler, Scott. "Crazy Glue." *Sport*, Feb. 1999: 28.

Pedulla, Tom. "For Barbers, It's Two for the Show." *USA Today*, 23 Jan. 2003.

Pompei, Dan. "The Value of Vick." *The Sporting News*, 28 Jan. 2005: 18.

Sandomir, Richard. "Bradshaw as Commentator: Comedy Isn't Pretty."

Sawchik, Travis. "McNabb in His Own Class." *Chicago Tribune*, 10 Oct. 2004: 22.

Shapiro, Leonard. "Limbaugh Quits TV Job Under Fire." *The Washington Post*, 2 Oct. 2003: A01.

Silver, Michael. "Fight to the Finish." *Sports Illustrated*, 9 Feb. 2004.

———. "Together Forever." *Sports Illustrated*, 24 Jul. 2000: 56.

Smith, Timothy. "Made in the U.S.A.: Steelers vs. Browns." *The New York Times*, 7 Jan. 1995: A31.

Vecsey, George. "Kurt Warner Gives Hope to Others." *The New York Times*, 1 Feb. 2000.

Vick, Michael. "How's This for Starters?" *Sports Illustrated*, 20 Sep. 2004.

Weintraub, Robert. "Favre from Heaven." Slate.com, http://slate.msn.com/id/2112019, 7 Jan. 2005.

Weisman, Larry. "For Toughness Over Time, Brett Favre Is No. 1." *USA Today*, 19 Feb. 2004.

Web Sites

National Football League: www.nfl.com

Pro Football Hall of Fame: www.profootballhof.com

BASEBALL

Books

Kelley, James. *Baseball*. New York: Dorling Kindersley, 2000.

Leventhal, Josh. *Take Me Out to the Ballpark*. New York: Black Dog & Leventhal Publishers, 2003.

Smith, Ron. *The Sporting News Selects Baseball's Greatest Players*. St. Louis: The Sporting News Publishing Co., 1998.

Williams, Ted, and Jim Prime. *Ted Williams' Hit List*. Chicago: Contemporary Books, 1996.

Articles

Aaron, Henry. "The Trailblazer: Jackie Robinson." *Time*, 14 Jun. 1999: 104.

———. "Baseball is 'Lucky' to Have Had McGwire and Sosa This Season." *The New York Times*, 23 Sep. 1998.

———. "Bonds Excuse Has the Scent of Snake Oil, Not Arthritis Balm." *The New York Times*, 7 Dec. 2004.

———. "Bonds, the Babe and the All-Time Hitters." *The New York Times*, 12 May 2002.

Anderson, Dave. "When Sold, Babe Wasn't the Babe Yet." *The New York Times*, 23 Feb. 2004.

Angell, Roger. "Digging Up Willie." *Literary Cavalcade*, April 2003: 24.

———. "Sammy's Sin." *The New Yorker*, 30 Jun. 2003: 33.

Antonen, Mel. "Mark McGwire Speaks Out." *USA Today*, 24 Feb. 1999.

Ardolino, Frank. "Lou vs. Babe in Life and *'Pride of the Yankees.'* " *The Baseball Research Journal*, 2002: 16.

"Augusta Officials Nix Plan to Name Field After Ty Cobb." *The Associated Press*, 17 Mar. 2004.

"Babe Ruth Dethroned?" *The Baseball Research Journal*, Annual 2002: 102.

Baker, Russell. "Moralizing About Pete Rose in a Gamblin America: What Rot!" *Chicago Tribune*, 28 Jun. 1989: 19.

Berkow, Ira. "Much More Than Just a Hall of Famer." *The New York Times*, 14 Aug. 1995.

Boswell, Thomas. "Softened Splinter, Splendid Goodbye." *The Washington Post*, 6 July 2002: D01.

Buck, Joe. "How to Make an Exit." *The Sporting News*, 19 May 2003.

Callahan, Gerry. "Hank or Ted or Willie . . ." *Sports Illustrated*, 19 Jul. 1999: 27.

Callahan, Tom. "For Pete's Sake, He Cried." *Time*, 23 Sep. 1985: 60.

Carter, Jimmy. "It's Time to Forgive Pete Rose." *USA Today*, 30 Oct. 1995.

Castellaneta, Michael. "Riveting Rivalry." *Chicago Tribune*, 23 Jun. 2002.

Cole, Wendy. "Hey, Guys, Watch Your Backs—Here Comes Sammy!" *Time*, 27 Jul. 1998: 46.

Coleman, Murray. "Baseball Great Lou Gehrig." *Investor's Business Daily*, 28 Jun. 2000: A04.

Corliss, Richard. "A Little Respect for the Splendid Splinter: Ted Williams, 1918–2002." *Time*, 15 July 2002: 72.

———. "April 15, 1947: Breaking the Color Line." *Time*, 31 Mar. 2003: A25.

———. "These Are the Good Old Days." *Time*, 14 Sep. 1998: 90.

———. "The America That Ruth Built." *Time*, 27 July 1998: 50.

Cramer, Richard Ben. "The DiMaggio Nobody Knew." *Newsweek*, 22 Mar. 1999: 52.

Curry, Jack. "McGwire Is King, but Sosa Is Prince." *The New York Times*, 9 Sep. 1998.

"Cy Young Is Dead, Famed Pitcher, 88." *The New York Times*, 6 Nov. 1955: 19.

———. "In Tribute to Roberto Clemente." *The New York Times*, 2 Jan. 1973: 47.

Daley, Arthur. "The No. 1 Pitcher." *The New York Times*, 6 Nov. 1955: S2.

Davidson, Donald. "He's Still the Same Henry Aaron, but No One Will Let Him Alone." *The New York Times*, 14 July 1974.

DeFord, Frank. "Frank Deford's Ode to Derek Jeter." (Commentary) *Morning Edition*, NPR, 7 Jul. 2004.

"Denton True Young." *Dictionary of American Biography*, Suppl. 5: 1951–55. American Council of Learned Societies, 1977. Reproduced in History Resource Center. Farmington Hills, MI: Gale Group, http://galenet.galegroup.com/servlet/HistRC/

DiGiovanna, Mike. "The Late, Great Festival of Hate." *Los Angeles Times*, 17 Sep. 2002.

"The DiMaggio Mystique." *The New York Times*, 9 Mar. 1999.

Diskin, Bob. "A Pitcher Worthy of a Trophy." ESPN.com, accessed 6 Jul. 2004.

Drebinger, John. "Captain of Yankees Honored at Stadium—Calls Himself 'Luckiest Man Alive.'" *The New York Times*, 5 Jul. 1939.

————. "Maris Hits 61st in Final Game." *The New York Times*, 2 Oct. 1961: 1.

Durso, Joseph. "A Man of Two Worlds." *The New York Times*, 2 Jan. 1973: 48.

————. "Aaron: Sleepless but Relieved." *The New York Times*, 10 Apr. 1974: 23.

Gates, David. "Theodore Rex: Ted Williams's Sad, Funny Saga, from Superman to Everyman." *Newsweek*, 5 April 2004: 62.

Grann, David. "Baseball Without Metaphor." *The New York Times Magazine*, 1 Sept. 2002.

Green, Janet. "The Perfect Player." *The Jerusalem Report*, 30 Dec. 2002: 47.

"Hank Aaron." *American Decades* CD-ROM. Gale Research, 1998. Reproduced in History Resource Center. Farmington Hill, MI: Gale Group, http://galenet.galegroup.com/servlet/HistRC/

Jenkins, Chris. "Major League Feuds." *Baseball Digest*, Oct. 2003: 48.

Jenkins, Lee. "On and Off the Baseball Field, Bonds Prefers to Go for Distance." *The New York Times*, 20 Apr. 2004.

Kashatus, William C. "Cobb's Last Stand." *American History*, Jun. 1999: 36.

————. "A Cornucopia of Delights." *The Sporting News*, 14 Sep. 1998: 86.

————. "A Man Among Children." *The Sporting News*, 15 Dec. 1997: 14.

————. "A Small Piece of Forever." *The Sporting News*, 2 Jul. 2001: 62.

Kindred, Dave. "Joe DiMaggio, 1914–1999." *The Sporting News*, 22 Mar. 1999.

————. "Koufax and Rose: There's No Comparison." *The Sporting News*, 7 Oct. 2002: 72.

————. "The Class of '98." *The Sporting News*, 21 Dec. 1998.

Knisley, Michael. "Prodigious." *The Sporting News*, 14 Sep. 1998: 56.

Kogan, Rick. "Does Baseball Still Matter?" *Chicago Tribune*, 20 Jun. 2004.

Kroll, Jack. "The Mantle of Greatness." *Newsweek*, 21 Aug. 1995: 54.

Ladson, William. "Q&A with Hank Aaron." *The Sporting News*, 8 Apr. 1999.

Leonhardt, David. "Baseball's New Generation of Benchmarks." *The New York Times*, 25 Jul. 2004.

Mahler, Jonathan. "Shining a Light on the Shadow Man." *The Wall Street Journal*, 22 Oct. 2002: D8.

McGrath, Ben. "Nothing but the Best." *The New Yorker*, 1 Mar. 2004: 34.

McGrath, Charles. "Whether Sweet or Cranky, He Was Always a Slugger." *The New York Times*, 7 May 2004.

"Mickey Mantle." *DISCovering U.S. History*. Gale Research, 1997. Reproduced in History Resource Center. Farmington Hills, MI: Gale Group, http://galenet.galegroup.com/servlet/HistRC/

"Mickey Mantle." (editorial) *The New York Times*, 15 Aug. 1995: A16.

Nack, William. "The Colossus." *Sports Illustrated*, 24 Aug. 1998: 58.

Newberry, Paul. "Randy Johnson: Aged to Perfection." *Associated Press*, 19 May 2004.

NPR. "The Pete Rose Controversy." (transcript) www.npr.org, 19 May 2003.

Olney, Buster. "The Confidence Man." *New York*, 5 July 2004: 46.

Pearson, Richard. "Baseball Loses Its Last .400 Hitter." *The Washington Post*, 6 July 2002: A01.

Popper, Steve. "Jeter Hits, Walks and Runs Yanks to Victory." *The New York Times*, 25 Aug. 2004.

————. "A Gentleman in a Pinstripe Suit." *Sports Illustrated*, 12 Jul. 2004.

Reilly, Rick. "Chillin' with the Splinter." *Sports Illustrated*, 2 July 2003.

————. "Pride of the Yankees." *Sports Illustrated*, 28 Sep. 1998.

————. "You Had to See It to Believe It." *Sports Illustrated*, 14 Sep. 1998.

Roberts, Selena. "Maris Did Not Need Performance Enhanced." *The New York Times*, 7 Mar. 2004.

Rose, Pete, and Rick Hill. "Pete Rose's Confession." *Sports Illustrated*, 12 Jan. 2004.

Rosenthal, Ken. "One on One with Mariano Rivera." *The Sporting News*, 16 Aug. 2004.

Rubinstein, William D. "Jackie Robinson and the Integration of Major League Baseball." *History Today*, Sep. 2003: 20.

Rushin, Steve. "Living Legends." *Sports Illustrated*, 30 Jul. 2001.

Schulman, Henry. "Willie Mays; Birthday Celebration." *The San Francisco Chronicle*, 6 May 2001: B1.

———. "Jackie Changed the Face of Sports." ESPN.com accessed 6 Jul. 2004.

Schwartz, Larry. "Joltin Joe Was a Hit for All Reasons." ESPN.com, accessed 4 Jul. 2004.

———. "Koufax's Dominance Was Short but Sweet." ESPN.com, accessed 7 Jul. 2004.

———. "Lovable Ruth Was Everyone's Babe." ESPN.com, accessed 4 Jul. 2004.

———. "Mantle Was First in Fans' Hearts." ESPN.com, accessed 6 Jul. 2004.

———. "Mays Brought Joy to Baseball." ESPN.com, accessed 4 Jul. 2004.

———. "The Say Hey Kid." ESPN.com, accessed 4 Jul. 2004.

Smith, Gary. "Heaven and Hell." *Sports Illustrated*, 21 Dec. 1998: 54.

Smith, Red. "Death of an Unconquerable Man." *The New York Times*, 25 Oct. 1972: 53.

Simon, Paul. "The Silent Superstar." *The New York Times*, 9 Mar. 1999.

Stein, Joel. "The Fun Is Back." *Time*, 27 Jul. 1998: 40.

Stravinsky, John. "Spoilsports of the Century." *Village Voice*, 17 Aug. 1999: 181.

Taylor, Phil. "A Shot to the Heart." *Sports Illustrated*, 19 Apr. 2004.

"Ty Cobb, Baseball Great, Dies." *The New York Times*, 18 Jul. 1961: 1.

———. "An Imperfect Baseball Deity." *The New York Times*, 14 Aug. 1995: A1.

Vecsey, George. "Mays Pays Homage to Jackie Robinson." *The New York Times*, 7 Apr. 1997.

———. "Hello, New York." *Sports Illustrated*, 23 Feb. 2004.

———. "Ten Reasons Why Baseball Is Back." *Sports Illustrated*, 5 Jul. 2004.

Verducci, Tom. "The Left Arm of God." *Sports Illustrated*, 12 Jul. 1999: 82.

———. "The Rocket." *Sports Illustrated*, 2 Jun. 2003.

———. "The Toast of the Town." *Sports Illustrated*, 6 Nov. 2000: 60.

———. "Splendor at the Plate." *Sports Illustrated*, 17 July 2002: 10.

———. "Sosa: So, So Fun." *Sports Illustrated*, 7 Sep. 1998: 21.

———. "What Really Happened to Ted Williams." *Sports Illustrated*, 18 Aug. 2003: 66.

Walsh, Joan. "Willie Mays." Salon.com, 13 Jul. 1999, accessed 4 Jul. 2004.

Weiner, Richard. " 'Say Hey' Again to Willie Mays." *USA Today*, 31 Mar. 2000: 3C.

Whitley, David. "Teddy Ballgame Made Fenway Memories." ESPN.com, accessed 6 Jul. 2004.

Will, George F. "The Numbers Game." (book review) *The New York Times Book Review*, 15 Aug. 2004: 10.

"Willie Mays." *U.S. News & World Report*, 29 Aug. 1994: 96.

Williams, Ted. "Humility and Pride." *Sports Illustrated*, 17 Jul. 2002: 84.

Zani, Andrea. "Maris 'Asterisk' Might Go but Ruth's Name Won't." *The Sporting News*, 12 Aug. 1991.

Web Sites

Baseball Almanac: www.baseball-almanac.com

www.baseballlibrary.com

The Coaching Corner: www.thecoachingcorner.com/baseball/baseballglossary.html

The Language of Baseball, An Enlexica Dictionary: http://www.enlexica.com

Major League Baseball: www.mlb.com
National Baseball Hall of Fame: www.baseballhalloffame.org

HOCKEY

Books

Dryden, Steve, ed. *The Top 100 NHL Players of All Time*. Toronto: McClelland & Stewart, Inc., 1999.

Falla, Jack. *Sports Illustrated Hockey*. Lanham, MD: Sports Illustrated Books, 1994.

Harari, P. J., and David Ominsky. *Ice Hockey Made Simple: A Spectator's Guide, 4th ed.* Los Angeles: First Base Sports, Inc., 2002.

Hughes, Morgan. *Hockey Legends of All Time*. Lincolnwood, IL: Publications International, Ltd., 1986.

McDonell, Chris. *Hockey's Greatest Stars*. Ontario: Willowdale, 1996.

McKinley, Michael. *Legends of Hockey: The Official Book of the Hockey Hall of Fame*. Chicago: Triumph Books, 1996.

Articles

Allen, Kevin. "Magnifique! Mario Lemieux Exits Game Surpassing All Expectations." *USA Today*, 16 Apr. 1997.

Associated Press. "Brodeur Poised to Write Another Success Story." SI.com, 19 Dec. 2003.

————. "Devils Clinch as Brodeur Wins No. 400," *The Washington Post*, 24 Mar. 2004.

Bradley, Mark. "Lemieux NHL's Something Special." *The Atlanta Journal-Constitution*, 31 Jan. 2001.

Booth, Clark. "Bruins' 75-Year History Woven Around Three Greats." *The Boston Globe*, 9 Oct. 1998.

Caldwell, Dave. "They Shoot, but Don't Score (Much) Against Brodeur." *The New York Times*, 26 Dec. 2003.

Cannella, Stephen. "Flyers Friction." *Sports Illustrated*, 27 Oct. 2003.

Chad, Norman. "Couch Slouch." *The Boston Globe*, 16 Feb. 2004.

Chidley, Joe. "Still Mr. Hockey." *Maclean's*, 21 Mar. 1994.

Curtright, Guy. "Rule Changes Find Few in Favor." *The Atlanta Journal-Constitution*, 15 Feb. 2004.

DeFord, Frank. "Myriad Problems Put Hockey's Future in Doubt." SI.com, 26 Feb. 2003.

Diamos, Jason. "Messier All but Says Goodbye to the Garden as a Player." *The New York Times*, 1 Apr. 2004.

"Doug Harvey, 65; Hockey Defenseman in the Hall of Fame." *The New York Times*, 27 Dec. 1989.

Dryden, Ken. "Farewell to the Rocket." *Time International*, 12 Jun. 2000.

El-Bashir, Tarik, and Thomas Heath. "Capitals Cut Prices for Season Tickets." *The Washington Post*, 21 Apr. 2004.

Elliott, Helene. "Ice Charade." *Los Angeles Times*, 18 Oct. 2000.

Farber, Michael. "Code Red." *Sports Illustrated*, 22 Mar. 2004.

————. "Comedy Central." *Sports Illustrated*, 11 Feb. 2002.

————. "Loud Start to the Quiet Revolution." *Sports Illustrated*, 29 Nov. 1999.

"Gone the Great Gretzky." (editorial) *Chicago Tribune*, 20 Apr. 1999.

Gordon, Alex. "Rivalries Stoke the NHL's Flames." *Hockey Digest*, Feb. 2002: 6.

"Gretzky Leaves Stage at Time When Few Do So." *Times-Picayune*, 25 Apr. 1999.

"Hull's Success Understandable: Skates Fastest, Shoots Hardest." *The New York Times*, 13 Mar. 1966.

Lapointe, Joe. "Is the N.H.L. Skating on Thin Ice?" *The New York Times*, 25 May 2004.

———. "Lemieux Makes Return into N.H.L.'s Void." *The New York Times*, 12 Dec. 2000.

Luecking, Dave. "The Great One Blessed Hockey." *St. Louis Post-Dispatch*, 18 Apr. 1999.

McGourty, John. "Beliveau Is a Player for the Ages." NHL.com, 8 Nov. 2002.

McGrath, Charles. "Ice Follies; Just a Little Violence Among Enemies." *The New York Times*, 14 Mar. 2004.

Neff, Craig. "A Pair of Battlers." *Sports Illustrated*, 8 Jan. 1990.

Nevius, C.W. " 'The Great One,' Gretzky Retires." *San Francisco Chronicle*, 17 Apr. 1999.

O'Donnell, Chuck. "Blood on the Ice." *Hockey Digest*, Feb. 2002: 50.

Reilly, Rick. "Punching Up Hockey." *Sports Illustrated*, 21 Jun. 2004.

Roberts, Selena. "Enforcers Are Irrelevant in the NHL Playoffs." *The New York Times*, 11 Apr. 2004.

Rogin, Gilbert. "One Beer for the Rocket." *Sports Illustrated*, 14 Mar. 1994 (reprint of 1960 article).

Ryan, Bob. "Bruins' Shore Skates Alone." *The Boston Globe*, 26 Dec. 1999.

Schultz, Dave. "Fighting, Not Penalties, Is Best Way to Settle Score." *The New York Times*, 21 Mar. 2004.

Seidman, Carrie. "Gordie Howe Retires at 52." *The New York Times*, 5 Jun. 1980.

Smizik, Bob. "Lemieux Serves as a Role Model for All." *Pittsburgh Post-Gazette*, 6 Mar. 1993.

Vecsey, George. "For Hockey and History, a Singular Star." *The New York Times*, 17 Apr. 1999.

Wickens, Barbara. "The Best Defense: Doug Harvey Helped Change the Game of Hockey." *Maclean's*, 8 Jan. 1990.

Wigge, Larry. "Goodbye, Great One: Wayne Gretsky." *The Sporting News*, 26 Apr. 1999.

Wilkinson, Alec. "First Period Slump." *The New Yorker*, 15 Mar. 2004: 62.

Yorio, Kara. "Getting a Handle on It." *The Sporting News*, 7 Apr. 2003.

Web Sites
Hockey Hall of Fame: www.hhof.com.
National Hockey League: www.nhl.com.

GOLF

Books
Vroom, Jerry. *So You Want to Be a Golfer*. Tigard, Oregon: Vern Perry Golf Publishers, 2003.

Articles
Brown, Clifton. "Mickelson Has Finally Made the Major Leap." *The New York Times*, 12 Apr. 2004.

———. "Singh Makes It to the Top and Would Like to Stay." *The New York Times*, 9 Sep. 2004.

———. "Tiger Is Human." *The New York Times*, 13 Jun. 2004.

Callahan, Tom. "Two Aces and a King." *Time*, 15 Sep. 1986: 83.

D' Amato, Gary. "All Work . . . for Singh, Gold Has Always Been a Love of Labor." *Milwaukee Journal Sentinel*, 11 Aug. 2004.

———. "Sportsman of the Year: Jack Nicklaus." *Sports Illustrated*, 25 Dec. 1978.

Deford, Frank. "Sportsman of the Year: Tiger Woods." *Sports Illustrated*, 18 Dec. 2000.

Herre, James P. "The Golf Plus Decade." *Sports Illustrated*, 23 Mar. 2004: 49.

Kindred, Dave. "The Golden Bear Roars Again." *The Sporting News*, 17 Apr. 2000.

Krauthammer, Charles. "The Greatness Gap." *Time*, 1 July 2002: 76.

Leonard, Tod. "Year of Renewal." *The San Diego Union-Tribune*, 11 Feb. 2004.

Potter, Jerry. "Singh: Golf Is 'All I Know.' " *USA Today*, 9 Sep. 2004.

———. "Different Tiger, Different Rules." *Sports Illustrated*, 28 Jun. 2004.

———. "Jack Nicklaus." *Sports Illustrated*, 19 Sep. 1994.

———. "Sportsman of the Year: Tiger Woods." *Sports Illustrated*, 23 Dec. 1996.

Reilly, Rick. "The Greatest Show on Earth." *Sports Illustrated*, 29 Aug. 2000.

Shipnuck, Alan. "Masterstroke: Mickelson Wins His First Major." *Sports Illustrated*, 19 Apr. 2004.

Smith, Gary. "The Chosen One." *Sports Illustrated*, 23 Dec. 1996.

Tarde, Jerry. "Jack Nicklaus, Still the 'Greatest' Golfer." *Golf Digest*, Dec. 2002: 14.

Towers, Chip. "The Masters: Popular Choice." *The Atlanta Journal-Constitution*, 12 Apr. 2004.

Web Sites

The Golf Insite Network: www.golfinsite.net.

Golf Today: www.golftoday.co.uk.

United States Golf Association: www.usga.org.

World Golf Hall of Fame: www.wgv.com.

BOXING

Books

Oates, Joyce Carol. *On Boxing*. New York: Ecco, 2002.

Heinz, W. C., and Nathan Ward. *The Book of Boxing*. Kingston, New York: Total Sports Illustrated Classics, 1999.

Ricciuti, Edward R. *How to Box*. New York: Thomas Y. Crowell, 1982.

Roberts, James B., and Alexander G. Skutt. *The Boxing Register*. Ithaca, New York: McBooks Press, 1997.

Articles

Anderson, Dave. "Golota, the I.B.F. and Yet Another Disgraceful Caper." *The New York Times*, 23 Mar. 2004.

Berg, Emmett. "Fight of the Century." *Humanities*, Jul/Aug. 2004: 10.

Berkow, Ira. "A Sluggish Pursuit, Mostly by Fairth." *The New York Times*, 7 Jan. 2005.

Crouch, Stanley. "An American Original." *Time*, 24 Dec. 2001: 75.

Elliott, Victoria Stagg. "AMA Pulls No Punches, Reiterates Boxing Ban." AMEDNEWS.com, 8 Jul. 2002.

Frommer, Frederic J. "Ali Calls for U.S. Boxing Commission." *Associated Press*, 9 Sep. 2004.

Gloster, Rob. "Boxing Promoter Don King Accuses ESPN of Defamation." *Associated Press*, 12 Jan. 2005.

Gordon, Devin. "True Believer: Ali Was the First Muslim America Loved." *Newsweek*, 24 Dec. 2001.

Hoffer, Richard. "Too Much Heart." *Sports Illustrated*, 29 Dec. 2003: 104.

Hummer, Steve. "Iron Mike's Corrosion Is Complete." *The Atlanta Journal-Constitution*, 4 Aug. 2004.

"Injury Rates in Sports." *Journal of Physical Education, Recreation & Dance*, Nov/Dec. 2003:9.

Jordan, Gregory. "Lack of Regulation, Not Tyson, Is Boxing's Problem." *The New York Times*, 1 Aug. 2004.

Kindred, Dave. *Sporting News,* 4 Mar. 2002: 64.

Marino, Gordon. "Visionary or Huckster, Boxing Impresario Don King Won't Be Counted Out." *The Wall Street Journal,* 3 Sep. 2003.

"Oscar de la Hoya." *Contemporary Hispanic Biography.* Vol. 1. Gale Group, 2002. Reproduced in Biography Resource Center. Framington Hills, MI: The Gale Group, 2003.

"Prizefighting." *Dictionary of American History,* Suppl. Charles Scribner's Sons, 1996. Reproduced in History Resource Center. Farmington Hills, MI: Gale Group, http://galenet.galegroup.com/servlet/HistRC.

Puma, Mike. "Only in America." ESPN.com, 12 Jan. 2005.

Reilly, Rick. "Unlike Mike." *Sports Illustrated,* 17 Jun. 2002: 88.

Remnick, David. "Kid Dynamite Blows Up." Reprinted in *The Book of Boxing,* W. C. Heinz and Nathan Ward, eds. Kingston, New York: Total Sports Illustrated Classics, 1999.

———. "Boxing Will Remain on Its Feet No Matter How Many Blows It Takes." *USA Today,* 21 Jan. 2004.

Saraceno, Jon. "De la Hoya Gives Boxing Punch of Respectability." *USA Today,* 4 Jun. 2004.

———. "Sad Story of Mike Tyson Only at Beginning of Final Chapter." *USA Today,* 4 Aug. 2004.

Sielski, Mike. "Frazier Battled Ali in Timeless Trilogy." ESPN.com, 30 Jan. 2005.

Springer, Steve, "Boxing Reform Bill Faces a Battle." *Los Angeles Times,* 2 Apr. 2004.

———. *Los Angeles Times.* "Tyson Source of Fascination." *Chicago Tribune,* 30 Jul. 2004: 10.

Web Sites

International Boxing Association: www.ibamensboxing.com.

International Boxing Hall of Fame: www. ibhof.com.

World Boxing Association: www.wbaonline.com

CAR RACING

Books

Martin, Mark. *NASCAR for Dummies.* New York: Wiley Publishing, Inc., 2000.

Wright, Jim. *Fixin' to Git.* Durham, North Carolina: Duke University Press, 2002.

Articles

Adler, Jerry. "Chariots of Fire." *Newsweek,* 28 July 1997.

Anderson, Lars. "Junior Wins." *Sports Illustrated,* 23 Feb. 2004.

Bechtel, Mark. "Crushing." *Sports Illustrated,* 26 Feb. 2001.

———. "Just Racin'." *Sports Illustrated,* 18 Mar. 2002.

Caldwell, Dave. "Jeff Gordon Ties the Record for Victories at Indianapolis." *The New York Times,* 9 Aug. 2004.

Kaplan, Don. "In the Driver's Seat." *New York Post,* 10 May 2004.

Lipsyte, Robert. "NASCAR Reflects Americans' Lives." *USA Today,* 29 Oct. 2003.

Lopez, Steve. "Babes, Bordeaux & Billy Bobs." *Time,* 31 May 1999.

Lord, Lewis. "The Fastest-Growing Sport Loses Its Hero." *U.S. News & World Report,* 5 Mar. 2001.

Web Sites

Daytona International Speedway: www.daytonaintlspeedway.com.

Indianapolis 500: www.indy500.com.

Motorsports Hall of Fame: www.mshf.com.

NASCAR: www.nascar.com